THE
COVENANT
ENFORCED

THE
COVENANT
ENFORCED

Sermons on Deuteronomy 27 and 28

by
John Calvin

Edited by
James B. Jordan

Institute for Christian Economics
Tyler, Texas

Library of Congress Cataloging-in-Publication Data

Calvin, John, 1509-1564.
  The covenant enforced: sermons on Deuteronomy 27 and
28 / by John Calvin; edited by James B. Jordan.
     p.   cm.
  Includes bibliographical references.
  ISBN 0-930464-33-8 (alk. paper): $14.95
  1. Bible. O.T. Deuteronomy XXVII-XXVIII – Sermons
– Early works to 1800.   2. Reformed Church –
Sermons – Early works to 1800.   ·3. Sermons, French
– Translations into English – Early works to 1800.
4. Sermons, English – Translations from French – Early
works to 1800.   5. Law (Theology) – Sermons – Early
works to 1800.   6. Jewish law – Sermons – Early works
to 1800.   7. Covenants (Theology) – Sermons – Early
works to 1800.   I. Jordan, James B., 1949-   .   II. Title.
BS1275.C35   1990
252'.042 – dc20   90-32836
                                                        CIP

TABLE OF CONTENTS

PUBLISHER'S PREFACE

Gary North

I have several goals in publishing this collection of John Calvin's sermons on Deuteronomy. The first is to provide primary source evidence to answer the question: "Was Calvin a theonomist?" These sermons reveal clearly that the answer is *yes*. Second, I am interested in Calvin's social theory. This question interests me both as an historian and a social theorist. Was there something unique about Calvin's social theory that separated him both from the medieval theorists who preceded him and the Lutherans who were his contemporaries? Third, and less relevant to the broader social and historical issues, is theology as taught in contemporary Calvinist seminaries consistently covenantal and Calvinistic, or has it drifted off into other paths? I say *less relevant* because contemporary Calvinism is today a minor institutional eddy in the broad stream of evangelicalism, a movement identifiable by the shrunken condition of its seminaries and also of the denominations that still profess *and enforce* the historic Reformed creeds.

I note the title of this book, *The Covenant Enforced*. Where is the covenant enforced – the covenant preached by John Calvin? The answer is clear: almost nowhere. The systematic and self-conscious unwillingness of Calvinists to both preach and institutionally enforce covenant theology, beginning in the 1660's[1] and escalating ever since,[2] is at the heart of the spiritual crisis of the West.

---

1. The Restoration of Charles II in England in 1660 marks the beginning of the decline.

2. See my forthcoming book, *Rotten Wood: How the Liberals Captured the Presbyterian Church in the U.S.A.*

Was Calvin a Theonomist?

Because Calvin wrote the single most effective theological handbook in the history of the church, *The Institutes of the Christian Religion*, readers have tended to ignore the enormous compendium of writings that constitute his life's work. The 22 volumes of Bible commentaries published by Baker Book House only skim the surface of his total output. Most of his writings have yet to be translated from the Latin. His 200+ sermons on Deuteronomy appeared in English in the late sixteenth century and were promptly forgotten.[3] Yet it is here, in his sermons on Deuteronomy, that we find the heart of Calvin's covenant theology. It is in Deuteronomy that God's covenant is presented most comprehensively.[4]

What Is Theonomy?

The question, "Was Calvin a theonomist?", obviously demands a definition of theonomy. Theonomy, as Greg Bahnsen uses the term,[5] is a view of the Bible that argues for the continuing validity of God's revealed law in every area of life. Bahnsen argues that unless a specific Old Testament law has been abrogated by the New Testament, either by specific revelation or because of an application of a New Testament principle, its authority is still morally and/or judicially binding. "The *methodological* point, then, is that we presume our obligation to obey any Old Testament commandment unless the New Testament indicates otherwise. We must assume continuity with the Old Testament rather than discontinuity. This is *not* to say that there are *no changes* from Old to New Testament. Indeed, there are — important ones. However, the word of God must be the standard which defines precisely what those changes are for us; we cannot take it upon

---

3. These have been reprinted in the original small print by the Banner of Truth, Edinburgh.

4. Ray R. Sutton, *That You May Prosper: Dominion By Covenant* (Tyler, Texas: Institute for Christian Economics, 1987).

5. I told him in 1977 that *theonomy* must be a composite of the Greek words for "reduced sales." I was wrong, though not about the level of sales. It is a composite of *theos* (God) and *nomos* (law).

ourselves to assume such changes or read them into the New Testament."[6]

This position has produced a certain amount of exegetical bobbing and weaving. "There are," Bahnsen writes, "*cultural* discontinuities between biblical moral instruction and our modern society. This fact does not imply that the ethical teaching of Scripture is invalidated for us; it simply calls for hermeneutical sensitivity."[7] "Hermeneutical sensitivity" allows a degree of latitude – how much, no one can say in advance. But every intellectual and judicial system eventually adopts a similar qualification; the human mind is neither digital[8] nor unfallen. Nevertheless, theonomists are at a comparative disadvantage in terms of creating a systematic apologetic system, since they assert that the Bible is relevant for every area in life, not just in great shining platitudes, but specifically. This makes for a complex, detailed, and difficult apologetic.[9]

In general, however, the precision of the definition of theonomy supplied by Bahnsen has led to an extensive output of theological works that apply it to a whole host of biblical-theological issues, including social theory.

John Calvin, Theonomist

I have already given my one-word answer: *yes*. Now I need to prove it. The following extracts from sermons reprinted in this volume make his position plain. I begin with his view favoring the continuing validity of the Decalogue (ten commandments), the

---

6. Greg L. Bahnsen, *By This Standard: The Authority of God's Law Today* (Tyler, Texas: Institute for Christian Economics, 1985), p. 3.

7. Greg L. Bahnsen, "The Reconstructionist Option," in Bahnsen and Kenneth L. Gentry, *House Divided: The Break-Up of Dispensational Theology* (Tyler, Texas: Institute for Christian Economics, 1989), p. 32.

8. Modern computers "think" digitally; they are in fact giant morons, not giant brains. A. L. Samuel, quoted by Nicholas Georgescu-Roegan, *The Entropy Law and the Economic Process* (Cambridge, Massachusetts: Harvard University Press, 1981), p. 92.

9. It also leads to the multiplication of critics who do not read it before they go into print with their criticisms.

words of the law. He cites Deuteronomy 27:26: "Cursed be he
that confirmeth not all the words of this law to do them. And all
the people shall say, Amen." His comments do not indicate any
doubt on his part regarding the comprehensive claims of God's
law:

> For this cause, therefore, it is said, "Cursed be he who does
> not confirm the words of this law." He is not here speaking of one
> or two commandments, or of some part of them, but of the whole
> law, every part and parcel thereof without exception. And indeed,
> we ought to think of how St. James says that He who has forbid-
> den to steal, has also forbidden to commit adultery; and that He
> who has forbidden to murder has also forbidden false witnessing.
> We must not rend God's justice in pieces. In whatever way we
> offend, we violate God's law, and despise His majesty. But He
> will be acknowledged in His law throughout in all points, and not
> just in part, as I have told you before. [Below, p. 64.]

> But here is a dreadful sentence, and such a one as ought to
> make the hairs stand stiff on our heads: "Cursed shall he be who
> does not perform all the words of this law." Who says this? It is
> God Himself. It is, then, a definitive sentence, such as admits of
> no appeal beyond itself. God will have all men confess it so, yea
> He will have every man confess it with his own mouth. What,
> then, remains for us to do? Where is the hope of salvation? From
> this we see that if we had only the ten commandments of the law
> we should be utterly undone and perish. It is necessary for us to
> have recourse to His mercy, which outstrips His justice, as St.
> James says (Jas. 2:13). God's goodness, then, must be manifest
> towards us to deliver us from the damnation all of us would
> experience if this curse should stand and there be no grace to
> overcome it. [Below, pp. 66-67.]

For John Calvin, the Epistle of James was no "epistle of
straw," to cite Luther. It brings us the very hope of our salvation,
a guide to the binding law of God.

Did he take the details of the case laws seriously? Yes. He
went to Leviticus 18 and 20 in search of the definition of incest.
He writes that "these degrees of consanguinity should be observed. For without such order, what would become of things?

How would we differ from bulls and asses?"[10]

This comparison of a brute beast and a man without God's law is a familiar one in Calvin's ethical theology:

> How are we made the people of God except by being His Church, and by having the use of His sacraments, and that is all the same as if He appeared among us? For we may not expect that God should come down from heaven in His own person, or send His angels to us. Rather, the true mark whereby He will be known to be present among us is the preaching of His Word purely unto us, for there can be no doubt but that then He bears rule in our midst. So then, let this thing profit us, that we know that our Lord receives us to Himself and will have us to be of His own household. Seeing it so, let us take pains to obey Him in all our life, and to keep His commandments. Let us not wander like brute beasts as the wretched unbelievers do, because they never knew what it was to be of the house of God. [Below, p. 33.]

Calvin believed in the primacy of obedience. This is why his theology is intensely ethical.

> And we can see that the promise is not empty when we continue reading, "Keep the commandment I set before you this day," says Moses, "that You swerve neither to the left nor to the right to go after strange gods and to worship them." We see how God continually reminds us of obedience to His Word so that we should serve Him, though not in that hypocrisy to which we are so much inclined. Let us remember therefore this lesson: That to worship our God sincerely we must evermore begin by hearkening to His voice, and by giving ear to what He commands us. For if every man goes after his own way, we shall wander. We may well run, but we shall never be a whit nearer to the right way, but rather farther away from it. [Below, p. 128.]

Biblical law served the basis of Calvin's ethics. This is why he should be classified as a sixteenth-century theonomist. But it was more than simply his commitment to the requirement of obeying God's law that made him a theonomist. He also held a

---

10. Below, p. 54.

social theory that was essentially theonomist in approach.

Calvin's Social Theory

What is the nature of social change? This is *the* question of modern social theory.[11] Humanist scholars usually focus on the perceived dualism between mind and matter: ideas vs. history as the primary basis of social development. The Bible, in contrast, focuses on the question of ethics: covenant-keeping vs. covenant-breaking. This raises the key issue in biblical social theory: *God's sanctions in history.*[12]

Calvin's view of history was straightforward: God brings His sanctions — blessings and curses — in the midst of history in terms of each man's obedience to His law. Each man reaps what he sows in history. Calvin did not qualify this statement in any significant way, and he repeated it over and over:

> For if any one of us should reckon up what he has suffered all the days of his life, and then examine the state of David or Abraham, doubtless he will find himself to be in a better state than were those holy fathers. For they, as the apostle says (Heb. 11:13), only saw things afar off, things that are right before our eyes. God promised to be their Savior; He had chosen them to be, as it were, of His household; but meanwhile where was He who was to be their promised Redeemer? Where was the doctrine that is made so clear to us in the gospel concerning the resurrection? They knew the same afar off, but now it is declared to us in the gospel in such a way that we may indeed say, as our Lord Jesus Christ gives us to understand, that blessed are the ears that hear the things that are told us concerning Him, and the eyes that see the things that we see, for the holy kings and prophets longed for the same, and could not obtain it (Matt. 13:16f.).
>
> We therefore have a much more excellent estate than they had who lived under the law. This is the difference of which I speak, which needed to be supplied by God because of the imperfection [lack of completion] that was in the doctrine concerning the reve-

---

11. Robert A. Nisbet, *Social Change and History: Aspects of the Western Theory of Development* (New York: Oxford University Press, 1969).

12. Sutton, *Prosper*, ch. 4.

lation of the heavenly life, which the fathers only knew by outward tokens although they were dear to God. Now that Jesus Christ has come down to us, and has shown us how we ought to follow Him by suffering many afflictions, as it is told us (Matt. 16:24; Rom. 8:29), in bearing poverty and reproach and all such like things, and to be short, that our life must be as it were a kind of death; since we know all this, and the infinite power of God is uttered in His raising up Jesus Christ from death and in His exalting Him to glory of heaven, should we not take from this a good courage? Should not this sweeten all the afflictions we can suffer? Do we not have cause to rejoice in the midst of our sorrows?

Let us note, then, that if the patriarchs were more blessed by God than we are, concerning this present life, we ought not to wonder at it at all. For the reason for it is apparent. But no matter how things go, yet is this saying of St. Paul always verified: that the fear of God holds promise not only for the life to come, but also for this present life (1 Tim. 4:8). Let us therefore walk in obedience to God, and then we can be assured that He will show Himself a Father to us, yea even in the maintenance of our bodies, at least as far as concerns keeping and preserving us in peace, delivering us from all evils, and providing for us our necessities. God, I say, will make us to feel His blessing in all these things, so that we walk in His fear. [Below, pp. 100-1.]

Blessings in the Small Things

Calvin was not speaking merely of the great sweeping movements in mankind's history. He was speaking of the small things of each man's life. There is orderliness in a man's life because there is a coherent, predictable relationship between obedience and blessings. God does not limit His covenantal blessings to the afterlife:

> Let us therefore be persuaded that our lives will always be accursed unless we return to this point whereto Moses leads us, namely to hearken to the voice of our God, to be thereby moved and continually confirmed in the fact that He cares for our salvation, and not only for the eternal salvation of our persons, but also for the maintenance of our state in this earthly life, to make us taste at present of His love and goodness in such a way as may

content and suffice us, waiting till we may have our fill thereof and behold face to face that which we are now constrained to look upon as it were through a glass and in the dark (1 Cor. 13:12). That is one more thing we ought to remember from this text, where it is said that we will be blessed if we hearken to the voice of the Lord our God.

This is to be applied to all parts of our lives. For example, when a man wishes to prosper in his own person — that is, he desires to employ himself in the service of God and to obtain some grace so that he may not be unprofitable in this life but that God may be honored by him — let him think thus to himself: "Lord, I am Yours. Dispose of me as You will. Here I am, ready to obey You." This is the place at which we must begin if we desire God to guide us and create in us the disposition to serve Him, so that His blessings may appear and lighten upon us and upon our persons. So it is concerning every man's household. [Below, p. 107.]

The same thing is true concerning cattle, food, and all other things. For we see here [in this text] that nothing is forgotten. And God meant to make us to perceive His infinite goodness, in that He declares that He will deal with our smallest affairs, which one of our own equals would be loath to meddle with. If we have a friend, we should be very loath, indeed, and ashamed to use his help unless it were in a matter of great importance. But we see here that God goes into our sheepfolds and into the stalls of our cattle and oxen, and He goes into our fields, and He cares for all other things as well. Since we see Him abase himself thus far, shouldn't we be ravished to honor Him and to magnify His bounty? [Below, p. 108.]

A Covenantal Promise

God promised the Israelites that they would be blessed, so as to confirm His covenant with their fathers. "But thou shalt remember the LORD thy God: for it is he that giveth thee power to get wealth, that he may establish his covenant which he sware unto thy fathers, as it is this day" (Deut. 8:18). Calvin echoed this view: God's blessings in history point to His faithfulness in eternity:

Let us conclude, then, that when God says that He shall bless us in the fruit of the earth, and that He shall bless us in the fruit of our cattle, it is a most certain argument that He will not forget the principal thing. These things are lowly and of little count, and many times men despise them, and yet we see that God takes care of them notwithstanding. Since this is so, will He forget our souls, which He has created after His own image, which also He has so dearly redeemed with the sacred blood of his Son? Surely not. First of all, therefore, let us acknowledge God's favor toward us, in abasing Himself so far as to direct and govern everything that belongs to our lives and sustenance. And from there let us rise up higher, and understand that He will not fail us in the things that surpass this present life, but rather that in the chief things that belong to our life, indeed even in this world, God will stretch forth His hand to furnish us always with all things that are needful. [Below, pp. 108-9.]

A Visible Testimony to Our Enemies

These blessings of God will be visible to pagan enemies of God. He cites Deuteronomy 28:10: "And all people of the earth shall see that thou art called by the name of the LORD; and they shall be afraid of thee." The point here is: these blessings are not merely internal, "spiritual-only" blessings; they are public blessings. They are blessings that differentiate covenant-keepers from covenant-breakers, not merely in eternity, but in time and on earth.

Now He says moreover, that other people shall see that we are called by God's name, and they shall fear us (v. 10). It is not enough that God promises to make us feel that we are safe in His keeping; but He also says that even the pagans, our mortal enemies and the despisers of His majesty, shall be made to know the same. Now it is certain that the infidels do not know the arm of God in such a way as it ought to be known to us. They come far short of it. For though they see, they do not see. How then can it be possible for them to perceive that God has blessed us, that we live by His favor, and that we are nourished through His provision? After all, they are blockish, and do not recognize that anything comes to them from the hand of God. . . .

They will not know it through any persuasion of mind or through any such true understanding of it as we ought to have. But Moses says that they shall have it proved to their faces; as for example, we see the wicked grind their teeth when they behold the faithful prospering, and when they see that God upholds and keeps them. And how does this come about? Truly they will be astonished at it, and they will not be able to think otherwise but that God does indeed favor their adversaries — not that they take it to heart or have a proper attitude about it, but in that they are at least confounded in their own selves. [Below, pp. 117-18.]

Can Such Things Really Be?

Men who receive the blessings of God, even faithful men, will have doubts about the relationship between obedience and historical blessings. Calvin recognized this fact of life and warned against it. Unfortunately, his warning has not been taken seriously by those who profess to be his disciples today.

Now Moses repeats again what he had said concerning the fruit of the womb, of cattle, and of the earth. Surely it would have been sufficient to have promised once that all bodily blessings come from God. But on the one hand we see the mistrust that is in men, how when God speaks to them, they ceaselessly argue and reply, saying, "Yes, but can I be sure of it?" And therefore to give us better resolve, God confirms the matter He had previously spoken of. Again we see our unthankfulness to be such that we attribute things to "Fortune" or to our own skill and craft, which are actually done for us by God. Therefore He calls us to Himself, and shows that it is He who does it.

And on the other hand, He would have us to understand that if we intend to prosper in all points, we must hearken to Him and obey Him. For all men, yea even the most wicked in the world, desire to have issues of their own bodies, increase of cattle, and great revenues. But what? In the meanwhile we despise God, the author of all goodness, and seem as though we labored purposefully to thrust His hand far from us, which is as much as if I should ask a man for an alm and then reach up and box his ear, or as if he should come to my aid and I should spit in his face; even so deal we with our God. [Below, p. 119.]

Negative Sanctions, Too

There are not merely positive sanctions in life, but also negative sanctions. We can expect to receive these if we do not honor God as the sanctioning Sovereign in history:

> It is certain that God will threaten often before He finally comes to execute judgment. Let us therefore consider His long patience in tarrying for us (Ps. 86:15; Rom. 2:4). For if we abuse the same, it will result in nothing other than a heaping up and doubling of God's wrath toward us, so much so that it would have been better for us if He had rooted us out the first day than to have borne with us so long. Let scoffers say that respite is worth gold. There is no respite that we would not redeem with a hundred deaths, were it but possible, when we have been so stubborn against our God and so disobedient to His Word that we have made into a laughing matter His giving us some token of His anger.
>
> Let us therefore consider that as long as God is sparing us He is giving us leisure to return to Him, and that if our enemies have left us alone, it shows His favor to us, that we might act to prevent His wrath. But if we will neither hear Him when He speaks nor receive His warnings, then we will need to give ear to these His threats here set forth, and it becomes necessary for Him to send us off to another school. It is of the wonderful goodness of our God that when we have thus provoked Him (as we see we do), yet He forbears us and does all to recover us to Himself, not by forcing us with many strokes, but by attracting us after a loving fashion, being ready to receive us to His mercy, not standing as a judge to vex and to condemn us.
>
> But what? When we have shown contempt for all this, it must come to pass in the end (as I have said before) that our Lord will stir up against us other masters, so that the wicked will rise up against us and seek to make a slaughter of us by butchering and murdering us, being in very deed the executors of God's vengeance — of which we were warned long beforehand, though we chose to laugh at it, continuing in our sins and wickedness. That is why I said that as long as God speaks to us, and we condemn ourselves and acknowledge our sins and seek atonement with our God that we may live in peace in this world, then even if it is

God's will that we should have enemies and be kept occupied with wars, yet notwithstanding He holds us still in His keeping, and we are maintained and defended by His power and goodness. [Below, pp. 152-53.]

There can be little doubt that Calvin believed in a covenantal view of history in which the ethical character of men's lives affect their outward conditions. The judicial content of Calvin's ethical system was explicitly biblical. Without this belief in covenantal cause and effect in history, there could be no possibility of creating an explicitly biblical social theory. That such a view of history is rejected by most Protestant theologians today, and has been rejected as far back as 1700, explains why no Protestant group other than the Christian Reconstructionists have attempted to devise a uniquely biblical social theory. It also helps to explain the enormous hostility of modern Calvinist theologians and fundamentalist church leaders to Christian Reconstructionism: they hate Old Testament law with a passion. Even more than this, they hate the idea of God's sanctions in history in terms of this law, for such a view of sanctions would make Christians morally responsible for applying His law to the details of life, preaching the conclusions publicly, and enforcing them wherever legally possible. In short, it would make Christians responsible for what goes on in society. Responsibility on this scale is what modern Christianity for over a century has desperately sought to avoid.

Ethically Random History:
A Non-Calvinist Theology

We now come to the third aspect of this inquiry: the concept of history taught at Calvinist seminaries. Before beginning this inquiry, let us once again consider Calvin's view of the covenantal nature of God's sanctions. He insisted that this covenantal relationship did not end with the New Covenant era:

> Now Moses says that this people shall be an astonishment, a proverb, a byword, and a ridicule among the nations in which they will be dispersed. Here our Lord shows that as His goodness should be displayed among the people of Israel, so that every man

should rejoice in the seed of Abraham, so should the very same people be abhorred and detested. The promise to Abraham was thus: All nations shall be blessed in thy seed. Of course, it is true that we must look to our Lord Jesus Christ, who is the very bond of the seed of Abraham, or else this blessing has no place or ground to stand upon. Yet notwithstanding, they who were descended from the race of Abraham should have been blessed by God so that they might have been an example, that everyone desiring grace might say, "O God, take pity on me, as upon the children of Abraham," whom He had chosen and adopted. Such was the promise.

Behold here the threat that was laid against it: When men see how fiercely God smites the people whom He had chosen, they will be astonished at it and think thus with themselves, "Is it possible that they whom God chose should now be cast off and be persecuted and thrown under foot with all manner of reproach?" And upon this, men may say, "O God, keep me that I not fall to such a case as this people is in." Or else when they intend to curse, they might say, "God do to you as He did to those vile Jews." This much is to be understood from this place.

Now let us mark that just because the Holy Spirit spoke thus by the mouth of Moses, it was not His intention that this doctrine should serve only for two thousand years or thereabouts, which was the time the law lasted until the coming of our Lord Jesus Christ, but that we at this day must apply the same to our own use. Insomuch as God has come near to us, we must walk in His fear in spite of Satan, so that His goodness may shine in us and be perceived to remain upon us. And on the other side, when we are unthankful, and our God is as it were mocked by us, it is needful for us to think thus: "Well, we may shrink back from the way, but we shall gain nothing from all our plans, for in the end we shall surely come to shame."

In truth we see how it is said that the name of God will be blasphemed among the unbelievers because those who were counted faithful earlier have been so cast down that God may seem to have falsified His promise and to have deluded them, so far forth must the vengeance of God extend. Now, seeing that this is so, let us learn to submit ourselves to our Lord while He allures us to Himself with gentleness, and so hold ourselves under His obedi-

ence that we may not become a byword and a ridicule to all the
wicked, who seek nothing but to blaspheme God and to make a
mock of us. Let us, I say, look well to that. [Below, pp. 190-91.]

His language could not have been any plainer. Because of this,
we can say without question that what parades itself as modern
Calvinism is a far cry from Calvin in the area of the doctrine of
the covenant. In fact, it is the opposite of Calvinism, covenantally
speaking. It is one long denial of the ethical cause-and-effect
relationship in history that Calvin insisted on, again and again.

Modern Calvinism is generally either amillennial or premillen-
nial. It denies that covenant-keepers in history will receive sufficient external blessings of God to overcome the efforts of covenant-
breakers to suppress the gospel and the civilization that springs
from it. Similarly, they deny that God's negative sanctions in
history will weaken the covenant-breakers sufficiently to make
their resistance to the gospel successful in the long run. In short,
they deny Calvin's view of the covenant.

Calvin was a postmillennialist. He may not have been one
with the consistency that Bahnsen alleges,[13] but there was defi-
nitely a postmillennial strain to his theology, although he sometimes made amillennial-like statements.[14] The Puritans adopted
his postmillennial views, while continental Calvinism after 1800
adopted his amillennial elements. But there is no doubt that his
views on God's sanctions in history tended toward postmillennialism: the inescapable triumph of covenant-keepers in history, before Jesus returns in final judgment.

Meredith Kline vs. John Calvin

Calvinist theologian Meredith Kline, a consistent amillennial-
ist, is an equally consistent opponent of Calvin's ethics-based
social theory. He has fully understood the inescapable connection
between Calvin's covenantal view of historical sanctions and post-

---

13. Greg L. Bahnsen, "The *Prima Facie* Acceptability of Postmillennialism," *Journal of Christian Reconstruction*, III (Winter 1976-77), pp. 69-76.

14. Gary North, "The Economic Thought of Luther and Calvin," *ibid.*, II (Winter
1975), pp. 102-6.

millennialism. He therefore rejects Calvin's covenantal view of historical sanctions. He adopts a view of ethical cause and effect in history which is essentially random — "largely unpredictable," in his words — in the name of the doctrine of common grace. "And meanwhile it [the common grace order] must run its course within the uncertainties of the mutually conditioning principles of common grace and common curse, prosperity and adversity being experienced in a manner largely unpredictable because of the inscrutable sovereignty of the divine will that dispenses them in mysterious ways."[15] Compare this view with Calvin's view of *non-random, providential history:*

> Thus you see how we may possess and enjoy the blessings of God, which are set forth for us in His law. And when we see that our Lord interlaces these blessings with many afflictions and corrections, as though He had cursed us, we must realize that His purpose in this is to provoke us day by day to repentance, and to keep us from falling asleep in this present world. We know that our pleasures make us drunken and unmindful of God unless He constrains us by pricking and spurring us forward. Thus you see how things that at first sight seemed contraries agree very well in fact. And in that respect does Moses say that these blessings shall light upon us and encompass us round about, as if he had said that we will always be certain of God's favor — so certain of it that it shall never fail us if we serve Him.
>
> For the word "encompass," or to light upon us ["overtake," Dt. 28:2], indicates that the grace of God is not fleeting, *as though it fell at random* and as though we would not be able to catch it. No, says Moses, you shall be surrounded or encompassed with it. And therefore let us assure ourselves that the goodness of our God shall never fail us, so that we can never come to that goodness unless He draw us to Himself. And since we are subject to so many infirmities and vices, He, by bearing with us, shows us that we must have recourse to His free goodness for the forgiveness of our sins by the reconciliation that He has made in our Lord Jesus Christ, and that we, in straining ourselves to do His will, shall

---

15. Meredith G. Kline, "Comments on an Old-New Error," *Westminster Theological Journal*, XLI (Fall 1978), p. 184.

perceive that the goodness of God does not cease to be free to us, without owing us anything at all. [Below, pp. 93-94, emphasis added.]

To see the world in terms of ethically (covenantally) unpredictable events necessarily involves the adoption of either a deistic view of the world — a wound-up clock — or else the rule of chaos. Calvin understood this, and he rejected both views, but especially Deism's view:

You see then how we must understand that all the afflictions and miseries we endure in this world are indeed strokes from God's own hand. And along these lines it is said by the prophet Amos, "Is there any evil in the city that God has not done?" (Amos 3:6). That is to say, "Can there happen either war or pestilence or famine or disease or poverty or any other calamity whatsoever, that does not come to you from God? Wretched people, are you so foolish and beastish as to imagine that God, who created the world, has left it at random and has no care to watch over His creatures, or to bestow on them what He thinks fitting for them? Does He not sometimes show His goodness and sometimes make them feel Him as judge, punishing the sins of men, and making men know what His office is? Do you think that He lives idle in heaven, and that He does not set forth His power, or that the world is not guided and governed by His providence?" [Below, p. 140.]

Calvin's view of history was that the basis of history's unfolding is neither gnostic (hidden principles) nor Deistic (mathematical-mechanical principles). He did not think that we should despair of finding God's hand in history, either because of its supposedly hidden nature or because of its replacement by scientific laws. I wish that we could say as much for Kline's view.

Calvin also did not adopt an interpretation of Genesis 1 that denied its historicity — seven literal days — even though such a reworked interpretation (the "literary framework hypothesis") makes it appear that Genesis 1 can be conformed to pagan evolutionary scientists' very different timetable. He clearly recognized that scientific cause and effect is not a valid substitute for God's revealed causes and effects.

Now finally it is here declared to us that the course of nature, as we call it, is nothing but the disposition of the will of God, and that He bears such rule over both heaven and earth and over rain and fair weather, that He changes them at His own pleasure, and yet does not send either without cause. If there were a permanent order in nature, it would seem unto us that God never meddled with it; we would grant that He made the world, but we would then say that He does not govern it. We would think thus: "What? When the springtime comes, we see that the rest of the year goes on in the same course as did the year before. It is always the same." But in fact we see one winter is longer, and another winter later, and another earlier yet longer; we see one winter rainy, and another dry; we see abundance of snow in one year, and another year none at all; one year is hot, another cold. Now, does not such inequality make it manifest that God is at work? For the sun performs his office in one year as well as in the next, and always keeps his just course better than the best clocks in the world. How, then, do we get such variety of weather? It is God's doing, to call us to Himself.

Truly the philosophers (and scientists) do seek out causes as they term them. There is such a meeting of stars (say they), and this proceeds of such and such a conjunction. But where does all this come from, if not from the hand of God? We must always resort to the first cause. And indeed, such men are nothing more than beasts if they will not admit that!

Yet it is not sufficient to know that God guides all His creatures, and that He holds them bridled in order to make them bow, just as a horseman makes his horse to turn on this hand and on that, to stop, and to run. It is not enough to know that God looses and binds and sends such changes as He likes; rather, we must also understand that God does nothing without reasons. For if we say that God governs the world and do not know why He plagues us, we shall quickly be inclined to murmur against Him. And meanwhile we shall not profit under His chastisements and corrections, but continue dulled in our sins. So then, let us mark that in shutting up the heavens that it yields no rain, and in drying up the earth as if it were iron, He is showing us our sins and that

He is our judge. This is what we have to bear in mind concerning the course of nature, as it is here declared to us. [Below, pp. 143-44.]

Calvin paid more attention to the biblical concept of providence than he did to science. I wish that we could say as much for Kline.[16] On the question of historical cause and effect, to speak of Meredith Kline's Calvinism makes about as much sense as speaking of Calvin Klein's Calvinism.

Conclusion

The Covenant Enforced could have been called *The Forgotten Calvin.* John Calvin's theonomic legacy has been neglected by his spiritual heirs ever since the restoration of King Charles II in 1660. English and colonial American Puritanism became increasingly pietistic after the Restoration. Continental Calvinism also became pietistic. Both wings abandoned Calvin's respect for Old Testament law. Both wings abandoned Calvin's view of ethical cause and effect. Both wings abandoned his postmillennialism.[17]

There were ambivalent aspects of Calvin's thought. Like his postmillennialism, Calvin's theonomy was not rigorous. He did make statements against the legalistic, communistic Anabaptists that made him appear to be hostile to the Mosaic law, leading Rushdoony to criticise him for having taught "heretical nonsense."[18] We need to recognize that the social and theological issues of the

---

16. At least some of those of us who were attending Westminster Theological Seminary in the early 1960's recognized that Edward J. Young's *Studies in Genesis 1* was a rejection of Kline's view, although Young politely used Nic Ridderbos as a stalking horse. It is sad that Young's son Davis did not follow in his father's footsteps.

17. The postmillennialism of Jonathan Edwards and his followers was not theonomic; it was pietistic and emotional rather than cultural. Gary North, *Political Polytheism: The Myth of Pluralism* (Tyler, Texas: Institute for Christian Economics, 1989), ch. 7, subsection on "The Great Awakening." The postmillennialism of the Princeton tradition was also unconnected with considerations of biblical law. See Gary North, *Dominion and Common Grace: The Biblical Basis of Progress* (Tyler, Texas: Institute for Christian Economics, 1987), Appendix A.

18. R. J. Rushdoony, *The Institutes of Biblical Law* (Nutley, New Jersey: Craig Press, 1973), p. 9.

sixteenth century were less developed than today's discussions in many respects, despite the far greater intellectual rigor of the theological discussions of that era compared with ours. But this should not blind us to the obvious: *John Calvin's covenant theology was in fact biblically covenantal in structure.* He believed in 1) the sovereignty of a Creator God, 2) a God who reveals Himself in history, 3) a God who lays down fixed laws, 4) a God who brings predictable historical sanctions in terms of these laws, and 5) a God who (probably) raises up His people to victory in history. He did not adopt the six loci of seventeenth-century Protestant scholasticism, with its narrow definition of theology. His Calvinism was not narrowly theological; it was cultural in the broadest sense.

In this sense, Calvin was a Christian Reconstructionist. His is a legacy worth recovering or suppressing, depending on one's agenda. (When you find a Calvinist who appears to be involved in suppression, ask yourself this question: "What is his agenda?" Then seek the answer.)

EDITOR'S INTRODUCTION

by James B. Jordan

John Calvin preached through the book of Deuteronomy on weekdays from 20 March 1555 to 15 July 1556, totalling two hundred sermons in all. T. H. L. Parker describes the circumstances of their delivery as follows: "As senior minister in Geneva, Calvin had charge of the parish and church of St. Pierre, the former cathedral. This office entailed a considerable amount of preaching. By the *Ordonnances Ecclésiastiques* of 1541, two Sunday services were ordered, with three weekday services. In 1549, however, these latter became a daily service, held first thing in the morning before most people had gone to work. Calvin himself preached at both the Sunday services each week and, from 1549, every weekday of alternate weeks."[1] Parker goes on to way that it was Calvin's custom "to preach on the New Testament on Sundays (although occasionally on psalms in the afternoon) and on the Old Testament on weekdays."[2] An examination of the Deuteronomy sermons, fifteen specimens of which are included here, will reveal that Calvin seldom preached all six weekdays in his week. Others took his place from time to time, and sometimes he preached during the interim weeks, standing in for someone else.

Calvin preached without notes and thus did not write his sermons. Living in Geneva, however, was a French refugee named

---

1. T. H. L. Parker, *Calvin's Old Testament Commentaries* (Edinburgh: T. & T. Clark, 1986), pp. 9f.

2. *Ibid.*, p. 10.

Denis Raguenier. It was learned that he "was a skilful short-hand writer and that he was taking down Calvin's sermons verbatim, for his own spiritual profit."[3] The community of French refugees put up money to support him in this, so that he could devote himself fully to it. Parker describes Raguenier's labors: "Raguenier had to be there in church with his pen and ink and paper, not only twice on Sunday but also every morning of alternate weeks, at six o-clock in summer, seven in winter, taking down every word of Calvin's sermons, ranging from about three thousand to above six thousand words in length. He then had either to write them out in longhand himself or dictate them to another scribe, keep the sheets carefully in order until the series of sermons was completed and then get that set bound and delivered to the safekeeping of the deacons."[4] Raguenier died in 1560, but his work was continued by men trained by him.

Parker comments on the accuracy of these transcriptions: "That no little errors should be made would be asking too much of men writing short-hand with a quill and ink in an unheated church. Moreover, the transcripts were not checked by Calvin himself. But the errors are remarkably few, and are nearly always such as can be easily corrected by modern authors. Thus the manuscripts can be taken as faithfully reproducing Calvin's own words."[5]

Calvin began his Deuteronomy series on 20 March 1555, immediately after a long series on Job, which had begun 26 February 1554. After Deuteronomy, he went on to Isaiah (July 1556 to September 1559). On Sundays he was preaching 1 and 2 Timothy and Titus, and then 1 Corinthians, while going through Deuteronomy on weekdays. The fifteen sermons contained in the present volume were delivered while Calvin was in the middle chapters of 1 Corinthians on Sundays.[6]

---

3. *Ibid.*

4. *Ibid.*, p. 11.

5. *Ibid.*

6. See T. H. L. Parker, *The Oracles of God: An Introduction to the Preaching of John Calvin* (London: Lutterworth Press, 1945), p. 161.

It is helpful to take note of the historical context in which the Deuteronomy sermons were preached. Early in 1555 came the collapse of the so-called "Libertine" party, a political faction that had opposed Calvin and the unfolding reformation of the Geneva Republic. These men, under their leader Ami Perrin, had harassed Calvin and the work of reformation for a decade. After an election in February of 1555, Calvin's friends and followers found themselves in a majority in the Genevan government. Seeing that they were losing power, the Libertine party assembled a mob in early May, but the government stood its ground in favor of Calvin's reforms. On May 16, the leaders of the Libertine party became involved in a scandalous public disturbance, and fled the city. The Reformation had finally won peace in Geneva.[7]

All of this happened just as Calvin was beginning his series on Deuteronomy, and sheds light on the freedom with which he makes applications from the book. Calvin was enabled to make positive suggestions for the reform of Christian society in an atmosphere of encouragement and freedom that he had not previously known. As Farley puts it, "Throughout the series Calvin never tired of stressing the importance of a God-fearing and well-ordered state, supported by a responsible and decent citizenry, led by a pious and accountable magistracy."[8]

Translation

The sermons on Deuteronomy were issued in an English translation by Arthur Golding in 1583,[9] and reissued twice in the same

---

7. For a fuller summary of these events, see B. W. Farley's remarks in his introduction to *John Calvin's Sermons on the Ten Commandments*, ed. by Benjamin W. Farley (Grand Rapids: Baker Book House, 1980), pp. 14ff. The sermons on the Ten Commandments are extracts from the complete Deuteronomy series.

8. *Ibid.*, p. 18.

9. *The Sermons of M. John Calvin Upon the Fifth Booke of Moses called Deuteronomie:* Faithfully gathered word for word as he preached them in open Pulpet; Together with a preface of the Ministers of the Church of Geneva, and an admonishment made by the Deacons there. Also there are annexed two profitable Tables, the one containing the chiefe matters; the other the places of Scripture herein alledged. Translated out of French by Arthur Golding. At London, Printed by Henry Middleton for George Bishop. Anno Domini 1583.

year.[10] The Golding translation has been reissued recently in its original typeface by the Banner of Truth Trust (1987). While the complete Deuteronomy sermons have never been given a more modern translation, the sermons on the Ten Commandments were retranslated and published in 1980 by Benjamin W. Farley.[11]

The present effort is not a new translation from the French, desirable as such would be. I haven't the skill or training to do it, and the costs involved put such a project far out of reach for the present publisher. What I have done is modernize Golding's translation. This has involved the following:

1. I have translated older English words and phrases into modern English, using the *Oxford English Dictionary*.

2. I have smoothed out Golding's prose in places where it seemed more tortured than necessary.

3. I have broken up some extremely long sentences.

4. I have added a great many new paragraph divisions. Golding's version of Sermon 149 contains seven paragraphs; my version contains forty-five. Calvin did not speak in paragraphs, of course, so this is simply for the ease of the reader.

5. I have added titles to the sermons and sub-heads, neither of which come from Calvin or Golding.

6. I have placed Scriptural references in parentheses. Most of these come from Golding's marginal notes, but some are my own. Almost all of these are editorial, since Calvin seldom cited chapter and verse when he alluded to other portions of Scripture.

7. I have provided a few footnotes to explain obscure matters and to compare Calvin's remarks in these sermons with statements he makes elsewhere, particularly in his lectures on the five books of Moses.[12]

---

10. Printed by Henry Middleton for I. Harrison; Printed by Henry Middleton for T. Woodcocke.

11. See note 7 above.

12. John Calvin, *Harmony of the Pentateuch*. I refer to the translation by Charles William Bingham, originally published by the Calvin Translation Society in four volumes in the nineteenth century, and currently available in the set of *Calvin's Commentaries* published by Baker Book House of Grand Rapids.

8. At the same time, I have not taken the liberty of completely rephrasing Golding's prose, because I did not want to risk departing too far from Calvin's own style. Thus, the reader will find a certain "archaic flavor" even in the present volume.

Let me illustrate with a section from Sermon 157 (one of my short paragraphs). Here is Golding's original, with spelling of obvious words modernized but no changes in words and phrasing:

> Now let us come to that which Moses saith farther. *He saith that GOD will strike the despisers of his law with many diseases.* He hath spoken heretofore of fevers, and of the whotte [hot] disease, and of the yellow jaundice, and of such others: now he speaketh of the Itch and canker *and of other worms and scabs.* Where also mention is made of the Hemorrhoids, as some do expound them; all these foresaid things be the weapons of GOD, to punish the offenders of the Law. To be short, they be his men of war to encounter with us, when he seeth that we take heart of grass [grace] against him. And truly when we favor our own lusts to violate his righteousness, and to break the order which he hath established among us: and when he seeth our lusts to be so inordinate which are thieves and robbers: he armeth his people and substitutes which be the diseases that are here spoken of, and other sorts.

Now here is my updated rendering:

> Now let us come to what Moses says next, that God will strike the despisers of His law with many diseases (v. 27). He has spoken earlier of fevers and of inflammations and of the yellow jaundice, as well as of others. Now he speaks of the itch and canker and of other worms and scabs. Mention also is made of hemorrhoids, as some understand it. All these things are the weapons of God, to punish the offenders of His law. In brief, they are His men of war to fight against us, when He sees that we take courage against Him. And indeed, when we favor our own lusts to violate His righteousness, breaking the order He has established among us, and when He sees our lusts to be so inordinate as to be thieves and robbers, then He arms His people and substitutes, which are the diseases that are here spoken of and other sorts as well.

In this paragraph are two obscure older English phrases. The first

is "whotte disease." A search in the *Oxford English Dictionary* led
to "hot disease" and provided "inflammation" as a modern equivalent. The second is "heart of grass." The *Oxford English Dictionary*
states that "heart of grace" means courage, and "to take up a
heart of grace" means "to pluck up courage." "Grass" is an
alternate spelling for "grace," according to the *Oxford English
Dictionary*. Finally, the last sentence in this paragraph is a bit
obscure, so I added an explanatory footnote, which reads: "That
is, He arms His people (our enemies) to make war on us, or else
He sends substitute warriors (diseases)."[13]

In reading these sermons I recommend bearing in mind that
they were delivered orally. Calvin's spoken sentences are long,
and they build phrase upon phrase. If you read them aloud, or
"listen silently" instead of reading rapidly, you will find them
easier to follow.

Calvin and the Law

In his Publisher's Preface to the present volume, Dr. Gary
North addresses the question of whether or not John Calvin was
a "theonomist." As North recognizes, this is somewhat of an
anachronistic question, but circumstances within the Calvinistic
community today virtually force the question to be raised anyway.
If we distinguish between a theoretical and strict "Theonomic"
viewpoint on the one hand, and more practical and loose
"theonomic" viewpoint on the other, we might say that Calvin
was not a Theonomist but a theonomist. That is, an examination
of Calvin's theoretical writings on the judicial aspects of the Mosaic law will reveal that he believed that they were given to Israel
in a rather unique fashion, and are not binding on modern civil
governments.[14] Yet, an examination of Calvin's practical writings
and sermons (such as the sermons on Deuteronomy) will reveal
that he used the Mosaic law, including its judicial aspects, as the

---

13. See page 158 below.

14. Godfrey summarizes Calvin's position, writing that Calvin "believes that the
moral law of God undergirds all specific laws and that the specific laws of Moses
expressed that moral law for Israel in its unique historical circumstances. The civil

foundation for social, political, and legal wisdom, and generally favored imitating the Mosaic laws in the modern world.[15]

In viewing Calvin's thought in its own context, it would be better to view him in terms of the preceding thousand years of *corpus Christianum.* In this model, the Church exists as an institution of worship and as a sanctuary in the center of society, while around her is gathered the body politic, headed by a devout ruler whose job it is to guarantee Christian peace and to protect and support the Church.[16] In a rough way, we can say that the primary concern in this model is with the Godly ruler, rather than with the law of God in the abstract. The Church labors to produce Godly sons, who will be Godly magistrates, whose minds will be informed with Godly wisdom, and who will make proper applications of the fundamental principles of the Bible to their societies.

After all, in reforming the city of Geneva, Calvin did not deliver two hundred lectures on common grace or natural law, but preached two hundred sermons on the book of Deuteronomy. He made full and direct applications from Deuteronomy into his modern situation, without apology. He viewed Biblical law as foundational and as the starting point for legal and socio-political reflection.

The specific question before Calvin in Deuteronomy 27 and 28 is the question of God's providential manipulation of historical events to bring blessing and judgment upon His people. Many modern Calvinists hold that God does not make a visible distinction between righteous and wicked communities in history during

---

laws of Moses as a whole are abrogated in the New Covenant although the equity or moral foundation of those laws remains. . . . A key category for Calvin in distinguishing moral from civil law in the Mosaic economy is that the moral law is permanent while the civil is temporary." W. Robert Godfrey, "Calvin and Theonomy," in William Barker and W. Robert Godfrey, eds., *Theonomy: A Reformed Critique* (Grand Rapids: Zondervan, forthcoming [1990]).

15. For a full survey, see Jack W. Sawyer, Jr., "Moses and the Magistrate: Aspects of Calvin's Political Theory in Contemporary Focus" (Th.M. thesis: Westminster Theological Seminary, 1986).

16. This is very close to the Bible's own model of society, at least in the Kingdom and Restoration periods. See James B. Jordan, *Through New Eyes: Developing a Biblical View of the World* (Brentwood, TN: Wolgemuth & Hyatt, 1988), chaps. 12-19.

the present age, though of course He will make a radical distinction in the world to come. The view often advocated or assumed today in Reformed circles is that a system of historical blessings and curses, prosperity and judgment, was a unique aspect of the covenants of the Old Testament, part of the teaching devices God was using at that time. Thus, Deuteronomy 28 has no practical relevance for us today, except to display how God feels about obedience and sin, and to give us a verbal picture of heaven and hell.

This is not Calvin's own view. As the reader will see as he goes through the present volume, Calvin is sensitive to the fact that in the New Covenant believers are under a more "mature" system of rewards and punishments. Sometimes God rewards believers with suffering, in order to make them more righteous and to help them lay up treasures in heaven. Because of the greater "maturity" of the Church, God's blessings and judgments may be postponed longer, or be slower in coming into play. Because of the completion of the canon of Scripture, we are to live in terms of the Bible and rely less upon providential blessings and curses for indications of God's favor and displeasure.

Calvin is sensitive to such considerations as these; but he does not throw out the baby with the bath water. As a devotee of Augustine, Calvin reflects the classic discussion of rewards and chastisements found in Augustine's *City of God*, Book 1. Augustine writes, "For though, if obvious punishment should now be visited for every sin, it would be thought that nothing is reserved for the last judgment, yet on the other hand, if no sin were now plainly punished by divine action, men would believe that there is no such thing as divine providence" (sect. 8).[17]

Thus Calvin states, "Now let us mark that just because the Holy Spirit spoke thus by the mouth of Moses, it was not His intention that this doctrine should serve only for two thousand years or thereabouts, which was the time the laws lasted until the coming of our Lord Jesus Christ, but that we at this day must

17. Saint Augustine, *The City of God Against the Pagans*, trans. George E. McCracken. Loeb Classical Library (Cambridge: Harvard University Press, 1957), p. 37.

apply the same to our own use."[18] He concludes this section of his remarks: "Therefore, when we look at such a mirror [the history of the Jews], let us learn to make a good use of it, and let their example serve to seal this doctrine and to confirm it, so that we do not test God, and so that we not continue hardhearted so long that He decides to wrap us up in reproach with all the rest of the nations of the world."[19]

A Note on Calvin's Pessimism

The reader of these sermons will no doubt be struck by the fact that, despite the encouraging and optimistic tone of the Biblical passage under consideration, Calvin manages to turn his remarks mostly to a discussion of suffering and affliction. Indeed, Calvin assures us that earthly prosperity is less in view in the New Covenant than in the Old, since the main purpose of earthly prosperity is to cause us to look beyond this world to the next.

Consulting Calvin's remarks on Mark 10:30, which says that those who follow Christ will receive a hundred-fold "in this life," with persecutions, and in the world to come eternal life, we find that Calvin states that "in the greater number of cases, those who have been deprived of their parents, or children, . . . are so far from recovering their property, that in exile, solitude, and desertion, they have a hard struggle with severe poverty. I reply, if any man estimate aright the immediate grace of God, by which he relieves the sorrows of his people, he will acknowledge that it is justly preferred to all the riches of the world."[20]

Later Reformed thought, seeking to be consistent with other, more optimistic strains in Calvin's thought (and in Holy Scripture), noted that while individuals may not receive the precise promise of Mark 10:30, the church as a corporate body will someday inherit the earth. Moreover, the goal of redemption is

---

18. Sermon 159, p. 191 below.

19. *Ibid.*, p. 192. See other illustrations in the Publisher's Preface by Gary North, above.

20. John Calvin, *Harmony of the Evangelists*, vol. 2, p. 407. In *Calvin's Commentaries* (Grand Rapids: Baker Book House, [19th c.] n.d.).

not escape from this world, but the restoration of the cultural mandate originally given to Adam; thus, earthly prosperity is not merely a type of the new Heavens and Earth, but a proper blessing in itself. There is no need to pit such things against each other.

The reasons for Calvin's relative pessimism are not far to seek. First, at the time of the Reformation, so many pressing problems confronted the Reformers the they were unable to devote much systematic attention to the problems of prophecy and eschatology. Neither Luther nor Calvin took up an exposition of the book of Revelation, for instance. Second, there was so much persecution of the true, orthodox faith in Calvin's day, that it is easy to see why he focuses pastorally on this problem in his writings and sermons. Third, Calvin himself was much afflicted with illnesses of the body.

The second generation of Reformers was almost universally postmillennial, and this view was the standard Calvinistic view both on the continent and in Anglo-American cultures until the mid-nineteenth century and later. Did this represent a departure from Calvin, or a development and fulfillment of the basic conceptions in his theology? At the very least, we have to say that there is an incipient postmillennialism in Calvin's thought, though there is also an incipient amillennialism.[21]

Those wishing to investigate the matter will find Calvin speaking very optimistically about the earthly future of the Church in his Commentaries on Isaiah 60:4 and Psalm 110:3, for instance. A reading of the prayers that conclude Calvin's lectures will also show this optimistic strand, such as the prayers which close the 61st lecture in Daniel and the 34th on Hosea.

Calvin's outline of history is found in his comments on 2 Thessalonians 2, verses 3-8. First, the gospel is preached to all nations. Then there is an apostasy, resulting in the rise of the Papacy. The Papacy will be beaten back by the preached word (v. 8). The underlying principle of antichrist will finally be de-

21. See James B. Jordan, "Calvin's Incipient Postmillennialism," available from Biblical Horizons, P.O. Box 132011, Tyler, TX 75713.

stroyed at the second coming of Christ.[22]

Thus, while Calvin's pastoral application of the blessings and curses of Deuteronomy 27 and 28 often focuses most heavily on the blessings of the world to come, there is also abundant evidence in his thinking of a positive appreciation of external cultural blessings in this life as well, such as peace and prosperity.

---

22. See also Ronald Wallace, *Calvin, Geneva, and the Reformation* (Grand Rapids: Baker, 1988), pp. 37-40.

1

ALTARS AND ENSIGNS

Sermon 149. Thursday, 27 February 1556.
Deuteronomy 27:1-10.

26:18. And the LORD has today declared you to be His people, a treasured possession, as He has promised you, and that you are to walk in all His commandments;

19. and that He will set you high above all nations He has made, in praise, and in name, and in honor; and that you will be a holy people to the LORD your God, as He has spoken.

27:1. Then Moses with the elders of Israel commanded the people, saying, Keep all the commandments I command you this day.

2. So shall it be on the day when you will pass over the Jordan to the land the LORD your God is giving you, that you shall set up for yourself large stones, and plaster them with lime,

3. And you shall write on them all the words of this law, when you have passed over, in order that you may enter the land the LORD your God is giving you, a land flowing with milk and honey, as the LORD, the God of your fathers, has promised you.

4. So shall it be when you cross the Jordan, you shall set up these stones on Mount Ebal, as I command you this day, and you shall plaster them with lime.

1

5. And there you shall build an altar to the LORD your God, an altar of stones; you shall not use an iron tool on them.

6. You shall build the altar of the LORD your God of whole [uncut] stones, and you shall offer on it burnt sacrifices to the LORD your God,

7. and you shall sacrifice peace offerings, and shall eat there, and rejoice before the LORD your God.

8. And you shall write on the stones all the words of this law very plainly.

9. And Moses and the Levitical priests spoke to all Israel, saying, Be silent and listen, O Israel. This day you have become a people for the LORD your God.

10. You shall therefore hearken to the voice of the LORD your God, and do His commandments and His statutes, which I command you this day.

In yesterday's lecture, Moses, having exhorted the people to serve God, declared that the covenant He had made with them was to their great profit. The more God bestows on us, the more particularly we are bound to give ourselves over wholly to Him, if we are not devoid of all sense and reason.

But yet for all that, even though we see that God is so liberal towards us, are we moved to offer ourselves in obedience to Him? No indeed! For this reason Moses said to the Jews that they had been chosen to be in praise, in name, and in glory, as a people separated out from the rest of the world, and unto God (Dt. 26:18, 19).

Some expound this to mean that they were "in praise and glory" so that God might be glorified. This, however, is a hard and forced exposition. It is, of course, true that God has chosen His people for His own Name, as the end for which He created all things, as it is often said in Holy Scripture. And the Church was built especially for the purpose of exalting the Name of God, as it is said in the prophet Isaiah (42:8), and as St. Paul also leads us to understand in the first chapter of Ephesians (v. 6), where he treats this thing at greater length. It is,, therefore, true in itself that God adopted the Jews so that they might know His exceeding favor and goodness, and that the glory due Him might be given Him.

In this place, however, Moses has an eye to something we have already touched on, namely that the people might be moved and inflamed to discharge their duties, because God has called them for no other reason than to utter forth the infinite treasures of His mercies. And for this reason he says "God has placed you this day in praise, in name, and in honor," as he had earlier said (4:33), "What nation is so noble and of such dignity, which has its God so near to it, as your God has made Himself familiar to you, to govern you?" This, then, was a dignity God had bestowed upon the Jews above the rest of the world. This should have stirred them up all the more to be obedient to the will and the word of God.

All things considered, though, we shall find that God can hope for nothing at our hands, or receive anything from us, but that we have all things from Him. Consider: When we have taken great pains to exalt the Name of God, will He be increased at all by it? What can we do for Him? Surely we of our own nature cannot but blaspheme His Name, and we are the reason why it is blasphemed.

If He will draw any good out of us, He must first put it there. But, when God has granted us the grace to glorify Him, do we bring anything to Him, or does He receive any profit from us? Of course not. Yet, in the meantime, He continues to pour out His benefits, so that we have all from Him, as I have told you before.

So then with good reason Moses declares to the Jews that they were called to praise, to renown, and to honor. He upbraids them with their unthankfulness, if they do not endeavor to serve God with all their power, since He has been so liberal with them. And this also applies to us nowadays. For seeing that it pleases God to imprint His image in us, is this not a preeminence that He gives us above all other creatures in the world, calling us into the company of angels, and into the body of our Lord Jesus Christ? Since He goes before us with His goodness, what remains but that we should give ourselves wholly to Him, and show that, seeing He has filled us with His glory, we will not cause His Name to be made light of, nor will we permit the doctrine of salvation He has given us to be reproached that the unfaithful should make a scorn of it. Let us therefore give all diligence to this, as we see we are warned in this place.

And that is the very thing at which Moses aims when he adds that when the people have passed over Jordan, and have come into the land promised to them, and have it in full possession, they shall then set up great stones, and write on them an abridgement of the law (27:2, 3).[1] And secondly, that they shall erect also an altar, both to give thanks to God, and to testify that He had fulfilled the promise He had made in former times to their fathers. This, I say, is the intent and meaning of Moses, namely that the people should not only give thanks to God one time, but that they should also do it afresh when they come into the land promised them, and that they should ratify what they had earlier confessed, which is that they owed all homage to God for that land, because it was given to them of His free bestowed goodness, and not gotten by their own power or befallen to them by any kind of chance or by the gift or help of men.

Spokesmen for God

We have to note precisely what Moses says, that he and the elders of Israel commanded the people saying, "Do what I command you" (27:1). I grant that this might refer to Moses, because he was the chief servant of God in publishing the law, but it is certain that both he and the elders speak in the name and as it

---

1. The verses actually say that they are to write "all" the Law, not an abridgement of it. It is hard to conceive of Deuteronomy 12-26 in its entirety being written on large stones, and most commentators assume that some kind of summary is in view here. This is probably what Calvin had in mind by referring to an "abridgement" of the law. In his *Harmony of the Pentateuch* I:369 Calvin writes, "God would have its sum inscribed," again holding that some kind of abridgement was in view.

were in the person of God. And yet it would seem at first blush that this sentence is not well framed: Moses and the elders say to the people, "Do what I command you," the subject of the sentence being singular rather than plural. As I have mentioned before, however, it was needful that the Jews should be taught that these things proceed not from men but from God, who spoke through their mouths. We see then that Moses and the elders are not coming here in their own persons as attributing anything to their own worthiness, nor do they attempt to stand on their own ground to charge the people with any laws, but they stand as the instruments of God to set forth faithfully whatever is committed to them.

Now if Moses, who was preeminent among all the prophets as we shall see (Dt. 34:10), nevertheless restrained himself with such modesty that he would not usurp to himself the authority to speak in his own name, what shall we say of those who govern the Church nowadays? Do they claim to exceed Moses? Let us note, then, that pastors are not appointed to set forth whatsoever doctrine seems good to themselves, or to bring men's souls into subjection and bondage to them, or to make laws and articles of faith at their own pleasure; but rather only to bring about the rule of God, that His Word may be hearkened to. Let that be noted for one point. We see, then, that all the traditions of men existing nowadays in Popedom in the place of the pure word of God, are but vain things. They must all be beaten down, and the true government of God must be established again in His Church. And that government is that men hearken to Him, that they submit themselves to Him, that both great and small receive what is delivered in His name, and that men go no further. Let this be well noted.

But at the same time we must also note that when those who are appointed ministers of the Word of God perform their office faithfully, then they may speak with masterly authority. And indeed we hear how Moses with the rest of the elders says, "I command you this day, keep my statutes." It is not for a mortal creature to advance himself so high. No. But because Moses brings nothing of his own, but is a faithful minister of God, and does nothing but expound the law even as it is given and committed to him, therefore he does not refuse to speak as from on high, as one having all power and authority. Therefore, when we bring nothing but the pure doctrine of God, without falsifying it, without adding anything to it of our own, then we may bring into captivity all the loftiness of men, as St. Paul says (2 Cor. 10:4,5), so that no man can exempt himself from the doctrine set forth to him, but even those who are the greatest must submit themselves to it. The servants of God, then, must behave themselves in such a way that they are not of a fearful mind to yield to the world when it rebels, and must not let themselves willingly be subdued (2 Tim. 1:7). Rather, they must hold their own with invincible constancy, yielding to their Master the honor of sovereignty and the overlordship of all the world. This is what we have to bear in mind concerning this text.

A Temporary Altar

Now let us turn to what Moses said to them. The Jews are commanded to gather great stones and lime them over, and so to engrave the law of God upon them that the letters might easily be read. And secondly they are commanded to build an altar on Mt. Ebal, and there to sacrifice to God. Concerning the altar, we have already said that it was a special witness on the part of that people, doing homage to God for the land they knew they held from Him. For indeed the law was there engraved, to the intent that the remembrance of the law should be renewed, and so that its teaching should be laid open and made common to all men. Also, this was so that at their first entrance into the land they might have a marker to put them in mind, to say, "This is a land dedicated to God." And just as princes set up their arms and ensigns in the ends and borders of their dukedoms and kingdoms, even so the ensigns of God were set up in that place, that men might say, "Behold, it is the living God that has dedicated this people to Himself, and has chosen them for His service," that He might be honored and called upon by them. Thus you see in effect what we have to bear in mind.

But before we pass any further, let us consider why it is said that they are not to make or build the altar of carved or polished stones, and that they must not lift up a hammer or any other tool upon it, but that the stones must be taken as they come to hand, without any fitting of them, so that it should be a rude heap of stones. This place has troubled many men without cause. Many have not been able to find any meaning in it without resorting to allegory, saying that when God commanded to have the altar made of rough and unhewn stones, it was to show that He takes no pleasure in any inventions of men, and that He will have no curious workmanship in His altar. This was to warn us that to serve Him rightly we must never mingle in our own notions and works, just as we see it is not lawful for men to set up at their own pleasure any service for God, because He desires obedience above all things. So this sense of theirs is in itself true, though it has nothing to do with this particular text. Moses is concerned with something else, which is that there should be but one altar to sacrifice to God.

We see that when the two and one-half tribes returned home after the conquest of the land of Canaan, and erected an altar, they were in danger of being utterly destroyed and rooted out (Josh. 22). For when news of it reached the rest of the tribes, they said, "What does this mean, making a second altar to God?" Thereupon they went forth to battle, intending to destroy the tribes that dwelt beyond Jordan and to put them to horrible slaughter. This was because God had commanded that they should make only one altar. And the reason for that was to maintain the unity of faith and agreement among the Jews. We know that although the law contains the perfect teaching of salvation, yet it is at the same time dark, as we have seen. Therefore, it behooved the Jews to be tied to the teaching, that they not wander. For we see how fickle men are, so that they are easily turned aside to make various sects, and every man has his worship apart by himself. God, therefore, minded to prevent that mischief, which He saw men were given to by their sinful natures, insisted that there be only one single altar.

But now, if they had made an altar of hewn and squared stones, it would have lasted forever. And what would men have said about it? "This is the altar on which they sacrificed to God." And thereupon they would have thought it proper service to God to sacrifice on it anew. And those who came long after would have thought that the sacrifices offered there were worth more.[2] This would have overthrown the order God had established among that people. It would have brought in general confusion.

We see what befell the hill of Samaria, as the woman who spoke to our Lord Jesus Christ declares: "Did not our fathers sacrifice on this mountain?" (John 4:20). Because Abraham, Isaac, and Jacob had dwelt there, the Samaritans thought that their temple was more excellent and more holy than the temple of Jerusalem. But it was built against the will of God. It was a heathenish place. It was more full of filthiness and uncleanness than any brothel. Of course, the people thought they were doing well, but we must always consider whether God likes what we are doing, and if He does not, woe be to us! So then, because men always seem without reason to follow the examples they hear of, it was requisite that there should be no altars made of polished stones, for they would have remained in place and there would have been sacrifices offered on them.

Now we can see what abominations proceeded from this in Israel. Jeroboam, intending to maintain his estate, erected an altar in Bethel (1 Ki. 12:28f.), and wanted God to be worshipped there and sacrifices to be made to Him there. He said to the people, "Behold, we sacrifice to God, who brought us out of the land of Egypt." He protested that he was not serving idols, but he actually was serving them. He certainly was, for it was God's will to have His Temple built in Jerusalem, where it was; and

---

2. The sacrifices would be worth more because the altar was of greater antiquity than the altar in Jerusalem. During the Renaissance, when Calvin lived and worked, the notion that older was better was the operative rule among most humanists, resulting in the myth that the ancient Greeks had a high and noble civilization, a myth still common today.

we have seen already that He reserves authority to Himself to say, "You are to call upon Me in that place I have chosen to have My Name called upon." (Dt. 16:2); for it is not for men to say, "Let us worship God in this place" but men must keep themselves to what He has commanded in that regard. Jeroboam therefore, in making a second temple, brought the service of God into corruption. He distorted and falsified the true religion. Of course, he made a fair protestation, as I have mentioned, that he would change nothing in the service of God.

So we see what the meaning of God is; namely, that when they arrived in the land of promise, they should sacrifice to Him on Mt. Ebal, and there set up an altar with such stones as came to hand, without using any workmanship, so that in time the altar would deteriorate, and that no mention of it should remain to draw into an everlasting rule something done but for one time only.

Temporary Ordinances

Now although this ceremonial law does not directly apply nowadays, yet we may gather a very profitable teaching from this place. First of all, let us note that we must not ground ourselves upon something God commanded only for a certain time, as if it ought to be observed forever. For under the law it was God's will that men should sacrifice brute beasts to Him, but nowadays there is no such thing. He required that there should be incense compounded, and lights set up, and fire always burning on the altar. These things are now done away, and if any man renew them, they are but dung. We see how they are used in Popery. When the Papists come and perfume their idols' noses, they think that it is an acceptable sacrifice unto God. And when they have consumed much wax on their torches and tapers and candles, they think they have exercised a wonderful devotion. And yet all this is but a mocking of God, for it was His will to be so served under the law.

But if we should now go and try to light the sun; that is to say, if now after the coming of our Lord Jesus Christ into the world, we should yet still use those lights as in the night and in the dark, it would be a perverting of the whole order of nature.[3] The ancient fathers walked under dark shadows, and therefore they stood in need of those aids. And when they had a light, it was to show them that they were not coming to worship God by accident or at random, but that they were guided and directed by the Word of God and by His Holy Spirit. And so they were kept in line, so that they should not presume upon anything out of their own fancies. But now we have no need for all these things. Why? Because the veil of the Temple is rent asunder, and God shows us His face in the gospel, even in the person of His Son, so that we may now walk as at noonday. So then, let us consider what is everlasting, and what is but temporary, that we make no fond and foolish confusions as the Papists do.

For that is the fountain from which so many superstitions arise. When the Papists baptize, they take spittle. Why? Because Jesus Christ did so (Mark 7:33). Yes, but did He draw as a consequence that men should make a rule of it, and that His miracle should be mocked at in baptisms? Will they make a young infant to speak, by their spitting on his lips?

Again, they have the healing of the sick, and it is a sacrament to them. Why? Because the apostles used oil when they healed the sick (Mark 6:13; James 5:14). Yes, but that gift was only for the beginning of the gospel age, and afterward miracles ceased.[4] Should

---

3. Just as in nature we use lights during the night, but have no need for them once the sun has risen, so in the typology of the Old Covenant, lights were perpetually maintained in the darkness of the Tabernacle and Temple, but these are gone once the Sun of Righteousness has risen with healing in His wings (Mal. 4:2). Notice, for instance, that Nicodemus came to Jesus at night (John 3:2), and of course Nicodemus was "in the dark" concerning what Jesus said to him.

Obviously Calvin is not opposed to the use of lights in church buildings. He is opposed to the idea of keeping a perpetual "altar lamp" burning in the church, however, for the Tabernacle with its perpetual lamp has been replaced by the light of Jesus Christ.

4. James 5:14 certainly seems to indicate a permanent practice of calling on the elders to pray over the sick, and anoint with oil. Though agreeing that special miraculous gifts such as tongues and prophecy ceased with the completion of the canon and the destruction of the Temple, not all Reformed expositors have agreed

we use these signs still, knowing this? Is this not a mocking of God? I suppose, then, that the truth and substance of things must depart and the signs must remain! What a brilliant idea! Again, they hold to other things, such as Lent. This is the fast that is to be kept, say the Papists. The reason is because Jesus Christ fasted. Yes, but did He who is the Fountain of all perfection and the Mirror of all holiness, fast every year? No, He fasted but once in His life.[5] The Papists say that we must fast every year, and that there is great devotion and holiness therein. But in doing so they would exceed Jesus Christ. Surely this is a devilish superstition, to fast forty days after this manner, on the opinion that by this means we may make ourselves like Christ. For we know that our Lord Jesus meant to show by this that He was at that time excepted from the general condition of all men, as the same was done to Elijah by miracle, and likewise to Moses when he published the law. And did the Jews follow Moses and Elijah therein? Did any of the many holy prophets ever fast that fast? No, for they knew well that it was not commanded them of God, and that He made no common rule of it; and they knew that He did not want them drawing into the force of law matters He had ordained for one time only.

So then, we see that it is very profitable to consider what God has commanded for one time only, so that we do not pervert everything, or desire to do whatsoever is contained in Holy Scripture without making any distinction, without knowing first whether the matter concerns us and is spoken to us or not. This is one point to be noted.

The Unity of the Faith

A second point to be observed is that we ought, as much as

---

with Calvin on this particular point about anointing with oil. Calvin bases his interpretation on the clearly miraculous manifestation of this practice in Mark 6:13. For a discussion by the editor, see James B. Jordan, *The Sociology of the Church* (Tyler, TX: Geneva Ministries, 1986), pp. 283ff.

5. That is, He fasted for forty days only once in His life. Lent is an annual forty-day semi-fast, observed in the Roman Catholic Church, and in some other churches.

we possibly can, to maintain unity and agreement among ourselves, as we shall declare by and by. It was God's will that there
should be only one Temple. Why? Because He wanted it to be a
bond to hold the people together in the purity and soundness of
the faith: "We have only one God who is called upon among us,
and we must come into one certain place to sacrifice to Him, and
all of us must gather together there." It is indeed true that we are
not nowadays tied to any such a system, but no matter what the
circumstances are, yet the substance remains for us. Let us therefore take heed unto every aid we have to hold us in this communion of faith, and in this unity that God requires; let us keep them
well, and let no man turn aside from them.

Concerning the outward order of things, we know that our
Lord Jesus Christ would have men to assemble themselves together. I grant that we are not bound all to be in one place, and
men also preach in various churches in one town. Why? Because
the whole world cannot be present to hear one sermon. Yet for all
that, because of our slowness we are so bound that we must gather
ourselves together in the name of God. He who wants to stay at
home, despising the common order, and says, "I can read at
home and edify myself sufficiently there," that man breaks asunder the unity of the faith and tears in pieces the body of our Lord
Jesus Christ, with all his strength.

We know that baptism was ordained to serve as a common
seal that we are the Church of God, and are governed by His
Spirit. Now if every man wants to have his baptism performed
separately, what a wicked disorder that would be![6]

The Holy Supper of the Lord is also distributed as a common
food so that we should all communicate of it. We are warned by
it that we are one body. And as one loaf is made of many grains
of wheat, which are so mingled together that they make but one

---

6. The Bible, of course, does not insist on baptisms' being performed in the
course of a worship service, any more than circumcisions had been. The Protestant
Reformers were anxious to restore the reality of congregational worship, and thus
sought to bring baptism into it.

substance,[7] even so ought we to be knit together, if we want to be counted as the children of God. Therefore, if every man wants to have his own separate, private supper, is this not a withdrawing of themselves from the community and brotherhood that Jesus Christ would have us to keep?

In Popery every man must have his altar and his chapel. Indeed, they were of the opinion that God was much bound to them for so doing. There should have been one common table (I shall not go on to point out that they have turned the communion table into an altar to sacrifice upon, which thing in itself is a devilish abomination), but in the mean time, although they retain the terminology, yet they will not have a common table for all the Church.[8] For every man thrusts himself in, saying, "Oh, I will have a chapel, and there I will have my devotions by myself." When men have come to this point, it is a horrible wasting of the Church of God, and the building of so many altars has been the cause of the creation of so many sects and divisions. Even if the Papists had placed no idols in their churches, and even if they did not have such a number of superstitions and idolatries as we see they have, yet in doing this one thing they have broken the unity Christ has solemnly set among His members, and in the whole Church.

What must we do then? Let us endeavor to keep ourselves in brotherly agreement and under the signs and tokens God has given us, and let us continue in them and make use of all those means He has given us to serve to that end. That is the teaching we have to gather from this place.

The Duty of Praise

But let us now return to what we said in the beginning, which

---

7. Compare Leviticus 23:9-21. The offering of first sheaf is followed by the offering of the first loaf, on Pentecost. The Spirit's coming on Pentecost bound the individual grains of the disciples into the united body of Christ, which is the loaf.

8. "Church" here means a local church. Obviously, Calvin realizes that a common table for the world-wide church is physically impossible. In any given locale, however, there is a church, and that church should be united.

is that God here required of His people a solemn acknowledgement of how much they were bound to Him. We are therefore exhorted to acknowledge the benefits of God, and to occupy ourselves therein, so that we never forget them. The people had already given thanks to God after they had come out of Egypt, in the wilderness, where they sacrificed continually to Him; but all the same, after they passed over Jordan, they were to begin to give thanks again. Why? Because men tend always to discharge their duties to God by halves, and they soon forget them altogether, and no longer think about what they owe God. This is the reason why they are required to be occupied continually in God's service.

So then, let us note well that during the entirety of our lives we are to devote our whole endeavor to magnify and set forth the name of God. For although we are not lodged in this land of Canaan, yet the favor of God ought to be esteemed as highly by us, and indeed more so, than any earthly inheritance that was given to the children of Israel. For God, having plucked us out of the dungeons of death, and out of the bondage of Satan, declares that we are blessed by Him and that we are a royal priesthood. Who among us can discharge himself in magnifying so great and so inestimable a goodness of God? So then, because we are slow and slack to give that glory to God which is His due, and because when we have once done it, we think it enough and we are loath to do it again, let us bear in mind the lesson taught us here, which is that just as God increases His gifts to us, and just as He confirms and ratifies them, so we on our part ought to be so much the more moved and stirred up to yield Him praise, declaring thereby how much we are bound to Him, and protesting that we are wholly His and that we will dedicate our whole life to Him. This, I say, is what we have to bear in mind concerning this passage, where mention is made of sacrificing to God.

Gratitude

Now, after Moses mentions the whole burnt offering, he adds, "You shall offer also peace offerings to the LORD your God"

(v. 7). Earlier on in the books of Moses, we are told that the peace offerings served for thanksgiving, so that if God delivered His people, if He gave them any victory against their enemies, if He delivered them from famine or any other calamity, they sacrificed in witness that this benefit deserved not to be forgotten. We see then that Moses aims wholly at something we have already declared, namely that the people should make an acknowledgement of this benefit to God, after they came into the land of Canaan. And when Moses says that it is a land flowing with milk and honey, it is (as we have already seen heretofore) for the purpose of stirring up the people to give glory to God, when they see that the land is so fertile, and that God has shown Himself so liberal towards them.

We know that at this present time it is not so fruitful a land, nor was it so fertile before their coming to it,[9] and this is a wonderful thing. And yet notwithstanding, the wicked have taken occasion from this to blaspheme, as that wicked heretic who was punished here mocked both Moses and the prophets, saying that when they praised the land of Canaan they were but setting out a fable.[10] This man shows himself (as do all despisers of God and such enraged persons as are possessed by Satan) to scorn God's benefits, which men may see with their eyes. Nor did he consider that God expressly threatened to salt that land (Ps. 107:34), which is to say, to make it barren, so that at this present day men see it desolate and waste; and he maintained his false opinion despite the fact that the matter was explained to him. At any rate, it is a dreadful thing to behold the condition of that country at the present time, in comparison with what it is known to have been

---

9. This is a bit speculative on Calvin's part, especially in the light of Genesis 13:10, "The whole plain of the Jordan was well watered, like the garden of the LORD." The area around Sodom was like Eden, but was cursed with salt for its sin, though it is symbolically restored by the gospel in Ezekiel 47:8-10. The history of this region can be seen as a type, and the same pattern is played out in larger scale with Canaan as a whole, and larger still with the history of the world as a whole.

10. Michael Servetus had been executed on 27 October 1553, a couple of years before this sermon was preached, though Calvin might be referring to someone else.

like previously. The meaning of this, as said in the psalm (107:37), is that when it pleases God to bless a land with fruitfulness, it will be fat and full of all manner of fruits, and contrariwise when He lifts up His hand to make it barren, it will be totally withered. We see this to be true in the land of Canaan.

So then, let us note here that Moses meant to show more particularly the favor God showed to His people in nourishing them in a land that, a man might say, was flowing with milk and honey, showing by this figure that this was done by miracle. Now for our part, while it is true that we shall not be fed fat in respect to our bodies,[11] yet in feeling the spiritual benefits God so largely bestows on us, we ought to be moved and stirred up to this consideration: that when we have stated as solemnly as possible that we are His, and that we owe all to Him, yet we are not performing even the hundredth part of our duty of gratitude.

The Duty of Obedience

Turning now to the great stones on which God commanded His law to be written, which we have alluded to earlier, let us note that God intended to hold His people under His obedience by any means He might. For men by reason of their infirmities need to be kept in awe, and to be called back to God, so that they do not swerve aside from Him. I have already made a comparison to the ensigns of princes, instead of which God would have His law to be written. Why? Because His laws are His true ensigns, and His word is the lively image wherein we ought to behold Him. And that is why He says, "You shall come and present

---

11. Calvin is not saying that the church will never prosper; indeed, a study of the prayers Calvin prayed after his lectures and sermons reveals a most this-worldly optimism. While Calvin did not disparage material blessings, he did not expect to see much of them in Geneva during his lifetime, thus "we shall not be fed fat." Calvin always stressed the context of blessings over the sheer quantity of them. In his remarks on Mark 10:28-31 ("he shall receive a hundred fold in this life . . . and in the world to come everlasting life"), Calvin emphasizes that the Christian takes greater delight in a few good things than does the unbeliever with vast riches, because the Christian has his goods in the context of the joy of the Spirit, while the unbeliever has his goods in the context of the bitterness of sin.

yourselves before My face," when in fact they presented themselves before the Ark of the Covenant, in which the law was enclosed. For God refused to be represented to men by any other shape than the continual instruction of His word, as we have already seen in our sermon on Deuteronomy 4:12, where it is said, "Remember that you saw not the shape of a man or of any creature whatsoever, but you heard the voice of God." Take heed, therefore, lest you counterfeit anything in this regard.[12]

Now that we understand the text, let us note that when our Lord vouchsafes to have His Word preached in any place, and gives us peace and quiet as by His own hand, it is so that we might do Him double homage. All those who live in the world and are fed and sustained by God ought to confess that He is worthy to have all sovereignty over them; but we who have a special privilege from God, and who are separated from the rest of the world, and who have His Word preached to us, and who have freedom to call on His name in purity, shouldn't we enforce ourselves to do Him double homage for it? Surely this ought to be thoroughly considered nowadays.

How greatly has God favored us! We may use His sacraments with all liberty and we have our ears filled every day with the doctrines of salvation, so that He continually calls us to Himself. On the other hand, we see many wretched people who are held in bondage under the tyranny of the Pope, and dare not open their mouths or make the least endeavor to worship God in purity. They have neither churches to resort to nor any means to be taught. The whole world sees this. So then, we ought indeed to have the ensigns of God, whereby the law should be presented.

Unfortunately, we see the reverse; for as soon as any man comes near to us [here in Geneva — ed.], he should perceive a wonderful change in us, because we have withdrawn ourselves from the defilements of the unbelieving. But whereas men should see that God reigns and bears rule among us, and has His seat

---

12. A reference to the making of images of God for worship purposes, a violation of the second commandment.

and throne with us, they may actually see us as loose in living as the most ignorant people in all the world. Nay, a man may see that God is defied by some of them to whom the gospel is preached, and that there are worse devils and more wicked men among them than in the deepest dungeons of Popery. Surely this deserves a double woe, for it is not only to the Jews that Moses has spoken, but it is to show all in general that since God vouchsafes to us the favor to be His, we ought to remove all corruption from among us, that men may know that we are indeed His people.

This does not, of course, excuse those who live in Popery. No matter how much they are threatened, so that they are not able to make a free confession of their faith without danger of death, yet they are always guilty of offending God in that they have not honored Him. Now if there is no excuse for them, how much greater will be our condemnation? For there is nothing to hinder us from serving God except our own wickedness and negligence.

So then, let us be diligent to discharge our duty, not as touching the outward ceremony of great stones as commanded here, but in respect to the thing God had a special eye on, namely that every one of us should not only yield himself to His obedience, and dedicate himself to follow His will, but also that with one common accord we should show that He is our sovereign King and that we are under His government. And because He has put us in a place where His name is openly called upon and where there are churches for us to come together to make our common prayers and to confess our faith, let us also endeavor to walk in such a way that men may indeed know that those places are not defiled, but reserved to the glory of Him who has chosen them for His use.

The Ensigns of God

Now for the end and conclusion, let us note that our Lord does not want His ensigns to be blazed [published] in just any sort of way that men like, but He will have His own image to be set forth in it, and that is why He speaks purposefully of the law: "The words," He says, "of the law." The Papists have chapels, crosses, and bright paintings, and they think that God is represented by them, but God has no liking for those things. We must return to the Word, which is the means by which God opens Himself to us, and He will be known by it. Let men therefore content themselves simply therewith.

Now concerning the injunction, "Let those words be well engraved," hereby we are taught that God did not give His law for a few people, but meant that it should be a common teaching to all, both great and small, even to the most simple-minded, and that all should be instructed by it. And if this was the case in the time of the law, by greater reason it ought nowadays to be in force among us who live in the New Covenant. For it is said that the gospel is to be preached to all creatures (Mark 16:15). God will not allow His teachings to be locked up, so that none but the clergy should thrust their noses into it, but He wants all to be His scholars, and the law to be written so that every man may read it. Why? So that all men should receive instruction from it.

Let none therefore exempt themselves from the reading of it, as we see many do, saying, "Oh, I am no clerk; I never went to school; reading does not pertain to my occupation." I grant readily that it is not every man's occupation to be a teacher, but who may exempt himself from being a scholar in the word of God? A man might as well renounce Christianity as say, "Oh, as for me, I know neither A nor B [I am illiterate]; so how can I tell what the law of God or any of Holy Scripture means?" Nevertheless, the will of God as declared to us in His Word is written in letters big enough, and although nowadays we have no heap of stones set up for the law of God to be written and engraved upon, yet notwithstanding our Lord meant to show in this symbolism that when He delivered His Word it was so that we should be taught and ordered by it, and that the teaching thereof should be common to all.

And truly, we have no less need to nourish our souls with the word of God than we have to sustain our bodies with bread and other daily food. Seeing that this is so, let every one of us labor in the way, and let us be attentive to hearken to our God when

He speaks to us by the mouth of the minister; and when we have His Holy Scripture, let every man endeavor to be taught by it. Those who have no skills to read themselves, let them hear it read, that we may show that since our Lord speaks to us, we are ready to receive whatever He says, and desire nothing else except to profit under Him in such a way that His Word is not only engraved in stone and lime but also imprinted on our hearts, so that in our whole life we seek to follow it, and give ourselves wholly to it

Prayer

Now let us kneel down in the presence of our good God, with acknowledgement of the great number of faults and offenses that we cease not to commit daily against His majesty, praying Him to make us feel them better than we have, so that we may endeavor to amend them more and more until we are clean rid of them; and since we obtain pardon for them by our Lord Jesus Christ, we may also increase and be confirmed in all righteousness and holiness, that so we may indeed confirm our calling. And let us pray Him that since He has chosen us for His people, it may please Him also to withdraw us from all the defilements of the world, so that we may be to Him a holy people in the name of our Lord Jesus Christ. And let us pray that it may please Him to grant this grace not only to us but also to all people and nations of the earth; etc.

2

BLESSINGS AND CURSES

Sermon 150. Friday, 28 February 1556.
Deuteronomy 27:11-15.

9. And Moses and the Levitical priests spoke to all Israel, saying, Be silent and listen, O Israel. This day you have become a people for the LORD your God.

10. You shall therefore hearken to the voice of the LORD your God, and do His commandments and His statutes, which I command you this day.

11. Moses also charged the people on that day, saying,

12. When you cross the Jordan, these shall stand on Mount Gerizim to bless the people: Simeon and Levi and Judah and Issachar and Joseph and Benjamin.

13. And for the curse, these shall stand on Mount Ebal: Reuben and Gad and Asher and Zebulun and Dan and Naphtali.

14. And then the Levites shall answer and say to all the men of Israel with a loud voice:

15. Cursed be he who makes a graven image or a molten image, an abomination to the LORD, the work of the hands of the craftsman, and sets it up in secret. And all the people shall answer and say, Amen [So be it].

We saw yesterday how God intended that the favor He showed unto the people of Israel should be acknowledged first by solemn sacrifice, and second by the erection of a monument, so that it might be known that this land was not purchased by the hand of man, but was given by God to that people for an inheritance. But now we have another commandment, by which God meant to bind the people unto Himself in another manner. Indeed, He had done so already, but because men are so difficult to root down, and because they cannot be bound by too many bands and cords, to hold them to obedience, God had ample reason to add what is set down here, in order to keep them better under obedience.

The Usefulness of Blessings and Curses

We have already dealt with the fact that when God gave His law, it was a mutual covenant, and just as He bound Himself unto the children of Israel to be their God, so also the people of Israel bound themselves to be His people. Here, however, an additional confirmation is given, to ratify that first bond the better: God ordained that when they had passed over Jordan, the people should divide themselves into two companies, and that six tribes should stand upon Mt. Gerizim, and the other six should stand upon Mt. Ebal over against them, so that the Ark of the Covenant and the priests should stand in the midst; and that those who were on Gerizim should bless, and those who were on the side of Ebal should curse.

Now we shall look into the content of the curses and blessings later on, as we deal with the chapter. Note at this point, though, that God, in order to encourage the people, not only delivered His will to them and said, "You shall walk thus," but also added to it, "You will not serve Me in vain, and your pains will not be lost, for I will cause you to prosper, and it is for your own welfare that I would have you to be subject unto Me. I seek after no profit or advantage by this, but it is for your own benefit and ease that you should cleave unto Me in keeping My commandments." Behold what blessings God gave, intending that the people should serve Him with a willing mind and not through force or constraint. Again, because men are so stiff-necked that they cannot stoop down without raising a ruckus, and because on the other hand their lusts carry them away in such a headlong manner that they quickly forget what it is to serve God and act like wild horses that have broken loose, threats are here added: "Take heed how you offend Me, for vengeance is ready for those who despise My law." Thus you see the curses that we shall take up more fully in the twenty-eighth chapter, but Moses touches on them here by way of example.

Now it would have been enough for God to say, "Whoever will serve Me in keeping My law, he shall be blessed, and I will make his whole life prosperous for him." If God has once promised to recompense those who serve him, it ought well to suffice us. What would men need to say in their own behalf? Similarly, seeing that God pronounces a sentence of condemnation upon those who transgress His law — considering that the Judge has spoken — no man ought to reply. What need is there, then, for men to ratify what God has said, as if His Word were not of sufficient strength and authority in itself? True it is that God well deserves to be hearkened to, and whatever He says is an unchangeable decree. All the same, He wants men to witness outwardly that they accept what He wills us to follow. He wants us to acknowledge the favor offered to us, and to declare that we are assured by faith that He will not deceive us in promising us prosperity when we endeavor to live according to His Word. God, therefore, will have us to agree with Him, that we also confess in humility and fear that there is great reason why He should punish all those who despise and overthrow His righteousness and commandments.

And when He threatens them, we may not think that it is in vain, but that in the end they will feel the execution of the sentence. God therefore in this respect will have us to say "Amen" both to the promises He makes to those who keep His law, and to the threats He denounces against all those who are rebels and despisers of Him. So then, we have now made a good entrance into the understanding of this place. We shall more fully treat of the blessings and cursings when we come to chapter twenty-eight, and it is better to handle them there because that place is more fit for it. It suffices to know in a word that when God offers His favor to those who obey Him, it is to the end that they should serve Him, not through constraint, but of a free good will, knowing that it is for their own ease and welfare; and again that on the other hand such as are of their own nature given over to their lustful desires, and take to themselves a lawless liberty of living wrongly, must be restrained by such fear that they see they will not escape the hand of God, but that in the end they must come to account. So, you can see what we have to bear in mind, in a word, until we come to handle the matter more at large.

Blessings: Conditional and Unconditional

Let us, then, note well that God thinks it not enough to have spoken Himself, but He will have us also to agree as it were in one melody with Him, as we noted earlier. This is to show the faith we have in His Word, which consists in these two points: namely, that we embrace His promises and hang wholly upon them, and second, that we tremble as often as He gives us any sign of His wrath, so that we are not dense or drowsy, or so hardened that He must strike us with heavy blows before we feel His anger, but that we prevent this by endeavoring to obey Him, and avoid His vengeance as much as we can.

Now then, the blessings in this place are conditional. For example, blessed is he who observes the law of God, who maintains His service purely, who is not given to superstitions and idolatries, who does not abuse His holy Name, who observes the day of rest and all other ceremonies, who honors his father and mother. The blessing, I say, is matched with condition, so that if we serve God, He will show Himself liberal to us, and we shall not lose our time. But all these blessings depend on the fact that God of His free goodness had chosen this people, so that they were not to rest on this point as if to say "Blessed is he who serves God."[1] For after all, no man discharges himself of his duty, as

---

1. That is to say, they were not to rest on their own works and obedience, but on God's prior choice of them to be His people.

we have already declared, and as we shall see further in the end of this chapter.

Seeing then that we are all sinners, even including the faithful, so that when we endeavor to walk uprightly we still make many false steps, what will become of us? It is certain that we should all be deprived of the hope of salvation if we had nothing else to lean upon than our own righteousness. But as I have told you, the conditional promises here depend on the fact that God has received us for His people and wants us to take Him as our Father. This is grounded on nothing other than His mercy. So then, we must be thoroughly persuaded that God will take pity on us, even though we are wretched sinners and do not deserve to be pitied. He will receive us as righteous and accept us, even though we deserve to be rejected by Him. And although we can hope for nothing but utter confusion, yet notwithstanding we are assured of the inheritance of salvation because we are His children. We must be thoroughly persuaded concerning this point.

So then, seeing that God has chosen us out and set us apart for His service, we may not take license and indulge in all manner of wickedness but rather we must endeavor to obey Him. For this reason we must be quickened and pricked up by His promises to serve Him. In this way we can see how the conditional promises are not in vain with respect to us, when they are grounded on the freely bestowed goodness of God, by which He receives us even though we are not worthy to be received, not imputing our vices to us. Although there are many stains and corruptions in us, yet He hides them and does not call them to account.

And so we see now how God encouraged the people of Israel to be of good comfort. For if He had begun in this manner with them, saying, "Serve Me and you shall be well recompensed for your labor," if God should speak this simple word to us, alas! what could we do? For even when we should try to serve Him, we should be very far from the perfection that He commands. Those who should run best would be but in the middle when they should have come to the end. All of us would be discouraged rather than have a good heart. But we must join both these things together: one, that He will not deceive us in any thing; and two, that He binds us to serve Him and declares that He will bear with us in our infirmities and not deal severely with us to pay us as we deserve, but will use a fatherly goodness.

Now on this basis we may be of good comfort to serve Him, when we may say, "Surely it is true, Lord, that I do not discharge myself of the hundredth part of my duty towards You, but no matter what, You will not fail to accept me because You do not respect what I do, but take a pleasure in me as in Your own child." You see, then, how God pardons us, and does not regard our faults and imperfections, which are in the service we yield to Him. When we serve Him of a sincere good will, and not hypocritically, He likes all we do and rewards us for it. Since we hear this, let us take pains, and receive the bridle into our mouths (as they say) and press on; and even though we are hindered by the vices of our flesh, yet let us force ourselves to go further. And why? Because we shall not lose our labor.

Thus you see what God means. We perceive His inestimable goodness in that of His own good will He offers His promises to us, although He is in no wise bound unto us, as we have seen heretofore; His will is to win us to Himself by all the means that He may. Now He repeats this point again, and that is done because of our sloth and negligence. For that reason He adds this aid; and all for our profit, for what is He advantaged thereby? Will He gain anything by our service? Let us defy Him to the utmost, what will that hurt Him? But, He will possess us for our own welfare.

The Rewards of Faithful Works

And with this He shows us also what mind is requisite for observing His law properly, which is that we come willingly and yield ourselves to Him, and place our whole felicity and joy in serving Him, and put this sentence into our hearts, that where our treasure is, there will our hearts be also (Matt. 6:21). You see what we have to notice touching the first point on the blessings. In effect, then, what is it that we have to do? Although nowadays we do not have the ceremony spoken of in this place, yet the substance of it must be in force among us, which is that in seeking to serve God, we must have an eye always unto His promises. Behold! Our God calls and allures us unto Himself. And how does He do so? He might have commanded us in one word saying "You owe all to Me; see therefore that you discharge yourselves as I command." But no, He bears with us, and displays a fatherly goodness toward us in saying, "My children, I will not have your service unrecompensed. Indeed I owe you nothing, yet nevertheless I shall be so bountiful above all that you need, if you serve Me, that your life shall be happy, and you shall prosper in all things."

And besides that, there is a sovereign blessing for us concerning the life everlasting. For all that we can desire or look for in this world is nothing in comparison with the salvation we hope for through faith, and all the blessings God promises us and offers us concerning the life to come. Therefore, all this ought to make us the readier and better disposed to submit ourselves to God. Why? Because seeing that our Lord seeks nothing but our welfare in our obeying Him, and offers us a reward for so doing, are we not too incredibly wretched if we do not enforce ourselves to serve God? You can see then how we ought with our good consent to ratify all the promises contained in the Holy Scripture, that while others think it is only lost time to do well, we may always have this imprinted in our hearts: that there is nothing better than to cleave unto God.

The heathenish sort think themselves very happy in following their own lusts. When lecherous and covetous persons have scraped together money from all sides, they think that all is well and they rejoice in their deeds. If fornicators, who are brutish in their fleshly lusts, are allowed to enjoy their pleasures, they wallow in them; they are drunk with them; they are wholly bewitched by them. If a vainglorious man comes to any dignity and is advanced to any authority among men, he thinks there is no other joy or happiness but to be in high estate. At the same place are all despisers of God. And in the meanwhile, the poor faithful ones are mocked; they are poor persons; they are set at naught; they hang their wings down; they do nothing but drop and pine away in this world. These wretched souls, say some, are not well advised to take so many pains over things they do not understand, for what profit do they have for all their travail? It seems, therefore, that they who seek to serve God are greatly beguiled, and that the wicked bear sway everywhere.

But we must be thoroughly resolved on the other side, as it is said in the prophet Isaiah, "Say to the righteous that it shall be well with them, for they shall eat the fruit of their actions" (Is. 3:10). The prophet Isaiah would have us to fight against this temptation. Even though the whole world should laugh the Godly to scorn, and the wicked triumph over them, yet for all that the faithful should not be astonished, but say to themselves, "No, no, the righteous man shall not lose his labor; he shall not be deceived of his expectation when he depends wholly upon the promises of God."

What we have to gather from this place, then, is that as often as we read the promises in the Scripture where it is said, "Blessed is the man who fears the Lord; those who walk in the obedience of His Word shall be blessed; blessed is he who walks uprightly and soundly with his neighbors, but especially those who renounce the world because they have a better inheritance in heaven" (Ps. 112:1; 119:1; Matt. 19:21); as often, I say, as we read these things, we must be confirmed in our faith, and answer with a good courage: "Amen, Lord; it is so. We do not dispute what You have said. We embrace Your promises in this place, and trust assuredly in them." Thus you see how every man ought to enforce himself to serve God, because He bears with us so gently, and commands us not so precisely as He might, having all authority over us, but applies Himself to our imperfection in order to win us and to enjoy us.

And above all let us be mindful of this general promise: that God calls us to Himself as His children; that He spares us and bears with us, and does not enter into an extremity of rigor with us; and that even though there are many faults in our works, He accepts them; that if we offend we always find pardon at His hand; that when we swerve aside he brings us back onto the way; and that none of our faults is imputed to us. You see what we have to keep in mind.

The Necessity of Threats

The threatenings of God are also very necessary for us. We can see that great pride and rebelliousness are in all of us, so that even though we are not rebellious on purpose, to set God at nought and to cast off His yoke, yet we are so dimwitted that we do not think of Him much, so that the enticements of the world seduce us to the extent that we are heedless of the warnings God gives us. If He calls us by gentleness, He can get nothing out of us, and therefore He uses threats.

From this we see that He uses every proper device, to hold us in awe under His obedience. On the one hand He uses mild and loving speech toward us (as I have already discussed), saying, "Come to Me, My children. Indeed, I owe you nothing, but still I shall bind Myself to you. I promise you that if you serve Me, it shall be for your profit." Thus our Lord speaks to us, as a Father that encourages His child in order to win him to be ruled by Him and to employ himself in His service with a free-hearted affection. On the other hand God, perceiving that this is not enough to move us, uses threats and says, "Take heed. If you think to cast away My word and yet remain unpunished, you deceive yourselves. I must call you to account for it. I will not allow My children to mock Me. I must be their judge. Do not look for any pardon when you have abused My patience. I must double your punishments, and My vengeance must fall horribly upon you."

Therefore, when God declares that our sins are unpardonable, and yet we continue in them and make no account of submitting ourselves to Him, especially since He has applied Himself in every way to us so that we should remain in His obedience and not perish; since we see that He has such a care for our salvation, must it not be the case that we are entirely too stubborn, indeed very beasts, if we are not moved to better behavior by the fatherly care He shows towards us? Yes indeed.

And therefore, being stirred up by the goodness and gentleness of God, of which even now I speak, let us also wake ourselves up with His threatenings. When we see that our flesh is wanton, and that it draws us unto evil, let us say, "Alas, should we shake off His yoke like wild beasts? What has God said?" Let us therefore tremble when we hear the threats of our God. For if the anger of an earthly king is the messenger of death, as Solomon says (Prov. 16:14), what ought we to think of the anger of God when it is announced against us?

So then, let us learn to tame ourselves with fear. When the temptations of Satan start to prevail over us, and our sins act as baits to deceive us, let it come into our minds to say, "What? Shall I under the delusion of some pleasure that will soon vanish, go and provoke the anger of my God and so perish forever?" After that manner, I say, we ought to call God's threatenings to our remembrance, and then answer "Amen" to them, saying, "Indeed, Lord, it is even so; it is no children's game. When You pronounce condemnation upon the wicked, You are ready to execute it, and when You have once pronounced the word with Your mouth, it is all the same as if we saw the fire already kindled to consume us."

In this way, I say, we ought to receive all the threats God utters against us, for that is the best means to teach us to observe the law. I mean, as far as our weakness will allow it; for as I have told you it is not possible for us to come to total perfection as long as we are enclosed in this flesh of ours. All the same, we may well dedicate ourselves to God, and be held in His fear, if on the one hand His promises are in force with us, and on the other we give ear to His threatenings.

Instruction From God

Let us now look at the order here set out. Moses, together with the priests of the tribe of Levi, commanded the people that six tribes were to stand on Mt. Ebal, and six on Mt. Gerizim. And afterwards He said, "Keep My statutes and commandments, which I command you this day, for you are made a people unto your God." This has already been expounded, but it is good to bear in mind always what has been said concerning it, which is that God speaks by the mouth of His priests as if He were there visibly in His own person. And that is so that His words should be received with the greater reverence. For when we see men who are just as mortal as we are, we are of the opinion that whatever proceeds from them may very well be rejected, and if no account is made of it, we think that the matter is not very important. And thus we see that the Word of God is often esteemed lightly. For when we see no one speaking but creatures like ourselves, we think that their pronouncements are nothing but a sounding of words.

But God wants the majesty of His words to be known, and even though it is brought by men, He will not have its worth to be diminished so that men ignore it, but He will have every man to bow before it and receive the yoke He puts on him. God therefore speaks in this place of Moses and the priests, but in such a way and in such language as to cause the people to lift up their minds higher, to realize that although they are taught by the means and ministry of men, yet they ought to confess that God is the Author of the word that men preach to them, and they ought to receive it as from God Himself and so be silent in listening to it, making no reply or criticism of it. For such contempt is not aimed at the mortal creature, but God Himself is despised by it. Therefore, let us note well all the ways in which God authorizes His Word, that we may be held to it and be ordered by it, so that every one of us bows down his head submissively as often as men speak to us in the name of God.

And moreover, we also see the order God has appointed in His Church. He will have all the world answer "Amen," for we ought all to be partakers of His teaching. It must not be kept stored away only for great men, but the smallest also must be instructed by it, so that they might be edified and profited by it. But however the case stands, there were always priests to speak, who were ordained to teach the people, as it is said in Malachi

2:7, "For the lips of a priest should keep knowledge, and people should seek law from his mouth; for he is the messenger of the LORD of hosts."[2] We see then that God in all times appointed some in the office of teaching the people, and of bearing abroad His Word.

And so, we today also need such an order, and we know what St. Paul says on the subject, in Romans 12:6, 1 Corinthians 12:28, and Ephesians 4:11.[3] And it is proved to us also throughout all the Holy Scripture, that God will have certain laws established and certain men appointed to bear abroad His Word, to be teachers in His Church, and to instruct the people in His name. We gather from this that when God has appointed such an order, all those who cannot allow themselves to be taught by this common order with the whole body of the Church, though they may call themselves Christians, yet they are no more holy than horses, for they think that it is enough for them to grant in a word that the gospel is the Word of God. But on the contrary, we see here that if we want to be of the body of the Church, and have God take us for His children, we must hear the Word of God as it is ministered to us by the ministry of men. But because this point has been dealt with at large previously, I have only at this time glanced at it by the way.

The Privilege of Obedience

There is also this point: "Today you are made the people of God, if you keep His commandments" (vv. 9, 10). Therefore, just as our Lord receives us into His house, so must we also wholly

---

2. It is useful to note that the Levites were not only located in Levitical cities, but also in every Israelite town (Dt. 12:12; 14:27; Jud. 17, 19). These Levites conducted worship and instruction every sabbath (Lev. 23:3). This was the origin of what came to be called the synagogue.

3. These verses all teach that there are special offices in the New Testament Church. Romans 12:6: "Having then gifts differing according to the grace that is given to us. . . ." 1 Corinthians 12:28: "And God has appointed these in the church: first apostles, second prophets, third teachers. . . ." Ephesians 4:11: "And He Himself gave some to be apostles, some prophets, some evangelists, and some pastors and teachers."

give ourselves unto Him, knowing that to this end He has taken us out from the rest of the world, and will have us to be His own, as it were His peculiar inheritance. All men, of course, are bound to serve Him; but yet notwithstanding, when He calls us to Himself, and shows Himself our Father, does He not bind us to Himself with a double bond? Yes, surely. Are we not then bereft of all sense and reason, and wholly bewitched, if we are not moved to yield ourselves over to His will, so that He may guide us and bear rule over all our life? Let us, then, weigh well these words: "Today you are made the people of the Lord your God, and therefore keep His commandments."

How are we made the people of God except by being His Church, and by having the use of His sacraments, and that is all the same as if He appeared among us? For we may not expect that God should come down from heaven in His own person, or send His angels to us. Rather, the true mark whereby He will be known to be present among us is the preaching of His Word purely unto us, for there can be no doubt but that then He bears rule in our midst. So then, let this thing profit us, that we know that our Lord receives us to Himself and will have us to be of His own household. Seeing it so, let us take pains to obey Him in all our life, and to keep His commandments. Let us not wander like brute beasts as the wretched unbelievers do, because they never knew what it was to be of the house of God.

Curse on Secret Idolatry

But now let us come to the rehearsal Moses makes of the curses. First of all he says, "Cursed is he who makes any idol or any molten image, or any carved image; all this is abominable to God. And cursed is he who puts it in any secret place. And all the people shall say, Amen." Let us note that Moses does not specify in this place all the curses, each one by itself, but rather sets down certain examples to show that all those who swerve aside from the law of God seek nothing other than to run willfully into utter ruin and destruction.[4] The effect, therefore, of all this is that if we

---

4. It is in Deuteronomy 28 that we find the general discussion of blessings and

want to prosper, we must draw near to God, seeing that He is the fountain of all happiness and prosperity. Whereas, on the other side, all those who depart from Him go and cast themselves into utter destruction. All those who cast off the yoke of God, who do not yield themselves to follow His law and His Word, depart from Him and do as much as is in their power to banish themselves from His presence. And so it is all the same as if they had cast themselves into the bottom of hell, and sought nothing else in this life but to provoke the vengeance of God against them, and thus to seek their own woe. So, this is what we have to keep in mind.

Now God begins with His own service, and not without reason. For (as we have declared before) the law is divided into two tables[5] to show us that men ought first of all so to behave themselves that God might be honored. This is the first and principal duty that we ought to perform, because we are His creatures, and because He has fashioned us for His glory. Let us work toward that end, and let our lives be lived with reference to it, seeing that the first table shows us briefly how we ought to behave ourselves towards our God. This is the reason why God now says in these curses, "Cursed is he who makes any idol."

But as I have told you before, Moses only rehearses certain curses, so as to comprehend the whole in one part, as we have seen examples of. In effect, therefore, when it is said, "Cursed is he who makes any idol," it is the same as if Moses had in general pronounced a curse upon those who falsify and corrupt the service and worship of God. It is as if he should say, "You know how and

---

curses. The specific curses in Deuteronomy 27 follow after many chapters giving penalties, civil curses if you will, for visible sins. Now, so as to seal the people into private as well as public righteousness, curses are placed on secret sins. All the sins listed in 27:15-26 are either said to be performed in secret, or else in the nature of the case would not be visible to public view. See Calvin's remarks to this effect in his *Harmony of the Pentateuch* III:207f. and in Sermon 151 below.

5. Modern exegetical and archaeological studies have argued rather convincingly that the two tables of the law were two copies of the entire Ten Words; cf. M. G. Kline, "The Two Tables of the Covenant," in Kline, *The Structure of Biblical Authority* (Grand Rapids: Eerdmans, 1972). Of course, no one is denying the obvious fact that the Ten Words move from laws pertaining to the love of God to laws pertaining to love for the neighbor; the only question is whether or not the term "two tables" should be used for this division.

after what manner our God wants to be worshipped by us; whoever invents any manner of idolatry, whoever devises any manner of superstition, makes idols." And that is not to serve the living God, but rather to follow their own fancies and imaginations, and therefore they are all accursed. You see then how we ought to expound this place.

It was Moses' intention to set down for us here such a specific instance as would cause us to see most plainly an intolerable corruption of the worship of God. For when God is misshapen in any painting, or in any puppet,[6] or in any other piece of wood or stone that men use to represent His image and say it is a resemblance of Him; this is a thoroughly gross and outrageous affair. Unfortunately men do not share this opinion, as we see in Popery when men say, "Lo, yonder is God, even a remembrance of Him." It seems that they are so brutish that they think there is no Divine majesty in heaven unless it is represented in the shape of an idol. In contrast, however, those who have had a taste of what God is, and have heard any syllable of His Word – where it is said that God is an immortal and infinite spirit, the fountain of life – such men know that it does immensely great injury to Him to represent Him by a dead thing and by a corruptible creature, to give His name to a mere puppet as if He were but a creature, and less than even we.

Those therefore who have even a slight taste of this doctrine abhor the setting up of any idol and the notion of serving God by going to one. They abhor the notion that any should pray to a dead thing, or look for health from something that can do nothing, neither good nor bad. Therefore, if this were well marked, we should find that Moses intended in this place to make idolatry more detestable, according to the rule we have heretofore expounded.[7]

Yet notwithstanding, we have two things to note in this place. The first is that God cannot permit His infinite majesty to be

---

6. "Puppet" is a term of contempt for carved images, implying that such idols only speak as their human masters direct.

7. "More detestable" – that is, men who know the Scripture already detest idols, but the curse is added to make idolatry even more detestable.

represented under stone, wood, painting, or any other creature in the world.[8] This being the case, what must we do when the representation is introduced into the very worship of God? We ought to lift up our minds above the world, and know that we may neither attach to nor make any idol or puppet of Him, for He cannot abide it. This is one point to be noted.

Secondly, we must also note that God will not be served or worshipped after our fancies, but He will have us to walk according to His Word, without adding anything thereto or taking away anything therefrom, so that all the inventions of men are equivalent to so many idols. They think that God will be pleased with what they do, but this is simply a bare guess on their part, while they ignore what He has said He desires. Therefore, they are really serving their own selves and not the living God, for He has given them a rule to live by. In sum, all of their so-called worship of God, deviously drawn up after their own fancies without warrant from God (for they cannot say, "This He commanded me"), are but idols of their own forging. Let this be well noted.

Now let us consider how God says, "Cursed is he who forges idols." Papists take pain to trudge from altar to altar, mumbling their prayers before their images, decking them out with candles, and performing other rituals, and if a man tells them that God dislikes all this, it angers them and they fall to railing against God Himself. And although they think they are winning a score of

---

8. What the Bible actually forbids is any attempt to conjure the presence of God in art for worship purposes. An example of the violation of the second commandment is found in Judges 17. Micah thought that he could capture and manipulate God by setting up a house of idols and getting a priest who could work the images. Micah said, "Now I know that YHWH will prosper me, seeing I have a Levite as priest." In short, what the Bible forbids is idolatrous iconodulism, not religious art.

It is understandable that the Reformers, reacting against Roman iconolatry, should move in the direction of rejecting all religious art; and it is legitimate to fast from any proper aspect of life that has been grossly abused. In Scripture, however, God did show Himself in visible signs and images, and since all creation reflects Him, there is a sense in which everything in creation illustrates Him. Nothing in creation, however, can function as a mediator, so that we may never "bow down and worship" anything as a channel to God. God is very near to us, and we approach Him directly through Jesus Christ, who is Very God of Very God.

heavens, every step they set out is a casting of themselves into the gulf of hell. And why? Because no matter how fair their replies, yet the Judge pronounces this sentence on them: "Cursed are all they who make idols." Let them go and seek their wages at the hands of the devil; our Lord has already pronounced His sentence, which is contained here: Cursed are all idolaters.

Now, someone may say that it is no great harm when a man acts from a good intent, saying, "I think it is good; I believe it is well to do so." All the same, God detests every bit of it, because it is a forging of a new god when men turn themselves from the pure simplicity of the worship of God to devise this or that. Although they think to do well, yet they are accursed. And why? Because God dislikes and condemns what they do. After all, it is not for a mere mortal creature to promise this and that to himself, but God must promise and we must answer Amen. And similarly when He threatens we must be confounded, and every mouth stopped before Him. He must have audience, and we must receive His threats and confirm them, as I have told you.

And here mention is purposely made of a secret place, to show that although a man might not be convicted before the eyes of the world, yet he is surely guilty in the eyes of God, for the heavenly Judge will find him out well enough. Therefore, let us not beguile ourselves and think that we can escape and remain unpunished just because men do not reprove us and convict us of the evil we have done. For we may well seek refuge in a hiding hole, but God will find us out, seeing that He says, "Cursed is he who makes any idol and puts it in a secret place."

And again he says, "It is an abomination unto the Lord," to show that men must not beguile themselves by standing upon their own opinions or upon the judgment of the world. It is enough that God says, "Such a thing displeases Me." Even if the world likes us, we gain nothing thereby. So then, let us take heed that we frame ourselves to the will of God in such a way that this world cannot carry us away, and so that we serve neither our own lusts nor those of other men, but submit ourselves always unto our heavenly Judge. Thus you see what we have to bear in mind.

For when it comes to the service of God, we must not look to see whether there are any witnesses of our doings here below; for even though we may deceive the whole world, yet God sees us, and we cannot escape His sight. Whatever lurking places we may have, let us know that our condemnation is ready at hand. And so, let us order our lives so that God is served and honored, not only with our feet, our hands, and our eyes, but also with the service of our hearts, that is to say with all our affections, and with all our thoughts given over to Him. And (to conclude) we are taught that the service of God is called spiritual for a good reason (John 4:24). And we may understand from this that it is not enough for us to do Him reverence before men, by kneeling down and by using other such ceremonies,[9] or by abstaining from idols in the sight of men; but also in secret when every man is withdrawn into his secret place: even then we must avow Him for our God and all our affections must be held under His obedience, and we must have the purity that St. Paul speaks of, namely the obedience of faith (Rom. 1:5), by which every one of us may dedicate and consecrate himself wholly unto God.

Prayer

Now let us kneel down before the majesty of our good God, with acknowledgement of our faults, praying Him that we may be touched more and more with true repentance, to be displeased with ourselves, so that when we apply our whole mind to study both His promises and His threats, we may not be so rebellious as to cast off His yoke, but rather be held back always by such means as are necessary and proper to us. Let us pray that we may yield to Him as willing servants, so that just as He of His free goodness has called us to Himself, so also He may guide and govern us by His Holy Spirit, that we may give ourselves over to Him and serve Him in humility and fear, embracing His promises and trembling at His threats. And let us pray that in the mean-

---

9. Calvin has proper ceremonies, such as kneeling and standing for prayer in worship, in mind here. The Reformers would be amazed to see our modern churches with people sitting during prayer!

time He will make us feel that if we are thus given over to His service, He will make us prosper and we shall be most happy, especially happy because He has set before us the inheritance of the kingdom of heaven, which He purchased for us in the Person of His only Son. Let us pray that it may please Him to grant this grace not only to us but also to all people and nations of the earth; etc.

3

SECRET SINS

Sermon 151. Wednesday, 4 March 1556.
Deuteronomy 27:16-23.

16. Cursed be he who curses [dishonors] his father and
his mother. And all the people shall say, Amen.

17. Cursed be he who removes his neighbor's boundary
mark. And all the people shall say, Amen.

18. Cursed be he who misleads a blind (person) on the
road. And all the people shall say, Amen.

19. Cursed be he who perverts the justice due to the
stranger, the fatherless, and the widow. And all the people
shall say, Amen.

20. Cursed be he who lies with his father's wife, for he
uncovers the skirt [corner, wing] of his father's garment.
And all the people shall say, Amen.

21. Cursed be he who lies with any beast. And all the
people shall say, Amen.

22. Cursed be he who lies with his sister, the daughter
of his father or of his mother. And all the people shall say,
Amen.

23. Cursed be he who lies with his mother-in-law. And
all the people shall say, Amen.

24. Cursed be he who attacks his neighbor secretly. And
all the people shall say, Amen.

We have already seen what God was aiming at in appointing

this solemnity, that the people should meet together on Mt. Ebal, which is over against Mt. Gerizim, to pronounce the curses that are set down here. For when God has once uttered His will to us, that is good enough for us, and all of us should consent to it and confess that to cleave to His Word is the rule of all righteousness. For the chief honor God requires of us, as though it were a setting of our seals upon it (John 3:33), is to declare that there is no gainsaying or replying to what He speaks, but that it is altogether certain and ought to be adhered to.

Furthermore, we ought to mark also that the condition of men's agreeing to God's Word is such that if they do the contrary in their lives, they condemn themselves with their own mouths. For it is not good enough for us to profess that whatever God says is rightful and reasonable, but we must also show by our deeds that His teaching has full force and authority among us. So then, he who gives such a confession with his mouth is his own judge without any other process of law, if he does not follow what has been taught him and what he knows to be right.

Now we have seen how God spoke of idolatries and then of superstitions. And I mention then that it is enough for us to have some examples here touched upon, to show us that God requires the full obedience of His law at our hands, as the conclusion of the passage demands. You see then that God ratified His whole service.

Cursing Parents

Now He comes to the second table, and begins with the honor and subjection that is due to the father and mother. "Cursed shall that man be," He says, "who curses his father and mother" (v. 16). Now this curse is very important, for it includes all that is repugnant to the honor, obedience, and help children owe to their fathers and mothers. Therefore, whoever does not yield honor to his father and mother is here cursed by God. We have seen before the punishment that was appointed for them (Dt. 21:18-21), so that if any man had disobedient children, he could bring them before the judges and they were, upon his single witness, to be stoned to death, and so such evil was to be taken away. For it is an unkindly and accursed thing that children should set themselves against those who brought them into the world, and have brought them up, and have taken such pain and care for them. For we know that a father occupies the place, as it were, of God toward his own children and offspring. It follows then that he who lifts himself up against his father or his mother is manifestly despising God, even as if he were a despiser of all religion. Now here, by the way, God tells us that although judges and magistrates may not do their duty [of executing the rebellious youth], or if perchance the wrong done to his father and mother is borne with, yet he has not therefore escaped. Many crimes are buried in this world, but God reserves His judgment even so, and sooner or later they must come to account.

Let us mark well, then, that there is no more speaking here of the execution of justice by means of law [lawcourts], for that has been spoken of before. Here God declares that those who have offended through disobedience, even though they are not punished in this world, and even though their faults are not known, so that no examination is made of them such as they deserve, have still gained nothing thereby because there is a heavenly Judge, who forgets nothing but keeps all things registered before Himself; and in the end He shall perform His office. Therefore, let us think well concerning this teaching, and even if men find no fault with us, and no man vexes or troubles us, let us not fall asleep for that reason. Rather, let every man summon himself, according to what is told us here, and consider that we must come before the judgment seat of God.

And therefore let us learn to walk in such a way that He may accept us when we come there, and so that we do not stand in fear of the curse uttered here. Not that any of us can perform the law (as I have declared more fully in earlier sermons), but we are obliged to tend toward it, and to put our endeavor into it. For even though we are not completely clean before God, but are on the contrary guilty of many of the faults that are contained here, yet He does not lay them to our charge, if we hate them and do not give ourselves over to them or let the bridle slack. For this reason let us learn to restrain ourselves, and to be sorry, seeing we are not as perfect as is required. But with all that, as I have declared before, let us strain ourselves to please our Lord God and to obey Him, and let us have such a record in our own consciences that we may freely and with open mouth say, "Cursed be he who has not followed the teaching of salvation in such a way as it is showed to us."

To make any long discourse on the honor that every man owes to his father and mother is not needful at this point, because the law has been expounded already before this. It suffices now to know that in this text God declares that all disobedience, as well against fathers and mothers as against all superiors whom He has set in authority in this world, is intolerable in His sight. For He will not have us to live here in a disorderly manner like beasts, but He will have order and government observed among us. And that cannot be done unless we stand in awe of such as bear any office for the common government of men. Whoever, then, breaks God's order, let him look to be accursed, just as St. Paul also tells us (Rom. 13:4) that those who rebel are not resisting creatures or men, but make war against God Himself when they go about to overthrow the superiority He has ordained and commended to us. Mark that for one point.

Secret Theft

Now next is added, "Cursed be he who plucks up his neighbor's boundary marks" (v. 17). We must always bear in mind what I have told you already, namely that here under one heading God includes all similar kinds. I told you at that place[1] that if a man's lands are not kept secure, no man will be master of his own possessions, but all will go to spoil and chaos. And surely the maintenance of just weights and measures, of lawful money, and the keeping of boundaries unchanged, are things that are universally acknowledged. How can men buy and sell, or engage in any

---

1. *Deuteronomy* Sermon 114, on Dt. 19:14.

trade at all, if the coin is not lawful? Again, if weights and measures are falsified, we shall be cheated. What purpose will justice serve any more? And we can say the same for boundaries and landmarks. So then, under this saying God intended to show that it was necessary for us to observe equity and uprightness in dealing one with another.

It is true that laws are enacted to punish such offenses, so that if any man shift his neighbor's boundary mark, or remove it, it will not be enough for him to set it in the right place again, or make amends for what he has done, but he will also openly be punished as for a heinous crime. The same is to be done for the falsifying of weights, and for the maintenance of false measures. Concerning the counterfeiting of coin, if a man does so, it is not enough for him to pay back what he has wrongfully taken, but he must also die for it, and with good reason.[2] For otherwise, as I said, all laws would have to be abolished. And it would be better for us to be wild beasts than to live without those means that God has ordained, nature also having taught us the same thing.

But suppose some man defrauds his neighbor, whether by false measure or by some other wicked practice, seeking to advantage himself through another man's loss, and the magistrate does not learn of it [or cannot solve the case], so that it remains unpunished? Well, here we are shown that in the end it must come to account before the heavenly Judge. If a poor man is bereft of his right, or oppressed by an authority, by violence or otherwise, so that he dare not say a word about it, or finds no advocate to take his case in this world, yet God guarantees him justice. And those who think themselves greatly benefitted by enriching themselves by hook or crook will at length find that it would have been much better for them to have had but one bit of bread to eat, than to have had ever so much to glut themselves

---

2. The Bible nowhere enjoins the death penalty for counterfeiting. The penalty for theft in Scripture is double or multiple restitution, not prison and not death. Calvin does not call for the death penalty in Sermon 114 (on Dt. 19:14), and in his Commentaries at this point mentions that the Romans punished this crime severely. Calvin may go beyond Scripture here, or perhaps is only referring to local custom.

with, and that it would have been better for them to have heeded the curse here set down. For God has no need of the help of man. Suppose all men dealt wrongly here, so that all things were confused and put out of order, yet this saying will not fall to the ground: The man who removes his neighbor's boundary mark shall be accursed, when God performs His office.

It is true that He wants men to use the sword, those into whose hand He has placed it, and He has ordained that they do so. And, if they are slack and slow in doing it, He will show them that He appointed them not in vain to punish crimes and offenses. But mortal men cannot prejudice Him. When an earthly judge fails to discharge his duty, it does not follow that this weakens God's authority, or that He is bereft of fit means to execute His office, or that He is idle. For He is not like worldly princes, who trust to their officers and are well contented to act as blind persons when things go amiss. "As for me," they say, "I understand that all things go well; and concerning my officers, my will is that they should act faithfully to what I have commanded them." A prince thinks it is enough for him to have said the word, but in reality God is looking over them, and controlling them. And even though offenders and transgressors escape the hands of men, yet shall they be punished at His hands in the end.

So then, let us not be worrying [like the thief] that we might be seen, or that we might not do a quick job of our deceit; but rather let us be worrying about this saying, "Cursed shall he be who pulls up his neighbor's landmark." Men may not see it at all, but God sees it, and we can no more avoid His eyes than we can His hand. So, let us beware of all fraud and false dealings, assuring ourselves that our Lord watches over us, and that He watches in such a way that He will not permit the poor to be crushed or the simple to be outraged or devoured, without such things being punished. Rather, He will show in the end how it is with good reason that He claims to Himself the title of Judge of the whole earth.

Neighborliness

Next we find, "Cursed be he who causes the blind to stray

out of the way, or to stumble in the way" (v. 18). This is a cruelty even against nature. For the more need a man has, the more other men ought to pity him and aid him. Here is a poor blind man. Men see him ready to take a fall, and they do nothing to prevent it. Those who take pleasure in such things must be of a totally evil and corrupt disposition, so that there is not one drop of common kindness in them. In brief, they must be lovers of all cruelty and evil. For even the heathen greatly abhorred such things, so that in some places such a deed was as grievously punished as murder, theft, or other similar things. Commonly, however, men made no law for it, the reason being that it was held that every man ought to be sufficiently learned in his own behalf, so that it would be superfluous to have said, "If a man see a blind man, let him set him on his way."

Nevertheless, as I have said before, we have to note that God extends the matter and teaching further. In effect, His meaning is to say, "Cursed shall he be who allows his neighbor to go astray for want of good counsel." For just as a blind man rushes against things and stumbles, and goes astray if he is not led and guided in his way, so also when we lack counsel and good advice, we are surely in the same plight that blind men are in unless we are rescued. Indeed, although a man may have eyes, yet if he is in a strange and unknown country, and goes quite out of his way, so that he is running hither and thither, and men leave him alone, it is all the same as if they had made a blind man go out of his way. The heathens also considered this to be so.

It is not for us to seek excuses, and say, "Why so? God is only speaking concerning blind men." Indeed, but even those who had neither law nor gospel were able to see the duty, and show us our lesson, namely that whoever does not show the way to a traveller when he sees him out of his way, is a very monster, and a detestable creature.

And so is he also who is stingy with the light of his candle. I see a poor man whose candle is out, and he comes to me to light it again. Doing this for him costs me nothing, and yet I say to him, "You shall have nothing from me." Are such people worthy to live on earth? So then, let us mark well God's meaning, where He curses all such as set the blind out of the way, or cause them to stumble.

So, let us gather together what I have touched on heretofore, which is that here God makes us to understand that if any of our neighbors have need of our help, we must help him if we are of ability and have opportunity to do it, especially if it is of no cost or charge to us. Indeed, even if it should cost us something, yet we are bound to help such as are in need and distress; and so what are we bound to do when it costs us nothing, and we need only open our mouths to give counsel? In that case we are not called upon to disburse anything. We are not in danger of losing either time or money, as they say. The thing is to be done at free cost. Shall we then be so cruel as to let a poor man sustain harm through our evil? What kind of dealing is that? Do not such people deserve to be confounded?

But, as I said before, this place does not deal with open punishments, to be executed by earthly judges. God tells us that even though such dealings are borne with, and laughed at, yet it will come to account before Him.

Now since this is so, let every man look to himself. And first let us beware, that when our neighbors are in any extremity, we are also pitifully moved with compassion to assist them. If it looks as if a blind man needs our help, let us be pressed and ready to reach out our hand and lend it to him. And especially if our Lord grants us the grace to be able to serve our neighbor's needs without costs and without straining ourselves in the matter. Let us understand that He is doing us a great honor. For whoever relieves the needy is the minister of God. Thus God employs us in His service, and promises that our labor shall not be lost. Shouldn't this provoke us the more to it? Note this therefore for a special point, that such as are succorless are here commended to us by God.

And moreover let us realize that if we are bound to guide the blind lest they stumble or stray out of the way, we ought to be much more forward and ready to advise a man when we see he has need of counsel and is likely to fall into some danger for want of our advice. But indeed much more ought the way of salvation to be regarded, so that if we see a man pushing himself over the line and heading into destruction, we must not disdain to warn him, saying, "Wretched creature, where are you going? What are you doing? Do you desire to perish?" And especially when he does it in ignorance, if we then spare our tongues so that they are not used as instruments of salvation to the poor ignorant soul, who wishes to be taught, surely such recklessness will not go unpunished or be forgotten by God. Even though neither law nor justice proceed against it, yet will this curse be ratified upon it.

In brief, let us mark that our Lord meant by this threat to encourage us to pity and compassion, in succoring all such as have need of us, and especially in employing ourselves when we see poor ignorant persons destitute of counsel, and we ourselves are able to bring them back again to the right way. Thus much concerning that point.

Justice and Oppression

A second statement concerning cruelty immediately follows: "Cursed be he who perverts the justice due to the stranger, the widow, and the fatherless" (v. 19). It is true that to the utmost of our power we must maintain every man's right. Nevertheless, our Lord in this place, as He has before, speaks of widows, fatherless, and strangers, because they lie open to a great number of injuries and outrages, and no man sets himself in their defense. Indeed, few have any care at all of them, because they are not able to make any recompense. Men see a stranger, see how he can be fleeced, how he can be oppressed, how he can be wronged, yea and that openly, and yet it will be winked at. And why? Because every man will be friendly toward his own neighbor; but as for that man, he is not of the same country or of the same city – he does not belong to us. Thus you see how the poor man is left destitute.

In a similar case are widows and fatherless children. As for the fatherless child, men do not expect him to acknowledge what is done for him today or tomorrow. Sometimes he lies in his cradle, and does not know who does him good and who does him evil, because he has no discretion. He cannot requite the pleasure done to him, and therefore every man leaves him alone. In the same situation do widows stand, especially when they are poor and are of no great reputation in the world. Every man shrinks from them, and they are left as it were in a gob of spittle.

Now, because these things come to pass so commonly, God purposefully takes such people into His protection, saying that if any man wrests or hinders the right of the stranger, the widow, or the fatherless, he shall be punished. Even if it is not accounted of before the world, but rather such evil doers are well liked, yet will He call them before Him and show that He cares for those He has taken into His safekeeping. And so under one heading, God meant to show briefly that if we tread upon such as have no reputation, and no means to defend themselves, and no one to lean upon in this world, yet He reserves to Himself their avenging. That is what we have to gather from this text.

Now, perverting or hindering the right (v. 19) is nothing other than the unjust and causeless oppression of the feeble and weak, and such as have no one to support and maintain them. The manner or figure of speech here set down in Holy Scripture means the same thing as our expression, "to dash a good case to the ground," and in general means to disappoint a man of his right. Now therefore, if I rob a man, when I take to myself those things that belong to him, when I strip him out of his substance, when I thrust him out of all that he has, when I overmaster him and take more upon myself than is properly mine, then I do hinder his right. And so we see, as I said before, that in this text God shows that He shall be the judge of all the outrages done to such as have no means to avenge themselves, and are forsaken and forgotten by men.

If we were well advised, surely we would be more afraid to have God as our adversary, than all the world put together. And indeed, we show that we give small credit to God's Word, since if a man is of a great family and has many friends, if a man is rich or highly favored by the world, we dare not meddle with him. Even if he has molested us, yet we shall sweetly swallow it up and be very careful not to provoke him. In such a way men will put up with all such as have the wherewithal to maintain themselves in this world, even when those who are destitute are robbed and devoured. Yet notwithstanding, God is their defender, and He says that in oppressing such folk, we make war against Him, and therefore that He also will not be slow to lift up His arm in the maintenance of those whom He has taken under His protection.

But men do not heed that. And thus do we not betray our unbelief? For if we had a true and lively sense that God is not jesting here, when He tells us that His curse shall light upon those who mistreat the weak and such as have no champions, it is certain that we should quake whenever we were tempted to do evil to any poor creature that has no stay, credit, or authority in this world. I see that this man has neither relatives nor friends. I see that no man regards him. I see that he is undefended. Now, if I advance myself against him, or if I trouble him, God will set Himself against me, for He has set His mark upon the poor man and has told me that if I meddle with such a person, He will take the case to Himself, and I shall be regarded as having challenged and disparaged His own majesty. If we kept this in mind, it is certain that we should be much more restrained and held back by His fear, than we are by all the favors and displeasures of this world. Nevertheless, we see the clean contrary — we are very dull in this regard.

It is certain that such cruelty as is committed against poor folk who have no stay to lean upon, demonstrates manifest contempt of God, and an utter scorning of Him, as if to say that He is unable to execute the vengeance He has threatened. Now when God is so lightly esteemed, do we think He will put up with it? You see here first how this kind of outrage is even against nature. For if we were not so caught up in our wicked affections, surely every one of us would confess that it is much worse to have hurt or devoured a poor weak creature than to have done harm to a rich man who is well allied and has reserves and the power to avenge himself. All men will grant that. Therefore, it is one of the greatest and most outrageous faults that can be found among men.

Again, it is a scorning of God, a most devilish wickedness when we are not moved at this statement of God, "I have these people in My hand. I will maintain them. Whoever advances himself against them must prepare to have Me as his adversary party." If we make no account of this, as if God had never spoken it, is it not a token that we are too hard hearted? And therefore, as I have already said, let us learn to bethink ourselves better, and to have a better regard of Him. And when we have dealings with such people as are despised by the world, without alliance, without friends, without deliverers, let us beware that we deal in such a way with them that it may always run in our minds that they are God's children, and that the heavenly Judge shall not forget the wrongs that are done to them, especially since He has told us here that those who have been so cruel to the feeble shall not escape His curse.

Sexual Perversion

Now Moses adds further (vv. 20-23), "Cursed be he who lies with his father's wife, with any beast, with his own sister, or with his mother-in-law." This passage treats all the infamous sorts of lechery, even of the most loathsome kinds of them, whether incest or sodomy, or other such corruptions. And it is with good reason that God chooses out these particular kinds,[3] for it is to the end

---

3. Calvin's point in general is that these perversions are singled out for the purpose of striking fear into the hearer. Without necessarily contradicting Calvin's point, the principal reason for this section of Deuteronomy is to enumerate certain kinds of crimes that ordinarily would never come to the attention of the magistrate, and to assure the people that God Himself would avenge these crimes, no matter how well concealed they might be. Sexual sins such as these are not likely to be found out for several reasons: (1) In the nature of the case the actions are private. (2) Three of these are capital crimes, and the other (incest with a sister) requires excommunication (Lev. 20). (3) Persons who are the victims of sexual abuse frequently feel a humiliating sense of moral shame and embarrassment, and thus do not report the matter to the authorities.

Calvin does not deal here with the phrase in v. 20, "for he uncovers the skirt

that we should be touched with the more fear and terror when we go about any kind of lechery.

God could have said simply, in one word, "Cursed be he who commits any lechery," and indeed, this is the very mark at which this text aims. Nevertheless, He did not content Himself so, but as I said He chooses those examples that are most outrageous. Why? So that we should be touched the more to the quick. For we see how slow we are in hearkening to the things God tells us. We have His Word, but what about it? It passes out of our minds. We shall not tarry to say that it behooves us to keep ourselves from breaking the law. But, if vices are spoken of in only one or two words, will they be esteemed as they ought to be, which is as crimes before God that deserve endless death?

We see how every man excuses himself, so that the secret thief makes no consequence of filching, until he goes from being a petty thief to being a robber; and then it seems to him as if things are no different from the way they were before, until he becomes a murderer and a cutter of men's throats. Thus do men proceed in degrees of theft, and so also they do in lechery. Then they count it as nothing, until eventually they fall into the greatest extremities. Seeing, then, that we are so dull, and are not touched with the kind of fear we ought to have when God condemns sin and would pluck us back from it, therefore it is needful that He should set before us the examples that are most detestable, even such as are calculated to make the hairs of our heads stand on end when we hear them named, even if we clench our teeth against His Word. This is so that no man should beguile himself with fond flattery, but every man be careful to hold himself under the obedience of God.

Here then we see two things. The one that God has condemned all unchastity and all manner of lechery. The other is that He has purposely chosen the things that are most ugly, such as incest and uncleanness against kind, and such as bestiality.

[corner, wing] of his father's garment." In his *Harmony* at Dt. 22:30, which says the same thing, Calvin points out that this phrase generally denotes exposing the father to shame and humiliation; *Harmony of the Pentateuch* III: 105f.

And why? So that men should have occasion to set their minds the better, and not do as they are commonly accustomed, which is to listen to what is said and yet ignore it, as if to say, "All this is very true," and yet make no account of it, acting like people who have been dazed, as if a man had knocked them on the head with a sledge hammer. So much for the first point.

Incest

And we see how God is much concerned about incest, when He says, "Cursed be he who lies with his mother-in-law, the wife of his father, or with the daughter of his father or mother, or with his own daughter-in-law," and such other degrees.[4] And why? Because we see that men in all ages have overshot themselves in this manner. God is well skilled in applying remedies according to men's specific diseases. Therefore, it is not for nothing that He insists so strongly on such things. And why? Because He saw that men needed to be held in check, and that such kinds of wickedness would have reigned if He had not set Himself stoutly against them and cast barriers in their way, as if He had said, "Stop there, and don't play the loose colt." If He had not ordered beforehand that men were not to rush forth into such vices, surely all would have dissolved into chaos. And if this wickedness existed in those days, we may be sure that we are not exempted from it nowadays.

And therefore, let us understand that since our Lord uses so much earnestness in this manner, He is warning us to occupy ourselves in minding these things, so that we think on them day and night, early and late, so that we may walk in such chastity and sobriety that our lives may not break forth into such beastly sins, but that we may be given to God to serve Him purely. That, I weigh, is what we have to gather from this place.

And let us not flatter ourselves. For God knows well what is needful for us, or else He would not here have spoken of things that are so shameful that we are embarrassed even to name them. And what about that, then? Was not God aware of our sensibili-

---

4. Calvin is summarizing Leviticus 18 and 20 here.

ties in this area? Yes, of course; but He knew that the heart of a man is a dreadful dungeon, and that we must be restrained as it were by force, or else He would never be able to hem us in. So then, let this provoke us the more to look closely at ourselves, so that we do not overshoot ourselves in one way or another, but be vigilant to dedicate ourselves to the service of God with all purity, as I said before.

And moreover let us understand that lechery is in itself so loathsome a thing before God, that even if men make no account of the punishing of it, this will be of no help to us when we stand before the heavenly throne. For it is no small thing that God banishes all whoremongers and lechers out of His kingdom, as it is said both in 1 Corinthians 6:9 (as we have seen recently),[5] and also in Hebrews 13:4.

That is what we have to bear in mind: namely, that God will not have men to give rein to their fleshly lusts, by companying together like brute beasts, but that every man should live chastely in marriage, and be so honest in that regard that nature not be forgotten, as it is when the son-in-law companies with his step-mother, or the father with his own daughter or with his daughter-in-law, or when the brother marries his sister. Rather, these degrees of consanguinity should be observed. For without such order, what would become of things? How would we differ from bulls and asses? Thus you see what we have to gather concerning the first point we made earlier, which is that our Lord here condemns all manner of unchaste dealings, and will not have men to behave themselves lawlessly in such cases, but to dedicate themselves unto Him and consider that their bodies are the temples of the Holy Spirit, and members of our Lord Jesus Christ, and therefore that they must repress their wicked affections. Keep that in mind as the first point.

Coming, then, to the second point mentioned earlier, God has here set down such examples before our eyes as ought to make

---

5. From October 1555 to February 1557 Calvin's Lord's Day sermons were on 1 Corinthians.

us afraid, in that He speaks of those who, against nature, company with their own mothers, stepmothers, or sisters. He speaks expressly of them, so that from the one we should come to the other, as we see he does in all His law. We have declared this more at length earlier. When He wants to condemn hatred, He speaks of murder. Why? Because if a man tells us that no man ought to hate his brother, we easily grant it to be a sin, but yet we make no conscience to do it. But when God says that He who hates his brother is a murderer, then we are the more abashed and restrained.

Likewise in this text. When scorners jest at whoredom they show that they believe God ought not to call them to account for it. And this vice did not just arise yesterday; we have seen it in all ages, as Moses reports here. And therefore, God names the most detestable kinds of lechery, so that we should conclude from it that if we do not live chastely, we shall fall from one evil to another until we are fallen into such a bottomless pit as would be horrible to think about. That is what we have to keep in mind on this text. So, we ought to take benefit from this warning, considering our blockishness. We think of ourselves as sharp and quick-witted, yet we understand nothing of the teaching of God. We are so dull that He finds it needful to use shocking speech with us, or else we would not be moved by the matter. In brief, we have less wit and reason than young babes have. Let men commend themselves as much as they like, and let them glory in the opinion that they are very able; it is still the case that they are so dull that they would be just like brute beasts if our Lord did not speak in a shocking way to us.

And why is this? Clearly it is because we are so possessed by our fleshly desires. None is so deaf as he who will not hear, as they say. Since we see this, let us take better heed, and when men speak in a shocking manner to us, let us not think they do us wrong, as some do who are so nice that if a man uses a rough style with them they say, "Oh, I could have understood all this just as well if you had been nice about it. I am just like a little baby." In brief, they are upset if a man speaks sharply to them, for they fondly presume in their own imaginations that they know all that is necessary after the first sentence spoken to them.

But notice that God here speaks in another style and language. Why does He do so? Because He sees that there is need. So then, let us allow ourselves to be taught according to our capacity. And seeing we are slow, if our Lord wakes us up, let us receive it meekly and learn to do ourselves good by it. And so you see what we have to gather from all these texts.

Assault

Moving on to verse 24, which says, "Cursed be he who strikes his neighbor in secret," we find that this is spoken against all hatred and rancor, and may serve for a conclusion [for today's lecture]. A man might demand here how it comes to pass that God here is cursing those whose whole offense is in things of which no mention is made in His law; for I have told you before that it is enough for a man to observe the things contained in the Ten Commandments, and that the whole perfection of our life is set down there. But no mention is made there concerning the blind [as in v. 18 here]. So then, how does it happen that God here denounces vengeance against something not forbidden in His law? Well, we see from this, as I have mentioned at other times before, that our Lord in His law requires all things that concern charity, such as that we should aid one another, and that there should be such a common bond among us that every man should spend himself in helping his neighbor. Whatever, then, is contrary to this is forbidden and condemned by the law of God.

And that is why it is said here, "Cursed be he who strikes his neighbor in secret." Under this saying, our Lord has comprehended all the misusages that we can offer to our neighbor, so that if we give him only a flip[6] it is a kind of murdering him. And when we see how a man who only grinds his teeth at his brother

---

6. Golding has "insomuch that if we give him but a phillip, it is a kind of murthering before him." This seems to be another spelling of "phlip" or "fillip" or "flip," which at the time included the meaning of "a quick, sharp blow."

is condemned to hellfire (Matt. 5:22), what will become of him who lifts up his fist? Surely, even to stir up a man's tongue against his neighbor is a sin worthy of grievous punishment. If we so much as go "hmpf" in a scornful or disdainful way, it is forbidden. How much more, then, shall we be blamed if we go about trying to outrage them in some way. Let us therefore mark that here, under one particular, God generally comprehends all the outrage, violence, and misdeeds that we can do toward our neighbors.

And He says expressly, "in secret," or "privately," so that we should keep in mind something I have mentioned to you before, namely that in this case the matter is not determined by a yielding of account before men. Suppose we have broken all the commandments, and yet no man challenges us for it, and the public authority approves of our doings, and when we are accused of it we are acquitted so that no man dares to complain about the disorders we have committed; suppose that were the case, still we know that God speaks otherwise, saying that if we have done our neighbor any harm privately, his blood will cry out against us for vengeance, when we think we have escaped.

And we see what is said of Abel. Even though no man gave information against Cain, and no process of law went against him, yet the blood of the murdered man spoke. God does not say, "I have heard a report about this," but rather, "The blood of thy brother cries to Me against thee." Here, then, we see that God is not threatening us with some punishment to be suffered at the hands of men, but rather is telling us that we must walk before Him and in His presence. And even though we do not fear any earthly justice, yet we ought not to forbear to restrain ourselves. For when God exercises His office, then the vengeance He has spoken of here must be executed upon all such as have escaped by favor, or concealed their crimes, or offended so cunningly that no man could ever find it out.

Seeing that this is so, let us look to it that we enter into our own consciences, and have God's law written there. Let us not be so much concerned with what men think, saying, "I have not been blamed or reproved." Rather, let us consider that our God watches over us, and understand the office of His Word to be such as is written in the epistle to the Hebrews (4:12), that when it is preached out to us, then all things must come to trial, and it must enter in, even to the most secret thoughts of our hearts. Now if God's Word has such power, let us assure ourselves that much more it has the office attributed to it. For this reason let us be restrained by this means, and when we have served God with our hearts, let our lives be so answerable thereunto that when we shall come before our Lord Jesus Christ we may show that we are truly minded to serve Him, and not to please mortal men.

Prayer

Now let us all fall down before the majesty of our good God, with acknowledgement of our faults, praying Him to vouchsafe to give us true repentance of them. And moreover, that He would bear with us until He has rid us quite clean of all our sins, and of all our spots. And that He would make us so to profit by the things we hear, that we may learn more and more to renounce ourselves, and to repress our wicked lusts, until He has clothed us again with the purity of that righteousness to which He has called us. And so let us all say, "Almighty God, heavenly Father, etc."

4

THE CURSE AND JUSTIFICATION

Sermon 152. Monday, 9 March 1556.
Deuteronomy 27:24-26.

24. Cursed be he who attacks his neighbor secretly. And all the people shall say, Amen.

25. Cursed be he who takes a gift to strike down the blood of a guiltless soul. And all the people shall say, Amen.

26. Cursed be he who does not confirm the words of this law by doing them. And all the people shall say, Amen.

We understand from this text that what we spoke of earlier is very true, namely that God intended to teach the people of olden time that it was not enough for them to discharge themselves before men, or to escape blame or punishment here, but that they must look up higher and consider that there is a judgment seat in heaven before which we must one day answer and make our account. That is what we must keep in mind if we are to discharge our duty properly. We may well trick men by putting on a fair countenance, and we may even so order our lives that no man can find any fault in us concerning our outward deeds; and yet all the while, if our hearts are full of wicked lusts, if it grieves us to be held in awe,[1] if we grate our teeth against God, what obedience is that?

---

1. Possibly a reference to public worship.

Assault

Therefore let us note that when this text says, "Cursed be he who smites his neighbor secretly" (v. 24), God is not only condemning the faults that come to knowledge before men, but also condemning the crimes that lie hidden. And so, if a man has lived in such a way that he cannot be rebuked by the world, but is rather praised and commended, he must not use that as an occasion to fall asleep, but must continually examine his heart and consider well whether there be any hidden nook or cranny therein. For if such a man is thoughtless and does evil, though men do not perceive it, yet God will always perform the office of judge. And if our hearts reprove us (as St. John says [1 John 3:20]), God sees us even more clearly.

So then, this text serves well to humble us. And indeed, we ought to remember one other sentence of St. John, where it is said that whoever hates his brother secretly, even if he conceal his hatred so that it is not perceived and rather makes a show of love, that man shall not fail to be condemned by God (1 John 3:15). And so you see in effect what we have to bear in mind.

Let us not busy our heads about men's reports. Even if a man is well regarded here in this world, yet let him not flatter himself on account of it. Rather let him summon himself before God and consider whether he be at fault in his heart. Let not men bring before God their opinions and fancies, for all such things will be refused; they will serve no purpose. And therefore let us walk with unfeigned heart before God. For we know that He does not regard the outward appearance, as it is said in 1 Samuel 16:7, but He requires the heart and truth, as it is said in Jeremiah 5:3.

And looking at what is said here concerning murders and fighting, we must extend the same to all other crimes. For if God calls to account those who have done any outrage to their neighbors, even though these are not known to the world, do we think that robberies, treasons, frauds, railings, slanders, and the like will pass by unnoticed? So then, let us learn that we cannot by any means avoid the hand of God or escape His vengeance if we foster vices in our hearts, though these be not visible to men.

And so that we may get more benefit for ourselves from this doctrine, let every one of us examine himself properly in his heart when he comes to hear the Word of God. For it is proper for us to be reproved inwardly, as St. Paul says in 1 Corinthians 14:25. Every man, I say, must search his own thoughts and affections to the very bottom.[2] Also, it is the peculiar office of God's Word to be a sharp sword, and to separate our thoughts from all our affections and preferences, and to enter even into the marrow of the bones, leaving nothing undiscovered (Heb. 4:12). Seeing this is so, let us prevent God's judgment, and not tarry until He curses us and bans us for the innocent blood that cries out against us, but let every one of us condemn himself as soon as he has offended, and let him be sorry in his heart and beseech God of His infinite goodness and mercy to deliver us from the curse that is denounced against all such as have so misbehaved themselves in secret and have not been convicted thereof before men.

Taking Bribes

Next we read: "Cursed be he who takes a gift to strike down the blood of a guiltless soul" (v. 25). Thus Moses speaks word for word. Nevertheless, the word *soul* means *life*. And because the blood is the proper seat of life, it is therefore said "the blood of a guiltless soul." Certainly, even if a man is sinful, yet it is not lawful to buy and sell his life. But as I have mentioned to you already, God here has set before us those crimes that are most detestable, so that we wake up, because we are not sufficiently moved when He speaks of ordinary faults. Such things slip past us, and we think to ourselves that it is not difficult to obtain forgiveness for them.

Now since there is so much laxity in men, therefore in this place God has chosen some offenses that even by nature we ought

---

2. Calvin ought not to be taken in a perfectionistic sense here, as if he believed that men could actually understand themselves exhaustively. Rather, in the context of Calvin's thought on sanctification, we should understand him to mean that we should examine ourselves as carefully as we are able. For a discussion of this general topic, see Ronald Wallace, *Calvin's Doctrine of the Christian Life* (Tyler, TX: Geneva Ministries, [1959] 1982).

to abhor. For if the life of an innocent person is bought and sold, it is a horrible matter. Virtually anybody you talk to will grant that such a wicked design ought not to be allowed. Thus we can now see God's meaning. But even though this thing is commonly and sufficiently condemned with full mouth, yet men do not cease to put it to far too much use. And for proof of this, look at the practices that are used commonly to oppress the poor and the simple sort. It is true that they are not generally in danger of having their throats cut; but when men harm them in their persons and in their properties, they are still guilty of a form of murder in the eyes of God. And when it comes to the seeking of methods to wrest justice from the innocent, and the practising of devices against those who seek to live in peace and concord, we find that it is all too common a thing. And therefore this law is no more than necessary.

Now it is true enough, as we mentioned before, that at first blush we can say well enough that there is no reason why we should continue in so great and excessive wickedness, and everyone is willing enough to admit that such is against nature; but yet the common practice and custom is the clean contrary. And therefore let us note well the teaching here set down, namely that God cannot allow so great a crime to be unpunished, such as the disappointing of the right, whereby the party that has not offended is oppressed, against all right and reason.

And truly God speaks here also of judges who have been corrupted to oppress a poor man, just as much as He speaks of those who have sold themselves or have set themselves out for hire to murder, beat, or strike men, such as these belligerent ruffians who seek employment as bully boys[3] — all such as these God utterly condemns in this text. And so under one particular example He embraces all like crimes.

So what we have to gather from all this is that covetousness must never lead us to harm any man. We see now that this

---

3. Street gangs were hired to harass the Reformers in Geneva by opponents of the Reform.

doctrine extends itself very far. For why are so many frauds, oppressions, outrages, and injuries committed, if it is not the seeking of illicit profit? Men think, "I must give some pleasure to the man who is in authority, because he is able to requite me again for it. So, if necessary, I for his sake will oppress one and torment another. And afterward, if that is not enough, I must move on to other kinds of things," so that the matter grows out of all measure. So much the more, then, is it needful for us to mark well this teaching: "Cursed shall he be who takes a reward to do men wrong."

The fifteenth Psalm says the same thing; namely that if we want to be people of God's household and dwell in His Church, we must beware of taking bribes to hurt the innocent. If God banishes all such out of His kingdom and from the company of the faithful, punishing those who have gone about to misbehave themselves after that fashion by setting themselves to sale and to hire through their covetousness, what remains for them but utter cursedness? For once God has disclaimed us, and no longer acknowledges us any longer as His, we must be accursed.

Where does all our happiness lie? Just where the fifteenth Psalm says: happy are those people whose God is the Lord. The way, then, for us to be happy is to be taken by God into His flock. And if He casts us out, then of necessity all kinds of mischief must come upon our heads. Since this is so, let us learn so much the more to restrain ourselves, and let every one of us be contented with what he has. And let us not advance ourselves by unlawful means, lest the profit we have gotten to ourselves become cudgels or lacerations to the poor, whom we shall have wounded by raking so to ourselves by hook and crook. Therefore, let us learn to have both our hearts and our hands clean from all evil and misdealing, if we wish to be blessed by God and to be numbered among the faithful. Thus you see in effect what this sentence means.

The Law Is One

Now, for a conclusion is said: "Cursed be he who does not

confirm the words of this law by doing them" (v. 26). Here we see even better something I have set before you already, namely that God here meant to seal His whole law in general, not omitting any point of it, even though He has set down only some particular examples of it. The point of this solemnity on Mounts Ebal and Gerizim is that the people might know that this law is the rule of perfection, and that God, the Author thereof, is not to be dallied with; but rather this law is to be received with all reverence. Yea, and every man ought to protest with his mouth that there is good reason for God to be obeyed, and that all transgressors of His will should condemn themselves, without making any excuses, and willingly acknowledge themselves worthy of death and all misfortune, should they not submit themselves obediently to the service of God.

For this cause, therefore, it is said, "Cursed be he who does not confirm the words of this law." He is not here speaking of one or two commandments, or of some part of them, but of the whole law, every part and parcel thereof without exception. And indeed, we ought to think of how St. James says that He who has forbidden to steal, has also forbidden to commit adultery; and that He who has forbidden to murder has also forbidden false witnessing. We must not rend God's justice in pieces. In whatever way we offend, we violate God's law, and despise His majesty. But He will be acknowledged in His law throughout in all points, and not just in part, as I have told you before.

Seeing it is so, let us mark that God has knit His commandments together to show us that it is not for man to put them asunder, as we see many do who covenant with God to abstain from some one sin, and think to themselves that they are discharged when they can say, "Well, at least I have not offended at all points. I have indeed committed some sins, but in all the rest I have obeyed God." The thief will boast that he is not a whoremonger. The murderer will say that he is not a swearer. The whorehunter will likewise have his excuse, that he does not transgress in other things, that he is not cruel, and such like. But what is all this? As I said before, God will not have His law to be cut up after that fashion into pieces and fragments. It is righteousness that consists of ten commandments knit together in one bond. God therefore must be hearkened unto, both in the first word and in the last, as well in the fourth as in the second.

Since this is so, let us remember what is said here, that God will have us confirm the words contained in His law. So, it is not enough for a man to have discharged himself of some piece of it. God will not content Himself with that. Neither will He take such service for payment, but He will have men to give themselves wholly unto Him. And with what condition? Lord, seeing that Your will is contained in Your law, let our lives be conformed thereunto, for we do not have the liberty to part them asunder. Also, as I have declared before, it is too gross a folly to think that we have a good will to honor Him, and in the meantime despise Him in one thing or another.

Active Obedience

And it is said here, "to confirm the words of this law by doing them." Here Moses shows us the way we are to accept the doctrine delivered to us in the name of God. It is not in the hearing of the ear or in the confessing of the mouth. Though they are true and right, they are not enough. For all is but hypocrisy if our lives are repugnant to it, and it will fall out according to this saying of St. Paul, that while we confess with our mouths that we believe in God, we deny Him in our lives. For this reason let us mark well that the true trial of our faith and obedience is to have our lives answerable to His law, and to show by our doings that we have not been taught in vain. That is what we have to note from Moses' words, that we must confirm the words of this law by doing them, yet by performing them not only by affirming that they are good and right (for that is but a small matter), but also by straining ourselves to serve God by applying our whole endeavor in that way, and by fashioning all our works according to His will. That is the good confirmation. That is the way for us to affirm that God is righteous and that He has given us a good, sure, and infallible rule, such as we ought to observe.

Now we see in effect the contents of this sentence, from which we must understand that God has not enjoined in us a chopped up obedience, but He will have us to receive His law to the uttermost in all points without exception. We see likewise that it is not enough for us to say that God has not commanded anything that is not righteous, but that we must also show an accord and consent thereto in our lives, by framing them after all His commandments.

The Curse Extends to All Men

Moreover, it is well for us now to see what condition we should be in if this curse were to be visited upon us. Certain it is that here all men are denounced accursed. And this curse means the same thing as if it were said that all are damned, all are lost, or all are forsaken. Take, for example, the most righteous persons that ever have lived in the world, and by this sentence they deserve to be cast away. Neither Abraham nor any of the patriarchs, neither David nor all the prophets, can be exempted from this condemnation. God by His prophet (Ezk. 14:14) declares Job, Daniel, and Samuel [sic, actually Noah – ed.] as righteous, and in a manner blameless, and yet even they also must fall under this curse.

And as for David, he confesses it with his own mouth, saying (Ps. 143:2), "Lord, do not enter into judgement with Your servant, for no man living shall be justified in Your sight." There David is speaking not of the common people only, but is putting himself in the same category. It is true that in other places he declares that it was his whole desire to serve God, and that his heart tended that way. All the same, he acknowledged that he came far short of discharging himself, or of having such perfections as were requisite. If he admitted himself guilty as much as other men, what shall we do?

But here is a dreadful sentence, and such a one as ought to make the hairs stand stiff on our heads: "Cursed shall he be who does not perform all the words of this law." Who says this? It is God Himself. It is, then, a definitive sentence, such as admits of no appeal beyond itself. God will have all men confess it so, yea

He will have every man confess it with his own mouth. What, then, remains for us to do? Where is the hope of salvation? From this we see that if we had only the ten commandments of the law we should be utterly undone and perish. It is necessary for us to have recourse to His mercy, which outstrips His justice, as St. James says (Jas. 2:13). God's goodness, then, must be manifest towards us to deliver us from the damnation all of us would experience if this curse should stand and there be no grace to overcome it.

And certainly St. Paul in Galatians 3:10 proves by this text that we cannot become righteous by our works, but that it is needful for us to be made righteous by faith alone (that is to say, by the mere grace of God), because every one of us stands condemned if God enters into account with us. Why? "Cursed shall he be who does not perform all the words of the law." Suppose a man replies, "Yes, but if a man does perform them, why should he not become righteous thereby? And why should he not be paid his hire by God, according to his deserts?" But St. Paul presupposes that no such man has ever been found, and none can possibly be found who performs all the words of the law and everything God has commanded.

Indeed, it is a common saying: "God's law is not impossible to fulfill." At this present day, when the Papists argue against us, this statement is regarded as an invincible argument to prove free will. Why should God have commanded us to love Him with all our hearts, if we are not able to do it? It is repugnant to think that God would exact more of men than they are capable of, for in so doing He would be unjust and cruel. In this way do the Papists reason. But St. Paul says to the contrary, "Cursed shall he be who does not perform all the commandments" (Gal. 3:10). And he presupposes, as I said before, that no man does perform them, and that it is impossible to find any such man. From this he draws his conclusion: all mankind is undone if they enter into examination of their works, so that men must be punished according to their deserts; it is necessary for God to cast them off and utterly to damn them.

And so we have an excellent lesson in this text. It is just as if God had struck down all the children of Adam with one blow of a club, and had thundered down upon them to fling them into a dungeon of damnation, that they might perceive that in themselves they are all damned and perishing. But we need not tarry here. For once God has humbled us, He goes on to give us the means fit for deliverance from condemnation, as we shall see more clearly later on.

The Errors of Rome

But before we proceed farther, let us consider how the Papists deceive themselves. They see well enough that no man performs the law of God, and even though they come up with the fantastic arguments I have already mentioned, saying that God has not ordered anything that is not in the power of men to perform, yet they are convicted even by their own experiences that all men are sinners, that all men have done amiss (as the Holy Scripture also tells us), that there is no one living upon the earth (as Solomon says) who does not sin, and that all men have need of the grace of God. The Papists then, although they see this clearly, still wrangle about it, saying that this is true only before we are regenerated by God's spirit. Nevertheless, if they be pressed, they must confess in the second place that even the holiest of people are still not perfect, and that there is some frailty in them. And even if they will not confess it, yet the Holy Scriptures show it, and every man feels it in himself.

Now then, why do the Papists so firmly insist on the righteousness of works, and maintain that we well deserve to be recompensed, that we earn or purchase the kingdom of heaven? How does it come to pass that they are so brutish and so beastly? It is because they imagine that even if we do not perform the whole law, yet nevertheless we still can earn merit or desert, and this they term "a righteousness in part." They say that all men do indeed sin, true enough, and that in this respect they are at fault before God and well deserve to be condemned if God is rigorous. Nevertheless, they also maintain that when they have the "righteousness in part," that is to say when they do partly obey the law, such doing is worthy of acceptance and worthy to be put into the account and reckoning. And this is what they glory in so much. After that manner, then, there are deservings in men, though they may not perform the whole law. This is one point.

Again, they have another devilish imagination, which is that when they have erred, they can make amends to God by their own satisfactions, and can ransom themselves so that they go scot-free, at least in their own minds. They will well admit, in a word, "we are in danger, but it does not follow that we have no means of escape, and of making God accept in exchange whatever we bring to Him." On this they have founded all their "good devotions," as they term them, such as pilgrimages, masses, and Yeremindes,[4] with all their freewill devotions, such as fastings and diverse other things, going so far as even to put their shrift[5] among their works of satisfaction. Again the prattling of some paternosters,[6] the babbling before a puppet,[7] the chanting of some mass, the setting up of some tapers,[8] and such other things, are all of them regarded as recompenses that will cause God to regard them as faultless. And because they see themselves as overstocked with such things, they forge petty inventions with which to play with God.[9]

And therefore they have invented venial sins,[10] so that if a man is tempted to wicked deeds, yet he is not regarded as having

---

4. "Year's minds": annual commemorative requiem masses said for the dead.

5. Works done as penance for sin, under the direction of the priest.

6. Latin for "Our Father"; a reference to multiple repetitions of the Lord's Prayer.

7. That is, before an iconic statue of Christ, Mary, or a saint. Calvin uses "puppet" as a term of ridicule.

8. Wax candles burned for devotional purposes. Lighting one of these to burn in the church was believed (as is today believed) to be a good work, which merits grace.

9. A reference to indulgences. The church had stored up so much merit that it could manipulate God by bribing Him with it.

10. In Roman Catholic theology, if a man dies with a "mortal" sin upon his soul, which has not been sacramentally removed through Holy Eucharist or Extreme

offended God until he becomes willing and perfectly contented to the performance thereof. If a man is tempted in himself, moved to do evil, all this is no deadly sin, say the Papists. It is but venial sin, and one sprinkle of holy water is enough to wash it clean away. But to the contrary, we see that it is said, "O Israel, what is it that thy God requires of thee, but that thou shouldst love Him with all thy heart" (Dt. 10:12). Here you see what the righteousness of the law is: that a man love God with all his heart. But he that has offended is accursed. And all of us offend. So then, are not all of us in danger of death? There is no man upon whom God does not pronounce this curse.

Now, when men have thought evil, so that they have been provoked to do wickedly, it is no sin (say the Papists): they are righteous still for all that. See how the Papists do wholly mock God, in that they think by some fond ceremony, or by a *mea culpa*,[11] they are discharged of their sins, and thus make nothing of them. These are the loopholes they use to mock God as they would a young babe, which is a dreadful thing. Yet, it is put to use in all their schools.

We on our part dare not think after this fashion, but rather we must keep in mind what the apostle says, that "it is a dreadful thing to fall into the hands of the living God" (Heb. 10:31). Therefore, we must not ever break the bonds and yoke He has laid in our necks; we must not act like wild beasts; we must not think of beguiling Him by some hypocritical show of obedience, having all the while no real purity of intention to serve Him at all. For in the end He will show that His vengeance shall light upon all such as have lived as hypocrites and doubleminded deceivers before His face.

What shall we do then? We must straightforwardly reject this pretense of "righteousness in part," which the Papists have in-

---

Unction, he will go to hell. If, however, he dies with only little sins, called "venial sins," on his soul, he will go to purgatory, where these will be purged away.

11. *Mea culpa*: Latin for "through my fault." An ancient prayer of penitence, characterized by this phrase.

vented. It is a device of Satan. Indeed, even they themselves will admit that we cannot merit by any inward worthiness that is in our works. They say that all the worth of our works comes only from this, that God is acquainted with us, so that when men have done all that is possible, yet there will always be some fault that can be found with their works when they come before God. Not that all Papists are of this mind; there is not one in a thousand that thinks this way. But there is here a far finer and more subtle doctrine of Popery, which is that works are not worthy of themselves, but because of the promise of the law.[12]

But what is the promise? Let us come to the point. Behold, God offers himself to all men, and says that whoever performs the law shall be blessed, and on the other hand they shall be cursed who step away from it. Thus you see that the perfect righteousness is the performing of the law. But as I have told you already, no man performs it, and therefore God is quit of His promise towards us. Seeing that we, on our side, fail in the condition, He for His part owes us nothing. After the same manner also speaks St. Paul, saying, "If righteousness depends on the works of the law, then is the promise null and void" (Rom. 4:14). St. Paul in this place touches the matter to the quick. After all, who is it that has so performed the law? And so consequently we shall all be damned if we ground ourselves upon our works. After that manner he speaks here (Rom. 4), and also to the Galatians (Gal. 3).

And so let us mark that God denounces all of us to condemnation when He says, "Cursed be he who does not perform all the things contained in the book of My law." As for this carrying on that the Papists call "satisfactions," they are but mockeries. God wishes to be served by true obedience. Moreover, the releasing of our sins is freely bestowed, as the Holy Scripture teaches. And so for all the "satisfactions" (as they term them) that men have come up with, they serve no purpose, nor does God accept any

---

12. Calvin seems to be objecting to the view that God condescends to accept our good works, unworthy though they be, as meritorious. Elsewhere Calvin strongly insists on the necessity of good works for salvation, but as necessary accompaniments of faith, not as meritorious. On this subject, see Wallace, *op. cit.*

of them. When we start coming up with our own ideas out of our brains, He refuses every bit of it. Therefore, let us hold to the grace of our Lord Jesus Christ, knowing that we are washed and cleansed by His blood, and that this is the only remedy that God sets forth for us.

Salvation in Christ Alone

Thus we have two things to mark. The one is that if we should be judged by the law of God, there would not be needed anything more than this one sentence to damn us all, yea even the holiest man that ever lived. For no man has ever satisfied God's law, and therefore are we all condemned. For if the holy fathers, who had an angelic holiness in this world, were all the same at fault before God, what will become of us? Let us now make a comparison between us and them. How far removed are we from the holiness of Abraham, the purity of David, the rectitude of Job, and the perfection of Daniel? When these stand condemned, where do we stand? Let us, then, learn to pull in our horns, and let every one of us keep his mouth shut, as St. Paul says (Rom. 3:19) when he brings us to the righteousness of faith and to the mercy of God.

What we need to keep in mind, then, is that God has removed all self-righteousness from us, to rid us of all presumption and pride, so that we should no longer pretend to come to account with Him to bind Him to us, but that we should willingly condemn ourselves. That is the first thing.

Now from this we have to consider the remedy that God has left, which is that we can be righteous by means of our Lord Jesus Christ. For He has delivered us from the curse that was due against us, and for that reason He was hanged upon a tree, as St. Paul says (Gal. 3:13). We have seen already in this series, in the twenty-first chapter, that as many as were hanged upon a tree were all accursed (Dt. 21:23). Now when God made that law, did He not know what He had already ordained concerning His only Son, who was to be hanged upon a tree? Surely it was an unchangeable decree, made even before the foundation of the world. Seeing this is so, we are redeemed from the curse by our Lord

Jesus Christ.

And we must now match this sentence with the other that we saw in the twenty-first chapter. It is said here, "Cursed shall be the man who does not perform all these sayings," and you see clearly that when we do not perform them we are condemned and as good as damned. But we must embrace, with this, our Lord Jesus Christ, who was cursed for our sakes, so that if this curse is not in vain, we must now be set free. What a thing it would be if the Son of God should be cursed without cause, and yet no benefit redound to us; that He who is the fountain of all blessedness should be accursed, and yet we know not why except that it is worthless? Now then, seeing that the curse Jesus Christ suffered in His own person is not vain and purposeless, let us realize that by the same means we are delivered before God. And so you see how we ought to make these two texts agree.

Furthermore, we know that He became subject to the law (Gal. 4:4) so that He might perform all manner of obedience to the full, as it were in our own persons. And the righteousness He has in Himself is at this day credited to us, as if every one of us had discharged himself before God. The way, then, for us to be delivered from our cursedness is this: After we have been ashamed and as it were plunged in despair, we may take heart again, being assured of our salvation, and offer ourselves before the amnesty of our God with full assurance that He will accept us as His children and also love us; and moreover that seeing our Lord Jesus Christ has fulfilled the law, and not failed in any point or jot thereof, now we are clothed again with His righteousness, and the same is credited to us as our own.

And therefore let us go boldly before God, and call upon Him as our Father. Let us not ascribe purity to our own works, or imagine that God owes us anything, or pretend to bring any desert or merit of our own; but being utterly empty, let us call upon God to vouchsafe not only to fill up what is partially lacking in us, by means of our Lord Jesus Christ, but to give us that righteousness of which we are utterly destitute and unfurnished.

And let us mark further, that when we are once thus received into favor, then will our works also be accepted. The way for us, then, to serve God to His liking is that being justified by faith (that is to say, having obtained forgiveness of our sins because daily and all the time of our lives we have need of it) and also having recourse to God's reconciliation with us of His own free goodness by means of the death, suffering, and sacrifice of our Lord Jesus Christ offered up to Him — having these things, the way to serve God to His liking is to do so with this attitude of faith. For then shall we do well, and then will He accept the service we yield to Him. And apart from this we have no faith in Jesus Christ.

But when we endeavor to serve God, even though there may be things wrong, and our affections turn us now one way and now another, yet God does not take our lives. Why? Because our sins are not imputed to us. It is true that this curse will stand in force in full rigor, but behold! Christ is our ransom, and pays for us, delivering us from our cursedness, and making satisfaction to God His Father. For we know that His death and suffering are accepted as the price and ransom of our salvation, that by such means we should be reconciled to God.

You see then, that on the one hand it behooves us to feel our own cursedness, that we may be afraid of God's judgments, and that on the other hand we must take courage, not doubting, but seeing that since our Lord Jesus Christ answers for us, we shall be received for His sake, and God will accept us together with our works, even though they are not as good as they should be but have some blots and blemishes in them, so that they deserve to be condemned and utterly rejected. In brief, the faithful, being justified by the grace of God, have along with it this benefit and privilege: that God accepts their works and does not charge them with this curse that they have deserved. That is how we ought to put this text into practice.

Mourning and Rejoicing

But I have told you that on the one side we must mourn and be afraid at the sight of our cursedness before God, and that on the other side we must trust in the grace Jesus Christ offers us. For if we should become careless because God has forgiven our sins, what a thing that would be! We would wind up in the same mess men get into when they think to render only partial obedience to God. Now then, it is needful for us to be sorry for all our sins, and if we detect any vice in ourselves, we must not permit it to reign.

It is true that we come short. I say not in one part only, but in all. There is no point in the law wherein we do not fail. That man who thinks himself free of envy and to be a despiser of worldly goods, surely he still has some other affection in his heart that holds him back in the world. He that is chaste and honest in his body, still has some vanities that will carry him away. He who does not foster any hatred or rancor in his heart, is not so clear of all wicked affection that he lives as perfectly as he ought. In brief, we shall be found guilty, not in one or two points only [but in all], so that there is not any part or piece of the law from which God might not condemn us.

And therefore, as I said, seeing we perceive such imperfection in ourselves, we must not stand in our own conceits, but mourn before God. And having mourned, we must endeavor to give ourselves over to Him, praying Him to increase in us the power and grace of His Holy Spirit, that we may manfully fight against our sins so as to subdue them, overcome them, and get the upper hand of them, to triumph over them once we are clean rid of them. Thus you see how we ought to proceed in this affair.

And this ought to make the faithful rejoice, that although they perceive their own imperfections, yet they must not cease on that account to embrace God's promises with gladness, assuring themselves that they will not be disappointed. And why? Because they enjoy all those things in our Lord Jesus Christ, by whom and by whose means the curse that was due to them is done away. You see then that on the one side it is needful for the faithful to be cast down utterly, and yet on the other side that they be lifted up again in our Lord Jesus Christ, because they know that if they look for what they do not have in themselves, they will find it if they seek it at the place God sends them.

And therefore let us not beguile ourselves any longer with the fancies of Satan, which reign in Popedom, which lead us to offer our own merits to God and to covenant with Him as if we had performed His law. Let us assure ourselves that on our part, all the covenants that are made in the law are utterly vain, and that all the promises that are conditional on our good deeds and holy behavior will be unavailable to us and never come to effect, unless we resort to this free promise: "Whoever believes that Jesus Christ died for our sins, and that God by His power has raised Him again to make us righteous, believing the same in his heart and confessing it with his mouth, shall be saved."

This statement is, of course, what St. Paul brings us to in Romans 10:9, which is the passage that will give us the understanding of this place. The righteousness of the law shows us that we are all accursed, and that there is not any way to save us as long as we remain there. What are we to do then, that we may have access to God? Let us with our hearts believe unto righteousness, and with our mouths confess unto salvation, that we put our whole trust in Him who has acquitted us towards God His father. And let us embrace the righteous obedience that He has yielded unto God, and likewise His sustaining of the curse that was due to us, so that He might free us from it.

Prayer

Now let us fall down before the majesty of our good God with acknowledgement of our sins, praying Him to make us feel them better than we have done before, that we may be more and more touched with the true repentance that mortifies all our fleshly affections. May He draw us from the delights of this world, and lift us up into a true desire of giving ourselves wholly to His law, so that we may daily profit thereby, knowing that the true perfection of all faithful folk is to know how far they are from perfection. May He do this to the end that all mouths may be stopped, and none acknowledged as righteous except God. May it be that when Christ's righteousness once shines upon us, we shall not be bereft of it, assuring ourselves that therein lies our perfection. May it please Him to grant this grace not only to us but also to all people and nations of the earth; etc.

5

PROMISE, OBEDIENCE, BLESSING

Sermon 153. Tuesday, 10 March 1556.
Deuteronomy 28:1-2.

1. Now it will come to pass, if you will diligently hearken to the voice of the LORD your God, being careful to do all His commandments that I command you today, the LORD your God shall set you high above all the nations of the earth.

2. And all these blessings shall come upon you and overtake you, if you will hearken to the voice of the LORD your God.

We have seen earlier how God covenanted with His people, purposing to bind them so that everyone should know his duty and be the better disposed to perform it. It does not matter whether people plead guilty or not when they have done wrong, for God here gives His determined sentence whether they consent to it or not. Nor does He start off with a condemnation of those who offend the law, but rather He begins with friendly promises, thereby to lure and win the hearts of men to Himself.

Promise and Duty

And so He says, "If you hearken to My voice, to obey My commandments, and be careful to keep them, you shall be blessed in all manner of ways, and you shall be surrounded through My favor with all kinds of welfare and prosperity." I have mentioned before that God shows great goodness towards men when He endeavors by such means to win them. It would have been enough, after all, for Him to have said, "This is your duty"; and all creatures would have to tremble at His speaking. Therefore, when He adds any promises, He sets aside part of His right, and therein humbles Himself, that we should be the better disposed and more inclined to serve Him. When we have done all that we can, yea and more than we are able, is God bound to recompense us? Surely not.

We must always bear in mind what our Lord Jesus says in St. Luke 17:7, that if a man has a bond servant and he sends him to labor in the field all day long, when the servant comes home at night, will he say, "Well, now I must take my turn. You sit down at the table, and I shall prepare your supper and give you your meat and drink. You have labored for me all day, and now it is my turn to serve you"? Will the master say this? No, of course not. Rather when the servant comes home, the master will say to him, "Cover the table, fix my supper, and give me a drink." Even so says Jesus Christ, "When you have done all that it is possible for you to do, don't think in yourself that God My Father owes you anything at all, or that He is obligated to you, but proceed further on and acknowledge that all you can ever do is but your duty towards Him." And indeed, seeing that God has created us, where is the man that can do too much in His service?

We see then that God might say plainly, "This is what pleases Me, and this is My will. You follow this way." And therefore, when He tells us that we shall be blessed, and not lose our labor but have a reward for our service, it cannot be doubted but that in so doing He sets aside some part of His right.

So then we may see that He acts as the good and kindhearted father to win His children. For even though a father knows well that his children are bound to obey him to the uttermost, and that he on his part is not in any way bound to obey them, yet he will surely say, "I love you, and I only desire your own welfare. Do according to my wishes, and I shall never forsake you." A father will be liberal in his promises, saying, "Look, you know that all I have is for you. For whom else do I travail? And to what other end? And if I see you take to good ways, I shall reward you accordingly." Thus acts the father who humbles himself in his authority. And why? Because he wishes that his children should serve him of a free good will, rather than be compelled to it by rigorous extremities.

Let us mark, therefore, that all the promises contained in Holy Scripture are, as it were, so many testimonies of the fatherly love of our God, showing Himself to have a care for our health and welfare, in that He vouchsafes thus to apply and fashion Himself to us. By this means the law of God becomes more friendly to us, in that we see that in keeping it we shall not be disappointed of a good reward, one far greater than we should wish, for under this word of blessing is comprehended all manner of prosperity.

Moreover, when God makes us to prosper in this world, it is for no other purpose than to give us a taste of His love toward us. This, however, is not the main point He wants to get across to us, but He leads us ever onward, so that when we feel His goodness in this present life, and that He cares for us and that He reaches forth His hand to provide all things that are necessary, we ought to conclude from this much more strongly that when He has taken us out of this present world, He will then pour on us the riches of His goodness in another manner than we are now able to comprehend. Indeed, we have in this life some small indications thereof, but the abundant accomplishment of it will be in the kingdom of heaven. Thus you see what we have to consider, in that our God delivers forth His promises to train us the better to serve Him of a free goodwill.

The Efficacy of Promise

Nevertheless, no matter how the world goes, let us mark that all of God's conditional promises are of no help to us if we stand on them alone, as I told you yesterday. And why? Surely God is faithful, and does not speak to deceive us. True, but let us look at ourselves. Where is the man that discharges himself of his duties so well that he may hope to be blessed by God? It is not said, "You shall be blessed by keeping part of My law." Rather, the text reads: "If you hear My voice and be diligent in keeping all My commandments, and fulfill them all, then I will bless you."

Now when we see men endeavoring as much as possible to keep the law of God, this is not due to their own power or natural inclination. For so far removed are they who have not been regenerated by the Holy Spirit from attaining to the service of God, that they cannot so much as conceive a good thought. What is the inclination of man, but a striving against God and all His righteousness? As long as men follow the leading of their own spirits they do nothing but fight against God as utter rebels against His will. In brief, we are not able as much as to think to do well (2 Cor. 3:5). To think is a very small thing, and yet St. Paul here cuts us off even from that power, and shows that we are so corrupted and perversely bent that in all things we move contrary to what God commands us.

In so much that God has reformed us by His Holy Spirit, and changed our malice and rebellion, to which we were previously wholly inclined, yet still it cannot be said that we proceed to obey Him in all perfection, for there is always some infirmity to prevent us. So that instead of running we halt, and trail our legs after us. Instead of going straight forward, we reel from one side to another. And frequently we stumble, as every man can tell for himself. How then can we hope to be blessed by God, being so far from keeping His law?

This is why I said that all the conditional promises are utterly powerless, and will never come to their effect, if God should rest upon that point. Indeed, this matter was expounded yesterday, and this passage was expressly cited by St. Paul where it is said that if salvation comes by works, and the inheritance proceeds from the law, there will be no performance of the promises (Rom. 4:14). For we fail on our parts, and therefore the covenant is void that God has made with us. Yet we may not conclude that God is mocking us when He sets down these promises, as the Papists do at the first opportunity, breaking out of bounds, acting as madmen. For when we say that all the promises contained in Holy Scripture are not effectual except by means of the forgiveness of our sins through the free goodness of God, and that we are justified by faith alone, they reply: "What? Seeing it is said, 'I will bless you, if you serve Me and honor Me,' it seems that God is being hypocritical, and dallying with men. Why should God make such a promise?" Thus do the papists accuse God of falsehood, and blaspheme Him, if they are not able to deserve the promises He has made them [on their own merits]. For otherwise, they think, it is but a mockery, to make men believe that He would bless them.

But let us beware of such madness, and let us rather understand why God has given His promise to men, and we shall see that it is not in vain. I said before that God has showed His great goodness in humbling Himself so lovingly unto us. We pertain wholly to Him. We are altogether His. And yet He does not simply command, but commands with the promises and gentleness, to win us. If a man replies to this and says, "What does it profit us?" I answer, truly it profits us nothing at all if we stay here; but we must go further. When we hear the promises that God has offered to us, and see that His whole intention is to win us through necessity, then we are condemned if we are not thankful and if we do not bend ourselves wholly to Him. But we cannot do it. Well then, are we excused? No, for it is our own wickedness that prevents us. Every man will condemn himself, says St. James, because there is nothing that provokes us to evil except the concupiscence of our own flesh. Seeing then that the fault is in us, we must make no more allegations. And here you see we are confounded before God.

Thus you see that we have a double reason to be lowly. First of all, because we are so sinful that God's goodness does not move us to come near Him or to put ourselves under His leading. And second, because we do not search out the bottom of the sin that is in us, in such a way as this: "Alas, seeing I have every day so many innumerable thoughts, so many desires and motions, such a store of affections, which serve altogether to turn me away from that good to which God calls me, by reason of which I never cease to offend God in all things, so that nothing can be drawn from me except utter evil, all offense, and all iniquity; alas, what will become of me?" Men, when they see this, must feel themselves doubly confounded.

And when they have well examined themselves, they must be driven to think thus: "Well, God has laid before me all the means that I can wish, to attain my salvation, if I were not altogether corrupt and perverse. And now I cannot plead ignorance, seeing that the law is given to me and the way showed me, how I ought to govern myself and how to lead my life. And so that I should be the more willing to do it, God has trained me to it by gentleness, promising that I will be rewarded for serving Him. Is this so? What, then, is to be done? I must not, in this case, make any further protestation or stand pleading any more against God, for I am too much to blame already."

Now when men find themselves thus condemned, then they are forced to seek their salvation outside of themselves, and to resort to this second remedy: "Alas, Lord, if the case were such that I should obtain salvation by serving You, You have given me Your law, and have joined to it Your promises. These things, however, avail me nothing. I must therefore forsake myself, acknowledging that I have no hope of life unless I find some better help." See here, I say, how we are led to our Lord Jesus Christ and made to embrace the grace offered us in Him, that by obtaining forgiveness of our sins we may be sure to be blessed by God. When we have obtained that one favor, that God is at one with us by means of our Lord Jesus Christ, then He does accept our imperfect works as though we had accomplished all the law.

Although the good the faithful do is not worthy to be received by God, yet He accepts it as good. Why? Because He of His own goodness wipes away all the faults that are in them. So then, when we labor to do well, notwithstanding that it does not lie in our power to attain to perfection because of the exceeding frailty of our natures, yet God will receive our service as acceptable, as though He had nothing to say against it. And so are we made partakers of the blessings that are here mentioned. It is true that we have not fulfilled all the law, but yet God records it in His accounts as if all had been performed because we are made clean by the blood of Jesus Christ. And just as we are cleansed, so are our works also, and when they come before God, He accepts them as though they were thoroughly good, righteous, and perfect. Here, therefore, we perceive that the promises are not given in vain, but that they have their effect in the faithful, not at the first glance, but when we come to them by degrees and circumstances, for then we shall feel the effect and force of them.

Now concerning unbelievers, the promises avail them nothing except to make them the more unexcusable before God in the last day. For what will they be able to plead, seeing that God has so familiarly offered Himself to them, requiring nothing but to have the fruition of their entire lives that they might obey Him? And yet they continue hardhearted. Do you not see how they stand doubly confounded? And therefore the promises and threats of the law are always good and righteous. Nor are they unprofitable, if a man will take them as they should be taken. But this will be better understood by the discourse that will particularly concern this.

The Grace of Law

Now let us proceed to expound the words that Moses uses. "If you will hear the voice of the Lord your God, and be careful to fulfill all the commandments I command you this day, all these blessings shall come upon you and compass you round about." Concerning the first point, Moses shows what we saw before, namely that the first thing in living well is to hearken to God. For men must not have the rule over themselves, saying, "I will govern myself after my own liking." We must not take such liberty, for he that takes too much upon himself will at the last be rejected by God for not yielding Him His due obedience, which is the foundation whereon we ought to build. Let us mark, therefore, that all they which follow their own foolish devotions (as they call them) are disliked by God. For Isaiah 1:12 must be heard: "Who has required these things from you?"

Let us acknowledge, therefore, that it is an inestimable benefit when God shows us His will, and that the state of the Papists is accursed. For when they intend to do well, they do not know which way to turn themselves, but every one follows his own fancy, saying "I hope it will turn out well, for my intention is good. And after all, common custom permits it. And again, our holy mother Church commands it." But in the meanwhile, the law of God is forgotten. We may learn from this that there is nothing but confusion in the life of man, in which is nothing else than a mingling without order until they are taught of God, as we shall see hereafter. This is the way; walk in it.

Careful Obedience

It is said that we "must be careful." This phrase was set down once before by Moses, and with good reason it is repeated here again. For we are warned by it that unless men are very heedful in obeying God and force themselves thereto and set their whole study thereon in good earnest, they will never attain to keep the law. And we ourselves see what weakness there is in us, even though God does govern us, and even though we are reformed by His Holy Spirit. As for the unfaithful, they are so carried away and so furious in their willful stubbornness, that a man would think they should run madly against God. Indeed, and although we are governed by the Holy Spirit, yet we are so frail that it is a pity to see. God requires a great perfection when He wishes us to love Him with all our hearts, to eschew all the vanities of this world and all our fleshly lusts, and in brief to forsake ourselves and to be altogether changed. This is a matter overly high and difficult.

Now let us consider what Satan devises and practises to turn us away from the service of God. How many sorts of temptations are there? They are infinite. Again how severe are the assaults that Satan prepares against us? When we have given considera-tion to all this, we may well conclude that it is with good reason that God says we must be careful, that every one of us must strengthen himself, and gather all our forces together, and not think to set forth negligently to the service of our God. For when we think to march one step forward, we shall go a hundred backward if we are not very strong and courageous, holding ourselves in awe and restraining ourselves, and gathering our wits about us so that we bend our minds wholly thereto, and even, as one might say, labor for breath in travelling about it.

And moreover, seeing we are laid about with ambushes on every side and should be soon taken, so that we might fall into the snares of Satan before we are aware, let us take heed and be watchful. That is what we are warned about here. And would to God that we would carry away this lesson with care. For then, while we are now applying our powers and all our endeavors to things not only frivolous but altogether harmful, tending to none other end than destruction, then every one of us would be vigilant to walk in the obedience of God and to give himself wholly thereto. And seeing that we are warned about it, there is no excuse. Shall we then obey our God, and show that our affection is so inclined, without deception? Let every one of us incline to what is given him in commandment, namely to be careful, vigilant, and attentive.

Authority of Office

Now he adds, "to keep all the commandments that I [Moses] set before you this day," or that I ordain for you. Although Moses is the speaker of this, yet he takes the authority and power to command and to subdue men. This is not anything of his own invention, as if to say that it ought to be received without gainsaying because he said so. Rather it is from God, because God speaks by his mouth, and because he himself faithfully delivers the teaching that was committed to him. For that reason he speaks in such a strong way, saying that they should keep his [Moses'] statutes.

It does not lie in the power of a mortal man to bind the consciences of people. And yet that is the very thing that has wholly corrupted the Church, in that men have usurped the office of God in making laws and statutes for the spiritual government of men's souls. And it is a point of high treason against God for the creature to usurp to himself what pertains only to God, whom the prophet Isaiah termed the Lawgiver (Is. 33:22), and also St. James (James 4:12), so that we should learn to hearken to Him, and wholly to depend on His word. Let us mark well then, that it is not lawful for men to enjoin laws for the souls of other men.

But when Moses says, "I ordain to you," he presupposes that he is not setting out anything of his own or forging any law out of his own brain; nor is he adding anything to what God had committed unto him; but only that inasmuch as he performed his office faithfully, he might well say, "I ordain for you." Just as when we set forth the pure Word of God, the very same Word is a sovereign commandment. Now this does not mean that we should usurp any dominion or sovereignty over men's souls, but that in doing service to God, we may command in His name and in His person. Thus we see here what Moses' meaning was.

And indeed, does it lie within us to promise men life everlasting or to denounce against them the vengeance of God? And yet we do it nevertheless, but we go no further than the Word of God, as it is put into our mouths. We have His testimony that we are His witness and His heralds. By His "witnesses" I mean we assure the faithful of the grace and salvation promised to them, and as His "heralds" we pronounce and publish His sentence against all the unbelieving and against all rebels. Therefore in brief God meant to show forth the majesty of His Word when He appointed Moses to speak in that manner.

This was so that we should receive the Word of God with more lowliness and reverence when it is preached unto us, not respecting the person (as if someone should say, "He is but a man that is speaking; he is just like us; as we are, so is he"), but as though we thought thus with ourselves: "It is God who speaks by the mouth of this man; therefore, let us tremble at His presence. Let us stoop, and receive what He says, and seeing He calls us before Him, let it serve to bring us to such obedience that we do Him homage, to show thereby that we receive what proceeds from His majesty." Let us keep that in mind from this text.

Comprehensive Obedience Enjoined

Now here a question might be put forth, why it is said "When you have kept all His commandments." For it is impossible for us to fulfill the law as long as we stand clothed with this mortal flesh. As I said before, we shall always be full of vices and imperfections. It seems, then, that it is to no purpose for God to require such a fulfilling of the law, seeing it is impossible. But here we must remember what has been spoken before, which is that God in His law does not respect our might, power, or ability, but our duty, and after what manner our life ought to be governed. And the same ought to suffice us, inasmuch as we say a man will never attain to the perfect obedience of God, but that we are always far from the end of our way. The cause of this is our corrupt nature, which is so infected through original sin that when we think on God we are troubled with many evil fancies, and when we have any good motion we are by and by plucked back from it, and we do not need any other thing to draw us to the complete antithesis.

But, does the impossibility of our doing it discharge us of our service that we are bound to perform for God? No. For the evil comes from ourselves. It is no marvel, then, that God in His law should have no regard to man's ability or inability, but rather to the duty we owe Him. Nor is it surprising that He should require the right that belongs to Him, for where is the man that can deny it to Him? God cannot change His nature. If we are rebellious, what does He have to do with our stains and filthiness? But He sets forth such a righteousness that we are not able to reply against.

And in His law He sets down a righteousness of a sort different from what He has in Himself. He does not have respect to His own righteousness, but to the righteousness that ought to be in His creatures, namely such as is in His angels. If we had continued in our integrity, and not been perverted and corrupted through sin, then should we have been able to discharge all that God requires of us in His law. That is certain. Now then, we see how it is with good reason that God will have us to keep His whole law. And though it is true that we are not able to perform it, the default proceeds from the sin that dwells in us, as I have showed before.

Now, with all this we have to note that since God promises nothing except to those that have obeyed all the law, it would be too incredibly stupid to suppose that we can merit or deserve by doing this or that thing. We must first of all have kept all the law, which is impossible. The Papists, however, praise their merits, which they think enable them to purchase the kingdom of heaven. They think that when they have done anything good in their own eyes, God is bound to them. "Oh," they say. "I have been devoutly at Mass." It is certain that they provoke the wrath of God by so doing, for we know that it is a devilish abomination. Again, "I have served such and such a Saint, my patron. I have such and such a chapel." And they think that by so doing they earn heaven. Truly all these things are but a despising of God. They are Satanic superstitions by which the service of God is thoroughly defaced.

But let us suppose that the papists did well in their dallying with such garbage, would God be bound to them for it? It is needful for them to consider what court their evidence must pass before. For it is not for us to bridle Him, or to tie Him to the stake, or to subdue Him to our fantasies. It must proceed from His own good will. Now then, what has He said? "When you will have kept all My commandments, then shall these blessings come upon you." Let every one of us look at how he has kept the commandments of God. Let the Papists brag as much as they like, can they say that they have accomplished a hundredth part of them? If they have kept one of God's commandments, they have offended Him in a hundred sins for it; and if there be but one fault committed, though it be ever so small, they are faulty in all, as St. James says (James 2:10) that he who breaks the law in only one point is guilty of having broken all of it.

Seeing then that they are offenders, they are deprived and banished from all the blessings that God has set forth, even from those that concern only this present transitory life; and much less are they able to earn the kingdom of heaven (as they imagine), being not able to deserve one morsel of bread to put into their mouths. They are thus shut out of all. And why? Because God has not promised anything except to them that keep all of His entire law.

God as Judge and Father

How shall we live, then? We must hear God speak after some other fashion; that is, we must hear Him speak the free promises He offers to us in our Lord Jesus Christ. God in the Holy Scripture uses a double kind of speech, by which I do not mean that He contradicts Himself, or that He is contrary to Himself, or that one of His sayings is repugnant to any other, for God always remains the same and, as I have said before, He changes not. All the words that proceed from Him agree together very well, without any contradiction. Nevertheless, concerning His law, there He has spoken as a judge, and not as a father. In His law He speaks as a judge, saying: "He who lives as he ought will not be deceived. He will not lose his labor. For when you have done Me service, I will cause you to prosper." In such a way does God speak in the person of a judge. And when we have received this word, behold, we are confounded, no matter how things stand. And why? Because we do not have the ability to obtain the grace that is offered to us, and we cease not to kindle God's wrath against us, and therefore we shall all be damned.

What is to be done, then? God comes, speaking as a father, and says, "Well, I am content to forbear this rigor, which I might execute upon you by My law, even though that rigor is not overly great, for I have given Myself so far to you as to promise what is not your due. I have been willing, as it were, to entice you by friendly means, but I have won nothing thereby because of your perversity. What is the remedy, then? I come now to tell you that if you will believe in My Son, I will release you of all your debts. If you will receive Him as your Shepherd, that He may guide you quietly, you will perceive that I do not desire to win you in any way other than by gentle and friendly dealings. It is as if I should say, 'Come to me, and I will forgive you all your sins, and accept you into favor.' And although you are miserable creatures, deserving utter damnation, yet I will completely forget and bury all your offenses. And when I have done that, I promise to beget you anew by My Holy Spirit. And this grace shall be given to you by means of My only Son, if you labor to come to Him. And then, even though you are driven to strive against many temptations and at first encounter you will not have full victory over them but will be surrounded with many spots and vices, yet I shall not lay any of these things to your charge. I forgive you your sins, and the good that you do shall be acceptable to Me through My favor, even though it deserves nothing." See here the second kind of speech that God uses toward us in the Holy Scripture.

Let us note, therefore, that when we hear the voice of God and know what we owe Him, and hear the promises that He has made to us in His law, we must stand confounded and condemned since none of those things can avail us because of our unthankfulness. Thus, we must have our refuge in the free mercy offered to us in our Lord Jesus Christ, and hearken to God when He speaks to us, which He does both in the law and in the prophets as well as in the gospel, saying, "I of My own mere goodness have become your Savior, and you must seek your salvation from some place other than in yourselves."

After all, the Redeemer promised by God was always kept before the minds of men, that they might rest on Him. That is why the sacrifices were ordained in the time of the law. For although Christ was not yet displayed openly to the whole world, yet did the Jews understand that all the hope of their salvation depended upon their reconciliation to God by means of the sacrifice that was to be offered. They brought brute beasts to the Temple. Was that to cleanse the uncleanness of their souls? No, of course not. But under these figures the Jews saw how they would be delivered from the curse of God and admitted into His favor, and should be acceptable to Him. And now we have a more certain testimony of this in the gospel, for there we see the thing itself fully accomplished for us, namely that although we have not kept the commandments, Jesus Christ has kept them.

And why did He do so? Because He was subject to it? No, but He became subject to the law for our sakes.

So then, let us have our recourse unto our Lord Jesus Christ, and let us hear God speaking in such a way that He not only says, "These are the things that I command you, and if you do them then you shall prosper and be blessed;" but also where He says, "Behold, I am your Father. Come to Me, but come in the name of My only Son, whom I have appointed to be your mediator. And acknowledge that there is nothing else in you but corruption. And do not trust in your own power or in your own free will, but casting away all foolish fantasies of vain presumption, come with lowliness to see the grace of My Spirit. Then you will be sure that I always uphold you by My goodness, and from day to day confirm you in My fear and make you to walk in My ways, so that I will not lay to your charge the faults of your works; they shall not hinder My blessing towards you. Not that you should not confess your transgressions, and always acknowledge before Me that you are sinful, but that your sin shall not be laid to your charge, even though there might come occasions why they should be called to reckoning to be reproved by Me." Such is the second voice of God, to which we must hearken if we desire to become partakers of the blessings that are here contained.

Here by the way we must note as a conclusion that although the faithful are exempted from the curse of God, so that He will not deal rigorously with them but rather uphold them and make them to enjoy the blessings He has promised in His law as though they had fully accomplished the same, yet they cease not to suffer many stripes of His rod, and our Lord chastises them continually, exercising some after one manner and some after another so that all are smitten. And all the chastisements God sends us are curses, every one of them, at least to outward appearance. If we are sick; if we are hungry or thirsty; if we are tormented in this present world; if we are troubled and persecuted; all these are the curses of God. Our enemies scoff at us. We are in reproach, in poverty, in vexation, and in many anguishes. One is troubled in his house by his wife; another by his children; and another by his neighbor.

Finally, the faithful are in many ways deprived of the blessings of God. It is certainly so.

This, however, does not prevent us from being ever more blessed by Him, because we have a continual taste of His goodness, to allure us to Him. Let us note well, therefore, that when He cuts off His blessings and does not give them as we wish, this is for our profit because He sees that we have need of some quickening to make us come to Him. And since every one of us will fall asleep on our sins, God is determined to awaken us, and to make us feel that as soon as we withdraw from His service He will also absent Himself from us, and that His grace will be taken away from us and we stand dispossessed of it — never, however, so utterly that the blessings of God will not overcome so that we may rejoice therein, acknowledging Him to be merciful and waiting upon His fatherly goodness, which will be shown more amply when He will take us again to Himself.

Thus you see how we may possess and enjoy the blessings of God, which are set forth for us in His law. And when we see that our Lord interlaces these blessings with many afflictions and corrections, as though He had cursed us, we must realize that His purpose in this is to provoke us day by day to repentance, and to keep us from falling asleep in this present world. We know that our pleasures make us drunken and unmindful of God unless He constrains us by pricking and spurring us forward. Thus you see how things that at first sight seemed contraries agree very well in fact. And in that respect does Moses say that these blessings shall light upon us and encompass us round about, as if he had said that we will always be certain of God's favor — so certain of it that it shall never fail us if we serve Him.

For the word "encompass," or to light upon us ["overtake," Dt. 28:2], indicates that the grace of God is not fleeting, as though it fell at random and as though we would not be able to catch it. No, says Moses, you shall be surrounded or encompassed with it. And therefore let us assure ourselves that the goodness of our God shall never fail us, so that we can never come to that goodness unless He draw us to Himself. And since we are subject to so many infirmities and vices, He, by bearing with us, shows us that we must have recourse to His free goodness for the forgiveness of our sins by the reconciliation that He has made in our Lord Jesus Christ, and that we, in straining ourselves to do His will, shall perceive that the goodness of God does not cease to be free to us, without owing us anything at all.

Prayer

Now let us fall down before the majesty of our good God, with acknowledgement of our sins, praying Him to make us feel them more than we have done before, that being beaten down, and as it were drowned in despair, we may be drawn to faith in our Lord Jesus Christ; and knowing that we are altogether empty and naked of all goodness, let us beseech Him to renew us by His Holy Spirit, until we are fully changed. Let us pray that we be more and more increased in His graces, so that we may have testimony that God regards us, and is near to us, and dwells in us; and that we may be confirmed in His adoption, that we may always wait for the heavenly inheritance and not be weary in this world to walk in His obedience; that it may please Him to bestow this grace not only upon us but also upon all people and nations of the earth; etc.

6

BLESSING AND AFFLICTION

Sermon 154. Wednesday, 11 March 1556.
Deuteronomy 28:2-8.

2. And all these blessings shall come upon you and overtake you, if you will hearken to the voice of the LORD your God.

3. Blessed shall you be in the city, and blessed shall you be in the field.

4. Blessed shall be the fruit of your body, and the fruit of your ground, and the fruit of your cattle: the offspring of your herds and the lambs of your flocks.

5. Blessed shall be your basket and your kneading-trough.

6. Blessed shall you be when you come in and blessed shall you be when you go out.

7. The LORD shall cause your enemies that rise up against you to be smitten before your face. They shall come against you one way, and flee before you seven ways.

8. The LORD shall command the blessing upon you in your storehouses, and in all that you set your hand to, and He shall bless you in the land the LORD your God is giving you.

It is a thing to be marvelled at, that men cannot be persuaded that they will prosper if they do righteously. This, however, proceeds from unbelief, because they do not acknowledge that their lives are in the power and direction of God, and that it is His peculiar office to govern us. For if we were well assured that all creatures are in the hand of God, and also that He has care of us, it is certain that every one of us would rest in Him, waiting to receive all goodness from Him. This is something that should encourage us to serve Him, and to direct ourselves after His will. But although every one of us seeks and desires his own ease, yet we do not understand that God is the one from whom we must look for it. We can say it well enough, but our actions show that we cannot judge or conceive it to be so.[1] Everyone tries to become rich by evil practices; every man seeks his own happiness by offending God! We have to conclude that we are without sense and reason, since this doctrine, in which we should be resolved, cannot be imprinted in our minds; to wit, that all welfare proceeds from the hand of God, and that there is no way to prosper except by giving ourselves over to Him, and to His service.

Misery and Sin

Yet notwithstanding, God has always left this engraved on the hearts of men so that the pagans themselves had the same opinion common among them: that the wretchedness and miseries to which we are subject proceed from the corruption of mankind. It is certain that they were not taught about the fall of Adam, and that they did not understand how all mankind came to be cursed, for the Devil through his wiles had put them out of that knowledge. All the same, it was understood among them, and written down, and common to all of them, that all the sickness and wretchedness that men endure, all the famines and plagues and such like things, have come from this: that men have tried to rob God of more wisdom than belongs to them. They did not know that this came from the Tree of the Knowledge of Good and Evil; they knew nothing of that. Nevertheless, God did not permit that knowledge to be buried completely, so it remained among the

---

1. That is, our actions show that our profession is mere lip service. We look to our own craftiness rather than to God's blessing for prosperity.

heathen and infidels. They understood that because man tried to usurp to himself more knowledge than was lawful for him, all things are now confounded in this world, and the life of man has become miserable and subject to so many adversities as to make it horrible.

Now, this by itself is sufficient to make us altogether inexcusable. Yet, God will have us (by "us" I mean those whom God has chosen to be part of His household) to be more familiarly taught. Thus God speaks as it were mouth to mouth, and what the infidels had only by means of imagination, the same does He tell and testify to us. I say, He tells it to us that we might know it familiarly, and He testifies it to us that we should be assured thereof. This is why He says that He will make all manner of felicity to rain upon us: so that we shall hearken to His voice. By this He shows that though we do not deserve it, He is ready and forward to entreat us as a father does his children; and that He does not delight in vexing us with multitudes of evils, but intends rather to make us feel His goodness in all respects. Let us therefore be advised to walk in the obedience of our God, if we want Him to pour upon us the treasures of His grace in such a way that our lives may be blessed.

Why the Righteous Suffer

Nevertheless, we know that God often afflicts His people for reasons other than their sins, as we see it happened to Job, this being a notable mirror for us. We see the like in the holy patriarchs, who although they did endeavor and travail to serve God, yet were in as great troubles and griefs as could be. This is even more manifest in the New Covenant. For since God has revealed more fully what the perfect happiness of men is, it is required that the faithful be exercised under many adversities in this transitory life.

But let us note first of all that if God does not punish the sins of the faithful, yet He does chastise them in order to preserve them, just as a physician does not always wait until the sickness appears, but if he perceives any likelihood that a man is in danger, he will act to prevent it. God then, in not punishing the sins presently committed by His children, does chastise them in the interest of preserving them. It may be that there is a man who day after day obeys God, and does not offend Him in some particular sins. All the same, if he were always in prosperity, he would forget himself, so God acts to cure such diseases by withdrawing His blessings. He will not allow the fat to blind men's eyes or to hinder our coming to Him, lest it should hold us too long in this world. He will not allow us to become so entangled in our delights that we fall completely to sleep in the same.

There is a second point, which is that when God forbears to punish us for our sins, it is not because He does not always have just cause to do so if He wished. Pick out the most perfect folk you wish, yet if God were to deal with them in rigor, He should lay many hard knocks in them. But we may not think so, since we are not as clear-sighted as we should have to be to know the faults that God sees. But we must assure ourselves that God shows His patience and goodness in that He spares men, and does not punish them (and by this I mean the most righteous that can be found).

We may take as examples of this: David, when cruelly persecuted by Saul and by all his various enemies; and Abraham, who was stung and vexed in many ways, and also Isaac and Jacob; and all the prophets, who were afflicted by the wicked and by those who despised God, even to death; and finally the apostles and all the faithful, who were cruelly dealt with. This was not for their sins. No, indeed. If God had been pleased to call them to account, He might have punished them a hundred times more severely, and they would have had no cause to accuse Him of cruelty. He spared them, and in so doing He did them the honor of suffering for His name; or rather He tried their obedience, killed their carnal affections, and drew them near to Himself. For example, when God was pleased to make Job a mirror of patience, yet at the same time He made him acquainted with his own frailty. But whatever the case, He intended to make him serve as an example for us all. We perceive then that God has other meanings in afflicting His people than simply punishing their [specific] sins. Nonetheless, He never ceases to uphold them, even by His own mere grace.

We should, however, always come back to this point that the source of all the miseries that we suffer in this present world is sin. How so? Because if this corruption were not in our nature, condemned by God, and of which we also are convicted, we should enjoy here a blessed life. This entire world would be for us an earthly paradise. For we ought not to think that Adam was cooped up in a little corner for himself alone; rather, all the whole earth was blessed by God. We might have enjoyed it all until the end of the world. But where is this earthly paradise now? It is nowhere at all, for the earth is cursed. Such was the sentence that God pronounced on Adam and on all his offspring. And there we must understand that all the miseries to which we are subject in the present world grow from this root, because we did not continue in the perfection in which Adam was created.

We must realize that God reforms us when we have done amiss. He beholds the vices of which He intends to purge us by fit medicines, and does not wait until we have offended Him and provoked His vengeance, but goes before us and administers the remedy at the time He deems best. And further, when He afflicts us for some consideration other than our sins, it is a great honor and a special preeminence for us, and we have reason to praise Him in that He vouchsafes to mark us, and to make His adoption apparent in us by making us to suffer for the testimony of His truth and to receive wrongful persecution at the hands of men, under any pretext or occasion, whatever it may be.

Blessing and Adversity

Moreover, let us mark that is it not in vain that God promises that those who serve Him shall lead a happy life even in this world. Not that they will be exempt from all adversity, for that is impossible, and it is also against the interests of our salvation. But He will so dispose our lives that we shall perceive that He was not feeding us with an empty hope when He said that He will cause all who hearken to His voice to prosper. But by the way, we must remember that the blessings that are contained here are not designed to show what the ultimate felicity of men is, but to give us a taste of the heavenly life, to the end that we should seek for the celestial inheritance that is promised us and there to set our affections.

This must be set out more particularly, or else it will be unclear. It is true that there is a difference between us and the fathers who lived under the law. For God was at that time entreating them as little children, and it was fit that it should be so then. After all, they did not yet have our Lord Jesus, who has now set open the gates of heaven to bring us into the life and glory of heaven. Indeed, they had as much a part therein as we do, but it was necessary for them to walk in shadows and figures to understand it; therefore, they had need of some aid, of which we at this time have no need at all. And we must not think our state to be worse than theirs; not being like those who complain these days because God does not dandle them, and because they are not (as it seems to them) as much at ease as the old fathers were. Surely they deceive themselves in making this comparison.

For if any one of us should reckon up what he has suffered all the days of his life, and then examine the state of David or Abraham, doubtless he will find himself to be in a better state than were those holy fathers. For they, as the apostle says (Heb. 11:13), only saw things afar off, things that are right before our eyes. God promised to be their Savior; He had chosen them to be, as it were, of His household; but meanwhile where was He who was to be their promised Redeemer? Where was the doctrine that is made so clear to us in the gospel concerning the resurrection? They knew the same afar off, but now it is declared to us in the gospel in such a way that we may indeed say, as our Lord Jesus Christ gives us to understand, that blessed are the ears that hear the things that are told us concerning Him, and the eyes that see the things that we see, for the holy kings and prophets longed for the same, and could not obtain it (Matt. 13:16f.).

We therefore have a much more excellent estate than they

had who lived under the law. This is the difference of which I speak, which needed to be supplied by God because of the imperfection [lack of completion] that was in the doctrine concerning the revelation of the heavenly life, which the fathers only knew by outward tokens although they were dear to God. Now that Jesus Christ has come down to us, and has shown us how we ought to follow Him by suffering many afflictions, as it is told us (Matt. 16:24; Rom. 8:29), in bearing poverty and reproach and all such like things, and to be short, that our life must be as it were a kind of death; since we know all this, and the infinite power of God is uttered in His raising up Jesus Christ from death and in His exalting Him to the glory of heaven, should we not take from this a good courage? Should not this sweeten all the afflictions we can suffer? Do we not have cause to rejoice in the midst of our sorrows?

Let us note, then, that if the patriarchs were more blessed by God than we are, concerning this present life, we ought not to wonder at it at all. For the reason for it is apparent. But no matter how things go, yet is this saying of St. Paul always verified: that the fear of God holds promise not only for the life to come, but also for this present life (1 Tim. 4:8). Let us therefore walk in obedience to God, and then we can be assured that He will show Himself a Father to us, yea even in the maintenance of our bodies, at least as far as concerns keeping and preserving us in peace, delivering us from all evils, and providing for us our necessities. God, I say, will make us to feel His blessing in all these things, so that we walk in His fear.

The Purpose of Blessing

All the same, we must return to this point, that God in making us to taste of His favor here, does not intend that we should be so glutted with it that we forget the everlasting rest to which He invites us. And so all the benefits of God that belong to this transitory life must serve us for ladders to mount upward, and not for cushions to fall asleep on in this world. When God gives a man the wherewithal to live, endowing him with health, and permitting him not to be vexed by his enemies, what else should such a man do but be drawn to the grace of God and endeavor to serve Him so much the more and not misbehave himself in this world? He should go forward, using what God has given him as though not using it at all (1 Cor. 7:31), so that nothing stops him from keeping on his way to God.

But we do all things clean contrary to this, don't we? And therefore we ought to be more awake. When we hear the promises that are contained here, let us not think that God meant to pamper the people of the Old Covenant in their transitory pleasures, but rather that the same should be a means to draw them up on high, just as He intends for us today. All the good that we receive from Him has this end and intent, that our minds should always be raised up to the heavenly life. Does God give us bread to eat? He shows Himself therein to be our Father. All the same, even though we are His children, we do not cease to be as pilgrims in this world, having always one foot lifted up, and having here no rest. Therefore, let us have an eye to the inheritance of the kingdom of heaven, and let the bread we eat to nourish us be a means to direct us thither. After the same manner let it be with all other things.

The Perfection of the Promised Blessings

Now let us come to what is here contained in the text of Moses, and then in the end we shall understand better what has been said. Moses says here that God will bless His people in the city and in the field; He will bless them in the fruit of their bodies; He will bless them in their cattle; He will bless them in the fruit of their land; He will bless them in their baskets and in their stores and in their granaries; he will bless them in giving them victory over their enemies.

We know that the happiness of this present life, that is to say such happiness as may be in this world, is for men to have the wherewithal to maintain themselves in quiet, and to be preserved from their enemies. Here God sets down both the one and the other. Touching the one He says, "Blessed shall you be in the city, and blessed shall you be in the field. Blessed shall be the fruit of your body and the fruit of your land and the fruit of your cattle." It is certain that the chief blessing we can desire of God is in our own persons, that He provide us such things as are requisite for this transitory life. And that is the reason why He begins with our persons, and then comes to our children, and then descends to our cattle, to the fruit of the ground, and to all provisions.

It seems at first glance that God intended to pamper His people, as if he would set them up in a pig sty, and there cram their bellies, to let them sleep at their ease and in brief, that they should be here as in a paradise. But I have told you already it behooved God to bestow His benefits more largely upon the fathers that lived under the law, because they could not otherwise be drawn to Him, seeing that the promises of eternal life were not clear to them. In any case we have to note herewithal that when God speaks after this manner, He does not mean only to give men hope that they will be blessed in all respects, but also to admonish us that nothing prevents us from enjoying perfect felicity in this world, while we wait for the life of heaven, except the fact that we are wrapped in vices and corruptions.

And in this way God meant to train the faithful, that they should reason thus with themselves: "Let us serve God, and we shall lack nothing. And if we are vexed, and do not have all our desires, if the earth does not yield such fruitfulness as contents us, or if our cattle do not prosper as we wish, let us understand that this comes to pass because we are wretched creatures and cannot abide the perfection of God's blessings, so that He finds it fitting to withdraw His hand and to give us only a portion of His blessings, because if we should have more it would glut us, and in the end we should be choked with it."

This is the reason, then, why God here so greatly magnifies His blessings. It is done, not because men have ever been blessed in all manner of respects without feeling any vexation at all; this, I say, has never happened. So then, why does God promise it? As we have said before, it is to make us understand that whenever our life is not as blessed as we wish, we should consider that God knows us to be unable to receive the fullness of His benefits, and therefore finds it fitting to distribute them to us piecemeal, after the manner of feeding sick people or children, who because they lack discretion must be governed by others.

But we are even less well advised than sick folk or infants, for we would devour the blessings that God sends if He did not hold us in check, for our lusts are miserably corrupted. God bestows his blessings upon us sufficiently, but we, like sick folk, do refuse good meat, and fall to foul feeding, which cannot but hurt us. Thus are we carried away by our wicked affections and are never able to direct the use of God's benefits or to govern them as we should, for we should infect and defile everything if He did not take steps to prevent us. Let us mark, therefore, that God here is warning us to call our sins to remembrance, and to bewail them as often as we do not enjoy the fullness of His blessings, as is here mentioned. Nevertheless, He would have us to hope that by serving Him we shall prosper, and have enough for our contentment.

The Example of David

And indeed, we see how all the faithful have lived in this regard. It is certain, as we said, that David was in various kinds of tribulation. No man was afflicted more. But did he in all that time murmur against God? No. It is true that he uttered his griefs and passions, but that was with all meekness. And he did not omit to say that the anger of God lasted but a little while (Ps. 30:5), and that when He afflicted His people, He merely did it in the turning of His hand, while His goodness lasted a long time, and continues lifelong.

Lifelong? Well then, let us look at the life of David to see what we find therein. In his infancy he was brought up as a shepherd's son in the country, and God says that He took him from the flocks, as he was among his sheep. When he came to the court of Saul, it is certain that he was advanced to be the son-in-law of the king beyond all expectation and the opinion of the whole world. It might have been better for him to have remained a shepherd in the field than to have been in such travail and misery for the length of time we see he was in it. They sought his death by all means, and his life was not only hanging by a mere thread, it was also subject to reproach. So much so, that they counted him the most wicked villain in the world, a traitor to his prince, a man disloyal to his king. You can see, then, that David was, as it were, abominable to everybody.

And when God finally gave him peace [in that matter], then was he vexed with foreign wars, insomuch that he had no sooner finished with one people, than he was required to turn around and fight another. And to fill up the measure, his own natural son chased him out of his kingdom, intending no less than to cut his throat; and we see what other conspiracies he suffered, such as the conspiracy of Sheba.

Yet David always confessed without pretense that all the chastisements, miseries, and afflictions that God sent him were nothing to him, and that they lasted but the turning of a hand, or for a minute of an hour, whereas His blessings endure forever. How so? Because David did not have the kind of unthankful heart that we have. We embrace God's gracious dealings and make no account of them, but of every little harm we make a great mountain. When God chastises us we shrink down our shoulders, making great complaints and outcries. But let us learn better to esteem God's goodness toward us, in such a way that we are not found ungrateful for His grace.

This is the reason, I say, why we do not conceive the value of the blessings that are contained here [in this passage]. Why? Because if God sends us any vexation, we shut our hearts against Him. And though we may not murmur in speech, yet we do not fail to have some bitterness lurking in our hearts. There only needs to come one affliction into our life, and the grace of God is quite removed from our taste. And when He has done us all the good that can be devised, yet does it ever run in our remembrance? Rather, what we remember is "I have sustained such and such a harm," and our minds are never off of it.

Thus are God's benefits unsavory to us, so that we pass them over or let them slip. When things happen contrary to us, therefore, and our Lord afflicts us, let us receive the comforts that He gives us to moderate our affliction, and then we shall continue to walk on our way. And although we are called to endure many things, and even though by reason of our frailty and feebleness we are not able to overcome all temptations at the first blow, yet notwithstanding, through the grace of God we may get the upper hand. And when we are thus oppressed with our miseries, then we shall esteem God's grace in such a way that even in the midst of darkness we shall perceive what light God gives to us, so that we shall always feel Him to be our Father. For there is no doubt but that He will bless us sufficiently, to the extent that is fitting for our salvation. Thus you see what we have to do and to practise, if we want rightly to understand what God has said, that He shall bless His people if they hearken to His voice.

God, the Giver of All Blessing

Moreover, we are hereby warned not to seek anything we desire except from the hand of God. This is a very profitable admonition. For we see how men err when they desire to be at their ease. It is the natural inclination of all men to covet to be this and that, and what course do they hold in the pursuit of it? There can be no doubt about it: They turn their backs on God, and kick against Him. He that intends to become rich will use robbery and cruelty, deceit and wicked practices. He that desires to attain to credit and authority will practise treason, indirect wiles, and other sleights-of-hand. In brief, ambition rules such a man altogether. Finally, he that would give vent to any other of his lusts, cannot but provoke the anger of God. See at what point we are! And in this way our faithlessness uncovers itself in every way, as I have mentioned here before.

Therefore, we have need to be mindful of this lesson, which is that if we wish to prosper, even in this present life, there is no other means for it than to put ourselves under the guidance of God, who has all goods in His power to bestow on whomever He pleases. We may also hope that He will not be niggardly in distributing His gracious gifts unto us, at least if we hearken to

His voice. For as I have been saying, since we are His children, can we think that He takes pleasure in vexing us? Moreover, it costs Him nothing. No matter how liberal He is toward us, yet He is not afraid of having less for Himself as a result, or that He will feel any lack. For His is a fountain that can never be drawn dry.

Let us therefore be persuaded that our lives will always be accursed unless we return to this point whereto Moses leads us, namely to hearken to the voice of our God, to be thereby moved and continually confirmed in the fact that He cares for our salvation, and not only for the eternal salvation of our persons, but also for the maintenance of our state in this earthly life, to make us taste at present of His love and goodness in such a way as may content and suffice us, waiting till we may have our fill thereof and behold face to face that which we are now constrained to look upon as it were through a glass and in the dark (1 Cor. 13:12). That is one more thing we ought to remember from this text, where it is said that we will be blessed if we hearken to the voice of the Lord our God.

Specific Blessings of God

This is to be applied to all parts of our lives. For example, when a man wishes to prosper in his own person — that is, he desires to employ himself in the service of God and to obtain some grace so that he may not be unprofitable in this life but that God may be honored by him — let him think thus to himself: "Lord, I am Yours. Dispose of me as You will. Here I am, ready to obey You." This is the place at which we must begin if we desire God to guide us and create in us the disposition to serve Him, so that His blessings may appear and lighten upon us and upon our persons. So it is concerning every man's household.

When a man desires to live in peace and concord with his wife, or to have children in whom to rejoice, let him understand that all this is in the hand of God, and that it does not lie in our power or skill to order our households after our heart's desires. For they who think they can achieve it by their own power are very much deceiving themselves, and commit sacrilege in robbing God of the honor that He has reserved to Himself. It is said that the fruit of the womb is a special gift of God (Ps. 127:3), and so is everything else that pertains to the household. Accordingly it is said that it is vain for a man to build unless God also builds with him (Ps. 127:1). Those therefore who wish to possess a quiet state for themselves and their children, let them turn to God and commit themselves wholly to Him and to His guidance, knowing that there is no other means to attain to the same than by His blessing.

The same thing is true concerning cattle, food, and all other things. For we see here [in this text] that nothing is forgotten. And God meant to make us to perceive His infinite goodness, in that He declares that He will deal with our smallest affairs, which one of our own equals would be loath to meddle with. If we have a friend, we should be very loath, indeed, and ashamed to use his help unless it were in a matter of great importance. But we see here that God goes into our sheepfolds and into the stalls of our cattle and oxen, and He goes into our fields, and He cares for all other things as well. Since we see Him abase himself thus far, shouldn't we be ravished to honor Him and to magnify His bounty?

Let us conclude, then, that when God says that He shall bless us in the fruit of the earth, and that He shall bless us in the fruit of our cattle, it is a most certain argument that He will not forget the principal thing. These things are lowly and of little count, and many times men despise them, and yet we see that God takes care of them notwithstanding. Since this is so, will He forget our souls, which He has created after His own image, which also He has so dearly redeemed with the sacred blood of his Son? Surely not. First of all, therefore, let us acknowledge God's favor toward us, in abasing Himself so far as to direct and govern everything that belongs to our lives and sustenance. And from there let us rise up higher, and understand that He will not fail us in the things that surpass this present life, but rather that in the chief things that belong to our life, indeed even in this world, God will stretch forth His hand to furnish us always with all things that are needful.

Protection From Enemies

Then there is the second point, which is that we will be upheld against our enemies (v. 7). We have said that the first point is that God provides for us so that we lack nothing that is requisite for the passing of our life in this world. But if our granaries were fuller than ever, and our cellars thoroughly supplied, and our purses stuffed tight so that we want nothing, yet if our enemies are still able to scratch our eyes out and we are like a people set for the spoil so that we are daily afflicted and have no defense, what will our great abundance avail us? Therefore, it was God's will in brief compass to show here that His blessings extend themselves so far and wide in all cases and in all respects that nothing should be missing from such as do Him honor and service.

But let us mark that God has not exempted us completely from our enemies, nor did He exempt the people of olden time. Why? Because it is impossible for us to live in this world without some vexation at the hands of other men. It is true that as much as in us lies we ought to procure peace, for our part. But since the devil is prince of this world, he will not leave God's children in rest. And he has supporters enough to serve his designs; for all the despisers of God, all the wicked, and all the hypocrites that are in this world — the number of whom is infinite in manner — are Satan's darts, swords, and arrows.

Seeing then that we must dwell among those who despise God, and among the wicked, let us reckon that we shall be troubled and have enemies. Let us endeavor to appease them as much as we can, and let us give them no occasion of hatred. But in the meantime let us not be unprovided, however things go.[2] Thus much concerning that one point. For God has not said, "I will utterly root out your enemies, so that you shall have the world

2. In other words, we need to maintain a defensive military power in case of attack.

by yourselves, wherein to lead a happy and quiet life and to have all the felicity that can be wished." He has not said that. But He says, "Although you are compassed round about with your enemies, yet I will not permit them to have the upper hand over you."

Now he says further that if our enemies come forth by one way, they will flee seven ways. By this he gives us to understand that our enemies may well conspire by great numbers, so that it may be likely that we should be swallowed up by them, but yet they shall be filled with fear. This will be shown more largely at another text, but here we have to mark that the sustaining and maintaining of our lives are in the hands of God, and that our rest and quietness depend also on Him. And although men do continually devise ways to hurt and annoy us, yet God is ever strong enough to disappoint them when He has once received us into His protection, and to hinder them so that they will be able to attempt nothing against us but will be overthrown. That is what we need to remember.

Now when God permits us to have enemies, He is calling us thereby to Himself, and we ought to be the more provoked to call upon Him when we see ourselves driven thereto by necessity. For if this world should smile on us and rejoice at us on all sides, it would seem to us that we had no more need of God's protection. But when we are beset with perils and dangers and see that men lie in wait for us, seeking nothing else but to come in to vex us, it causes us to resort to God, to commit ourselves to His care, praying Him to be our Shield and Fortress, and our Defender. Let us therefore mark that God, in permitting us to have enemies, does thereby draw us to Himself, that we should pray Him always to succor and defend us.

But to conclude, we must remember that God is mighty enough to maintain us. How so? Well, if our enemies came upon us with great fierceness, it would be enough to daunt us and to put us out of courage. But however we fare, even if He allows them to rise up against us and to be as ferocious as wild beasts, yet they shall not know what to do but be astounded. And although they have tremendous advantage at the beginning, and be full of craft and wiles, yet God will blind their eyes so that they will cast themselves willfully into the snare and there be taken. Again, even when they are armed with malice and boldness to set upon us, God will in the end confound them, no man can tell how. He will destroy all their devices and attempts, and when they band themselves against us, and have great multitudes on their sides, yet will God scatter them. Just as when we see a cloud threatening rain, and it seems that all should be drowned, God scatters it and the tempest is gone – even so will He deal with our enemies. Thus you see in effect what we have to remember concerning this text, where it is said that we shall be defended against all such as set themselves against us, and that our God will make them flee before our faces if we do Him the honor to acknowledge him to be the Lord of hosts, and that His power is infinite, and that therefore the whole world can never prevail against Him in the least.

Conclusion

Finally, what have we now to do but submit ourselves to the obedience of God? Also, let us understand that all those who do not believe, and all those who despise God's majesty, although for a time their lives may seem happy, yet they are appointed of perdition, and all their goods shall become a curse to them so that they will be in a forlorn condition. Just as Psalm 69:22 says, their very tables will be turned into snares and artifices wherewith to trap them, and all the benefits of God will become deadly poison to them. Here is what we must keep in mind.

Moreover, as often as we are afflicted, let us humble ourselves and acknowledge our sins and bewail them before God. And in the meantime let us not omit to qualify our griefs, knowing that amidst the afflictions He sends us, there always appears a certain testimony of His goodness, and that it is necessary that He should so hold us in awe. Yet notwithstanding, we must not be cast down or discouraged when we are vexed and troubled, though we are encircled with never so many miseries. And why? Because God never fails, for all that, to show Himself a Father towards us. That is the thing whereon we must altogether rest, so that all the afflictions of this world may quicken us up to aspire to the heavenly heritage. And when we have bewailed our sins, let us not doubt but that God of His mercy will bless us, even in Jesus Christ the Fountain of all goodness and blessedness, by whom all curses are quite taken away. To prove that it is so: What may be the chief curse that is fallen upon mankind, if not death? And yet we see that the same has become an entrance into life. And how? In that the person of Jesus Christ is now made blessed. For this reason let us learn to rejoice, since we see that God has so provided for our salvation that although He makes us to feel our sins and would have us touched with some sorrow, thereby to bring us to repentance, yet He never ceases amidst all these to show Himself a Father evermore and by all means to advance our salvation.

Prayer

Now let us humble ourselves before the majesty of our good God, with acknowledgement of sins, praying Him to touch us to the quick more and more, that we may hate them, and that acknowledging the evil that is in us, we may seek His mercy, not only to forgive us the sins that we have already committed, but also to mortify us, and by the power of His Spirit to give us grace so to forsake ourselves that we may seek His righteousness and more and more profit therein until it be perfect in us, at such time as He will have taken us out of this world. And let us all say, "Almighty God, heavenly Father, etc."

7

SEPARATION UNTO BLESSING

Sermon 155. Thursday, 12 March 1556.
Deuteronomy 28:9-14.

9. The LORD shall establish you as a holy people to Himself, as He swore to you, if you will keep the commandments of the LORD your God, and walk in His ways.

10. So all the peoples of the earth shall see that the Name of the LORD is called upon you; and they shall fear you.

11. And the LORD shall make you abound in prosperity, in the fruit of your womb and in the fruit of your beast and in the fruit of your ground, in the land that the LORD swore to your fathers to give you.

12. The LORD shall open for you His good treasure, the heavens, to give rain to your land in its season and to bless all the work of your hand; and you shall lend to many nations, but you shall not borrow.

13. And the LORD shall make you the head and not the tail, and you alone shall be above, and you shall not be underneath, if you will listen to the commandments of the LORD your God, which I charge you today, to keep and do them.

14. And do not turn aside from any of the words that I command you today, to the right or to the left, to go after other gods to serve them.

Continuing the matter we spoke about yesterday, Moses shows us the condition that results from God's choice of us, when He takes us to be in His Church; which condition is that we should be separated and set far off from the common curse of mankind. It is true that God's goodness extends over all men of the world, so that we see how all are fed and maintained by His liberality; but meanwhile we also see how many miseries men are subject to. For this reason, it is good for us to be separated, and for God to watch over us and bear toward us a special love, as for His own children; for apart from all that, all our life would be confused, as we can see from the wretched infidels: Even though God bestows all kinds of blessings on them, yet they cannot profit by them, but always remain in doubt — and with good reason, for what can they rest their hopes upon, seeing they are not certified of the love of God? How can they hold to Him as their Father? Therefore, it is a word well worth marking, where Moses says that God has separated us from all other nations of the world.[1]

It is certain that this word "holiness" (see v. 9) indicates that the image of God should shine forth in us, and that we should serve Him purely in a virtuous lifestyle; but yet from there he proceeds farther, as he does in this text, showing that God will give unto His people a certain mark to show that they are privileged above all others. Therefore, in beholding what the state of men is in this present life, let us learn to resort always to this promise, that God has not only created us after the common curse of the brood of all Adam's children, but that He has also chosen

---

1. Christians are not to try to read tokens of salvation from providential blessings, for these are not signs of the Gospel, but normal results of it. Thus, providential blessings by themselves cannot give assurance of favor with God, and the pagans cannot get assurance from them. Christians have been "certified of the love of God" in baptism, which is the sign of God's promise to them. If a man does not persevere in the response of faith to that sign, then baptism is of no avail; but in and of itself it is a certification of God's favor. "As Baptism is a solemn recognition by which God introduces His children into the possession of life, a true and effectual sealing of the promise, a pledge of sacred union with Christ, it is justly said to be the entrance and reception into the church." This is from *Corpus Reformatorum* 9:116, as translated by Ronald Wallace, *Calvin's Doctrine of the Word and Sacrament* (Tyler, TX: Geneva Ministries, [1953] 1982), p. 176.

us to Himself for His heritage. And let us not doubt at all but that He watches over us and will make us to perceive that we are of His household and that He is near to us to aid us. Let us be well resolved in this.

Election, Promise, Preeminence

Moreover, Moses adds that all peoples of the earth shall see that the Name of the LORD is called upon over you, and they shall be afraid (v. 10). It is certain that the idolaters[2] can vaunt themselves, and claim the name of the God, even while they fight against Him and cast off all doctrine; insomuch that being as fierce as wild beasts they still look to be counted in the Church. But Moses here takes the term "call upon" to mean "naming." And indeed, he means that the people were truly and properly called by God after His own name, or named as His people. If we walk in the fear of our God and frame our life after His calling, then it will be seen how it is not in vain that He calls Himself our God and vows us to be His people.

Now it is certain that this teaching presupposes that we have our recourse to God, as being under His protection. For it is said that a man is called upon or named after the name of his prince where he is his subject and under his leadership. Even so it is said that the faithful have God's name called upon over them, signifying that they are His, and there they are all safe under His wings. And this cannot be unless we call upon God, and have our refuge in Him in all our necessities.

But where does such boldness come from, that we glory in this: that we belong to God more than others? For we know that the state of men is all alike by nature. Why then are we preferred before others who are descended from the selfsame race? It comes through God's election; for it cannot begin with us. For where is a man who can advance himself to come nearer to God than others? What can any man bring with himself to deserve such

---

2. A reference to Roman Catholicism, and the idolatry of worshipping images and sacraments.

preference? Nothing, obviously. Therefore, it is God who must make choice of us through His own mere goodness, and when He has declared Himself to be our God, then we may also for our part be bold in all assurance and without doubt call upon His name. Now we see what is the effect of this sentence.

Moses intends to declare the preeminence that God gives to those whom He has adopted as His children, which is that although they are mingled among men, and encompassed with many miseries, yet they are preserved, being under His hand and protection. This is because He holds them and avows that they are of His household, and not for any reason, except His own good pleasure. Let us therefore courageously defy Satan, when we see that he practises all that he possibly can against us, and let us count ourselves assured against all the dangers of this world, seeing that God has done such favor as not to leave us to fortune, as the unbelievers imagine. And why? Because we are unto Him a holy people.

And what do we get this preeminence from? We have it because He has testified to us that He is our God. If we had not gotten this word from Him, we should always be in perplexity. We should still doubt. We should be questioning this or that, and our life should hang as it were by a thread, as we shall see in this chapter. But seeing that God has uttered His fatherly love to us, and it has pleased Him to open His mouth to make us understand that He has given us familiar access to Him; seeing, I say, that we have such assurance, let us call upon Him. Let us not doubt, but glory in this, that He is our Savior, and that since we are His, we cannot perish.

All the same, let us beware that we do not call upon the name of God falsely, as all those who abuse it, making a mockery of Him, and despising His majesty. If we claim the name of God, let it be because we are grounded upon His promises and have received them through faith, and then let us call upon Him, let Him be our refuge, and let us not give ourselves to fond bragging as they do who think it enough for them to bear the bare name of Christian. No, let us follow the call of our God, as Moses shows here, saying, "If you will keep the commandments of your God, as I do set them before you this day" (v. 9). For there is good reason for us to yield ourselves to God's direction, seeing He has so bound Himself to us. And we should not only profess with our mouths that we are His people, but also show it by framing our whole lives agreeable to the same; and by keeping His commandments make it apparent that we have received the grace He offers to us. For that is the true evidence thereof.

The Heathen Shall Fear

Now He says moreover, that other people shall see that we are called by God's name, and they shall fear us (v. 10). It is not enough that God promises to make us feel that we are safe in His keeping; but He also says that even the pagans, our mortal enemies and the despisers of His majesty, shall be made to know the same. Now it is certain that the infidels do not know the arm of God in such a way as it ought to be known to us. They come far short of it. For though they see, they do not see. How then can it be possible for them to perceive that God has blessed us, that we live by His favor, and that we are nourished through His provision? After all, they are blockish, and do not recognize that anything comes to them from the hand of God. We see well how the infidels are fed and clothed; they enjoy the light of the sun; indeed, they have an abundance of goods. But as for the worshipping and seeking of God, we hear of nothing of the sort among them. And if besides their despising of the benefits of their God, they have no understanding whence they come unto them, how should they then know that God has named us with His own name?

They will not know it through any persuasion of mind or through any such true understanding of it as we ought to have. But Moses says that they shall have it proved to their faces; as for example, we see the wicked grind their teeth when they behold the faithful prospering, and when they see that God upholds and keeps them. And how does this come about? Truly they will be astonished at it, and they will not be able to think otherwise but that God does indeed favor their adversaries — not that they take it to heart or have a proper attitude about it, but in that they are at least confounded in their own selves.

He says that they shall perceive that God's name is placed upon us, and that it shall put them in fear (v. 10). For although they do not fear God, yet He bridles them secretly, insomuch that when they would practise anything against His people, they cannot do it, for they feel their courage broken. This is to be marvelled at, that God sometimes permits the wicked to cast out the foam of their rage against us, and they devise whatever they can, and work their spite; but once they have done that, then it will appear that they are His underlings, and cannot withstand Him. And why is this so? If God should permit the faithless to have their own way, it is certain that the world should not last three days, but that they would crush down all things before them. Therefore it is necessary that He should restrain them with some secret bridle, and not permit their desires to have full scope. And we see it before our eyes.

Why is it that we have not been swallowed up a hundred thousand times during these last twenty or thirty years? It is due only to God's defense, which consists not in signs that may be seen but in His secret restraint of the wicked as it were in prison, notwithstanding all the evil that is in them. By reason of this, when they have devised anything, they wash away like water, and all their thoughts vanish, and they lie as with their arms broken. And though they undertake great things, yet they cannot attain to their purposes. And so you see what Moses meant in saying that the wicked, in that they are our enemies, shall perceive that the name of God is placed upon us, and thereby be stricken in fear.

We see from this that there is no fortress or defense like having recourse to our God. As long as He takes the burden upon Himself to save us, let us boldly trust that we stand in safety; yea, although the wicked conspire against us, and lie in wait and watch for us, yet shall we be as an invincible fortress, since we can call upon the name of our God and be thoroughly assured in ourselves that He avows us to be His people; and we have good warrant of this if we do not break our faith that we on our parts have plighted to Him. But we must feel the protection of God in a way other than the wicked feel it; that is to say, in hearing His word we must embrace the grace that is presented to us, and rest wholly upon it. After that manner must we ascertain that the name of God is put upon us.[3]

Repeated Assurances of Blessing

Now Moses repeats again what he had said concerning the fruit of the womb, of cattle, and of the earth (v. 11). Surely it would have been sufficient to have promised once that all bodily blessings come from God. But on the one hand we see the mistrust that is in men, how when God speaks to them, they ceaselessly argue and reply, saying, "Yes, but can I be sure of it?" And therefore to give us better resolve, God confirms the matter He had previously spoken of. Again we see our unthankfulness to be such that we attribute things to "Fortune" or to our own skill and craft, which are actually done for us by God. Therefore He calls us to Himself, and shows that it is He who does it.

And on the other hand, He would have us to understand that if we intend to prosper in all points, we must hearken to Him and obey Him. For all men, yea even the most wicked in the world, desire to have issues of their own bodies, increase of cattle, and great revenues. But what? In the meanwhile we despise God, the author of all goodness, and seem as though we labored purposefully to thrust His hand far from us, which is as much as if I should ask a man for an alm and then reach up and box his ear, or as if he should come to my aid and I should spit in his face; even so deal we with our God.

God therefore, perceiving such malice in us, and that we

---

3. Calvin does seem to get off the subject here. Common restraint, after all, is not the point of the statement that the heathen will fear the name of God as it is placed upon His own people. Calvin might have called attention to the testimony of Rahab in Joshua 2:9ff., or of the Philistines in 1 Samuel 4:8. If Calvin wanders a bit from the text from time to time, that is not unusual in preachers; and it might be borne in mind that he was lecturing daily, rather extemporaneously, and frequently in bad health.

cannot simply be taught but stop our ears against what He says, repeats the same things again that He had spoken to us before. He warns us that if we lack anything, we must lay the blame for it on our sins, and not on Him. And why? Because He is ready, on His part, to bless us as much in the issue of our bodies as in revenue of land and in cattle; and He is liberal and rich enough for us; neither will He be stingy towards us regarding the blessings that are in His possession. Let us therefore acknowledge that the fault lies with us when He withdraws His benefits and does not give them to us as much as we wish.

Rain From Heaven

Moreover, it is noteworthy that he says that God shall open His good treasure, namely the heavens, and give us rain, that the earth may bring forth food (v. 12). Here Moses sets out the order of nature that we see with our eyes, that we might the better understand that God is our Father and Nourisher, and that although the sustenance whereon we feed is gathered from earth, yet it is God alone who sends all things. How so? The earth indeed has nature given to it to bring forth fruit, but if it should continue dry, what would come of it? We see that unless there fall both rain and dew, the earth will crack open as though it would cry out that it is thirsty, and it dries up for want of moisture. And therefore David, intending to utter his earnest desire of God's grace, uses this similitude, saying, "Lord, I am unto You as a dry ground" (Ps. 143:6).

We see before our eyes how the earth becomes barren and parched for want of moisture, and finally has neither strength nor substance. Had it so pleased God, could He not have given the earth the ability to have substance enough by itself? For as we read in Genesis 2:6, there was not such rain in the beginning as we have in these days, but God caused a certain vapor to rise up to moisten the earth. Cannot He do the same now, or else arrange matters so that the earth should have some kind of moisture proceeding from underneath? And indeed, where does rain come from? If you ask the philosophers [scientists today – ed.], they will say that rain comes from the vapors that ascend out of the earth, which being drawn up into the air, are sent down again upon the earth. Thus then, after the opinion of the philosophers, the vapors do ascend.

But now, how did it come to pass that God does not make the heavens yield rain except it come first out of the earth? Or why not let the earth retain the moisture it has so that it may always have strength and substance of itself? What is the cause of this rising up of the vapors, that when the earth has yielded them forth they are held up in the air as in tents, as is mentioned in the psalm (Ps. 18:11)? What is the reason for all this? It is because He sees us to be so stupid and idiotic that although He shows us with His finger that it is at His hand that we receive all goodness, yet He intends to make us to perceive it in a more visible manner.

And this is the reason also why He says that He will respond to the heavens, and the heavens will respond to the earth, and the earth will respond to the grain and to all the seeds that are committed to it (Hosea 2:21f.). When the husbandman sows his grain well, he lays it up as it were in prison, and it seems to be at the mercy of the earth. The earth then must conceive the grain, nourish it, and make it to spring up, and in the same way give it substance. But does the earth "hear" (respond to) the grain? No, it is deaf; that is to say, it has no power to make it prosper unless it is "heard" (responded to) by others. And how is that? The earth, as I have said, looks up to heaven, and after a fashion opens her mouth, for her mouth cleaves open when it feels extreme heat and is not watered as it wishes. The heaven then must answer the earth. The heaven? What can it do? Can the heaven give water? It has none to give except God draw it up into it by His secret power. Indeed, we shall see hereafter how God threatens to give a heaven of brass. It is needful then that God hear the heaven, and that we repair thither.

So then, as often as it rains we must understand that God opens His treasures, which are otherwise shut up. God, as I have said, could even without rain or dew cause the earth to bring forth fruit, but He uses such means as He knows to be convenient for our dullness, and He does so for the purpose of giving us less excuse. If we are unthankful to Him and close our eyes against so apparent a matter, we should be so much the more blameworthy at the last day, and be certain to yield an account for our willfulness in refusing to know the things that ought to be thoroughly known by us. Thus you see what we have to bear in mind.

St. Paul, speaking of the ignorance that prevailed in the old world before the gospel was preached (Acts 14:16), says that all people went astray like brute beasts. And why? Because that doctrine was not yet taught which is the true light to show us the way of saving health, as we shall see in the thirtieth chapter (Dt. 30:15). Notwithstanding, he adds that God nevertheless did not leave Himself without witness (Acts 14:17). And His statement, "He did not leave Himself without witness," is as if He had further said, "And how so? In that He has sent rain upon the earth in due time and season. He has also sent fair weather. These are God's witnesses, which declare that just as He has created the world, even so He upholds and preserves it. These are the witnesses that speak with a loud and clear voice, saying that we must look to God for all the nourishments that He gives us."

This is why I said that we should mark well this saying, that God shall open His treasure (Dt. 28:12). For although we see what great riches God has set in this world, what various sorts of beasts, what herbs, what trees, and what a number of all other kinds of things, yet all these things should decay and die if God did not send us daily from heaven the things that are requisite for the preservation of this life. Could we abide three days without the light of the Savior? If God did not give natural power to every seed, what would happen? We should rapidly perish. And if nothing else were involved except what I have been speaking about concerning the earth, it would soon dry up.[4] These therefore are the good treasures that God bestows upon us.

And when it is His will to show Himself a Father to us, He

---

4. In other words, God gives life to seeds. But even if we were to assume that the seed has life in itself, it still could not grow unless God gives rain, for the earth would dry up and the seed would die.

lays the heaven before us that we might see it there. It is just as if God should lift us up by the chin and say, "Poor creatures, when you seek food, you look to make sure you have planted enough seeds in the ground. Indeed, that is something you must look to, but you must first of all go higher, and lift up your eyes to Me; even nature itself compels you to do so. For you know that without rain the earth cannot prosper. Therefore, do not forget the things that I show to you day by day, which you have learned by experience."

This is the good treasure Moses is speaking of; and he expressly adds, "the heaven." Why? Because if he had said, "God shall show His bounty from above and from beneath," surely that ought to have been enough for us. But because of our infirmity, we see how God is careful to express the matter more plainly, so that He also shows that we must come to Him and look up to the heavens, because He calls us there, and has ordered matters such that He will have us to think ourselves to be barren and starving people except He pour His goodness upon us from above.

Now, having spoken of this good treasure he says, "He shall give you rain in due time, and shall bless the work or labor of your hands." By speaking of the due season, he shows to us that God's giving rain to us in due time proceeds from an especial care. After all, sometimes rain is very harmful, as we see before our eyes. From this we must conclude that if God did not have the power and skill to restrain the rain, the fruits of the earth and also the bodies of the men should rot. What does the rain do, if left to itself? It engenders only rottenness. On the other side, we see that the rain refreshes in season and gives strength to the ground, from which we see that it is the treasure of God, giving us sustenance. And why is that? Because God knows it is good for us that He cause it to rain.

Therefore when we see it rain out of season, let us mark how God shows us that it is very necessary for us that He watch over us, and that no drop of rain fall without His commandment, according to what we have previously seen, which is that He holds the waters above as it were in tents. The clouds are huge tents

(Ps. 18:11). The prophet[5] would have us to consider that it requires a most wonderful power to shut the rain up there, for otherwise we should be drowned out of hand, or at least we should be rotted by it, as I mentioned. And here, by the way, we are admonished, as we shall note hereafter, to consider our sins and trespasses, and to think that when God gives us extraordinary rains, they are as punishments for our offenses. Moreover, when the rain comes in season, let us acknowledge that there does not fall one drop but by God's appointment, assuring ourselves that it is necessary for us. That is the reason why Moses expressly adds this particular saying.

The Gift of Labor

Next he says that God shall bless the labor of our hands (v. 12). This is to make us understand, as he has already pointed out before, that it is not our own labor and travail that feeds us; as we have seen in the eighth chapter (Dt. 8:17), where he says, "When you are come into the land that God gives you, remember that during forty years you were fed with manna that fell from heaven, so that you should not say, 'It is my own labor that sustains me.'" Let us therefore learn by these texts that when we have travailed, and bestowed our labor to till the earth, and have considered everything that is requisite, yet nevertheless we must lift up our eyes and not stand in our own conceit so as to say, "I have done this; it is done by my own labor and wisdom." Let us rather acknowledge that it is God's doing to give increase, and that without Him, all our labor is in vain; so that even if we were breaking our arms and legs [backbreaking labor], yet instead of going forward we should be falling backward.

The sum of the matter is that we should labor in all lowliness, and when we have travailed for our living, we should understand that it is not in us to give the success, but that God must wholly

---

5. Assuming that the sermon was accurately transcribed, and Calvin did not really say "psalmist," then he is referring to the psalmist as a prophet in that all of Scripture is prophecy.

guide it and give it good issue, not only regarding the vegetation of the earth, but also regarding all things in general. So then, when a man applies himself to any kind of labor, let him not go about it presumptuously, but let him call upon God to help him, saying, "Lord it is Your pleasure that I should take pains. Well, I am doing so. But I know that I shall not prevail unless You guide me, and unless You give me good success. Through Your mere grace and goodness, let my labor prosper." This is the thing we were admonished concerning in this text.

Let us not then think that man's care and skill, or his travail and endeavor can make the ground fertile, but remember that the blessing of God rules all. All the same, this puts us in mind of our duty, for God will help us when we are not idle. We are not made of wooden logs, after all. Men must, I say, employ themselves when God promises them His blessing. These two points go together, namely that the Lord will bless us, and yet nevertheless that He will have us also to labor. It is certain that God could feed us if our arms were broken, and He could make us live without any care and without having to regard the maintenance of our own households. God, I say, could give us food free of cost, but it is His pleasure to exercise us with care and travail, and that every man according to his vocation should apply himself to what he sees fitting for him.

I say that God's matching of His blessings with our labor is to show that He will not have us to be sluggards, every man sitting on his own tail and not tilling the ground or occupying himself with any other trade, and taking the bridle in our teeth. Rather we should do this honor to God, saying, "Lord, although we have done what we can, yet it is nothing unless Your gracious goodness rule it." But men do not use this teaching properly, for we see how men are given to darkening the grace of God under pretence that they can do something for themselves; that is how they think of themselves.

And this demonic arrogance pertains not only to matters concerning the nourishment of our bodies, but also to the area of personal salvation. Is not this the foundation of the notion of "free will"? God requires men to study and labor to do good, to withstand temptation, to have such a fervent zeal as to give themselves wholly unto Him and to forsake themselves. And since God requires all these things, it seems that we can do them [in our own power]. Indeed, but we do not consider that God, for all His commanding, also said that He works by His Holy Spirit, so that He writes His laws in our hearts and engraves them in our minds, and causes us to walk according as He commands. Oh, this is very true, and yet we also must do our endeavor. And where does that endeavor come from? These wretches do not understand that it is God who drives us forward and stirs us up, and that all the endeavoring wherewith men endeavor comes from their being instruments of the Holy Spirit.

Now then seeing that under this pretence of working we seek nothing other than to darken the grace of God, so much the more diligently ought we to note this doctrine, by which God stirs us up and would have us to work, and yet shows us withal that we cannot profit unless He gives us good success. Truly there is a great difference between His handiwork and what the faithful do in endeavoring to live well. For as I have said, men are created to labor by nature, but we are so wicked and rebellious that instead of obeying God, we are born to nothing but to offend God until He has reformed us and made us new creatures. So then, God not only blesses our labor when we endeavor to serve Him through the grace of His Holy Spirit, but also we labor only through His power, according as He guides and governs us. This is the sum of what we have to bear in mind concerning this text.

The Promise of Dominion

Now it is also said that God shall make them the head and not the tail (v. 13). This means that those who endeavor to serve Him shall be set above, and not beneath. This is, as it were, the height of all prosperity. Now surely it was necessary (as was treated of yesterday) that the old fathers under the law should have more promises concerning this transitory life than we have. For they did not have such an opening of the heavenly life as is given us in the gospel. Therefore, it was God's will to draw them after that fashion, like little children. For, since an infant is not of capacity to understand the goodness of his father, therefore to encourage him the father will say to him, "I shall give you a nice new cap, or a gay new coat." This is agreeable to the capacity of the child, and because his heart is tender, such talk is used in dealing with him. All the same, the father's intention is to lead him on farther. Even so did God deal with the old fathers. He set forth His benefits that they should enjoy in this world, intending to draw them from hence to a higher hope, namely to the hope of the heavenly heritage.

And so, the Jews were made like a head when the kingdom flourished among them, when they overcame their enemies, and when God showed Himself to fight for them. Nowadays we must not look to have either kingdoms or principalities as they had, nor do we have in like manner the temporal kingdom of David;[6] it is sufficient for us that Jesus Christ is given us, and that we reign with Him, and that He is our King, who causes us to flourish under His government. I say, it ought to suffice us that we are a royal priesthood under our Head, who is the Son of God.

Nevertheless, our Lord has made a promise to all the faithful, that if they walk in His obedience, they shall not be oppressed by the tyranny of men, but shall be sustained in liberty, which is also a blessing as much as any that can be desired in this world. Knowing therefore that this is a special gift of God, as it is here showed, let us learn to serve Him and to give Him the whole authority over us, that by His governing of us we may be set free from bondage to men. We shall see hereafter in this present chapter (Dt. 28:17) how He threatens them that will neither fear Him nor shrink at His terribleness, according as it is said in the Psalm (105:38): God must lay the fear of men upon all them that will not fear Him and be His willing subjects.

---

6. Notice that Calvin carefully qualifies his statements here: "as they had; in like manner." Obviously, Calvin believed in the Christian reform of civil government; that was what he was doing in Geneva.

Let us mark, therefore, that when we yield to the reigning of God over us, we shall be maintained by Him in such a fashion that men will not be able to oppress us. And if at any time the wicked have their sway, and seem to set their feet as it were upon our throats, let us understand that God is bringing us low because we have offended Him and because we have not rendered to Him the praise that belongs to Him, and that He chastises us according to our deserts. But we must always come back to this point, that if we do not cast off God, we shall be received by Him in such a way that He will be to us as an army, and will make us able to walk with our heads upright, as it is said in the third psalm (v. 3). So then, this blessing served not only for the fathers that lived under the law, but it continues also unto the end of the world.

The Primacy of Obedience

And we can see that the promise is not empty when we continue reading, "Keep the commandment I set before you this day," says Moses, "that You swerve neither to the left nor to the right to go after strange gods and to worship them" (v. 14). We see how God continually reminds us of obedience to His Word so that we should serve Him, though not in that hypocrisy to which we are so much inclined. Let us remember therefore this lesson: That to worship our God sincerely we must evermore begin by hearkening to His voice, and by giving ear to what He commands us. For if every man goes after his own way, we shall wander. We may well run, but we shall never be a whit nearer to the right way, but rather farther away from it.

And God wills to be not only heard but also obeyed by all men without exception, and without adding anything to His Word or subtracting anything from it. And this is expressly said, because men dare to be so bold as to bring in their new manners of serving God, to do what they suppose to be good. Contrariwise, let us understand that when God has once showed what He will have us to do, we must simply hold ourselves there, without presuming to add thereto or to diminish therefrom by any means. But above all things He would have us to acknowledge Him to be our God. For the true reason that men stray, and altogether vanish into so many superstitions and idolatries, is that they know not what they ought to worship.

We have, therefore, greatly profited from the gospel, from the law, and from the prophets, when we have the skill to say, "This is the God who showed Himself to Abraham, the God who showed Himself by Moses, the God who lastly showed Himself fully in the person of His only Son, and the same is He who is our God." As it is also said in the prophet Isaiah (25:9), where he speaks of the manifestation of our Lord Jesus Christ: "Lo, this is He; lo, this is our God." Then let us have a settled faith, that we not be rovers. Let us not be like little children or like wavering reeds that are carried every which way; but let our faith be well grounded, by taking root in our Lord Jesus Christ.

Prayer

Now let us fall down before the majesty of our good God with acknowledgement of our sins, beseeching Him to teach us true repentance, so that we may bewail them and be heartily sorry for our corruption, to withdraw us from them more and more, and therein to reform us. And forasmuch as we are not only frail but also altogether rebellious, that it may please Him to bring us home again to Him and to prop up our weakness with His strength, so that we may overcome all the hindrances that serve to turn us from Him, and that we may with perfect constancy go on to the mark to which He has called us, until we attain to the perfection of all righteousness. And that in the meanwhile, it may please Him to uphold us in such a manner that even if we fail, yet He will cease not to take us for His children and make us to understand more and more that He confirms us in the trust of our salvation. That it may please Him to grant this grace not only to us but also to all people and nations of the earth; etc.

8

GOD'S THREATS

Sermon 156. Friday, 13 March 1556.
Deuteronomy 28:15-24.

15. But it shall come to pass, if you will not hearken to the voice of the LORD your God, to observe to do all His commandments and His statutes that I command you this day; then all these curses shall come upon you, and overtake you:

16. Cursed shall you be in the city and cursed shall you be in the field.

17. Cursed shall be your basket and cursed shall be your kneading-trough.

18. Cursed shall be the fruit of your body, and the fruit of your land, the increase of your cattle and the flocks of your sheep.

19. Cursed shall you be when you come in and cursed shall you be when you go out.

20. The LORD shall send upon you cursing, vexation, and rebuke, in all that you set your hand unto, until you be destroyed, and until you perish quickly; because of the wickedness of your doings, by which you have forsaken Him.

21. The LORD shall make the pestilence cleave to you, until He has consumed you from off the land to which you are going to possess it.

22. The LORD shall smite you with a consumption, and

with a fever, and with an inflammation, and with an extreme burning and with the sword and with blasting and with mildew; and they shall pursue you until you perish.

23 And your heaven that is over your head shall be brass, and the earth that is under you shall be iron.

24. The LORD shall make the rain of your land powder and dust; from heaven shall it come upon you until you are destroyed.

We have seen the past several days how God entreats His people with promises. Now on the opposite side, He adds threats. And that is not without a good reason, for we see how slow we are when it comes to submitting ourselves to obeying God. Our feet are swift enough to run to evil, as the prophet Isaiah says (59:7), and as it is spoken of in the Proverbs (1:16; Rom. 3:15), but God cannot make us set forth one step to behave ourselves properly, and therefore we must be compelled to it by force.[1] Nevertheless, God certainly begins with gentleness and goodness. And that is why He first sets forth His blessings to those that serve Him. He might very well have begun with threats, but He did not. In so doing He makes a test to see whether we are apt to be taught, by showing Himself fatherly towards us, and by making it to be seen that he seeks nothing other than our benefit, welfare, prosperity, and quietness.

Promises as Motives

Thus we see how God first tests us, and if that does not avail, He uses threats. These two belong together. Let us consider the

---

1. Did Calvin really say "God cannot make us set forth one step to behave ourselves"? Maybe; at least his translator did. If so, this shows that Calvin was not such a stickler for precise language that he refused to use common jargon to get across his ideas. Everybody knew that Calvin believed in irresistible grace. Secondly, Calvin is speaking of God's "inability" in a covenantal sense, not in a decretal sense. God is unable to get through man's sinfulness by means of covenantal promises and threats; obviously, God is fully able to change men by means of regenerating grace. Calvin is not so focussed upon decretal theology that he is unable to speak freely about the covenant.

matter: What good does it do if we do not serve God freely and willingly? Even if men are not able to find any fault with us, yet if we obey unwillingly, our whole life is detestable. After all, the main point is that we are to have a free and good will, to give ourselves over to God. For if we are not to obey merely with a view to the reward, how much more does it follow that if we obey simply out of constraint, all our life is cursed.[2] We can see that a desire to serve God because it is not lost labor [because it is rewarded – ed.] is not all we have to do. For when we have come to that point, we are only half way. Even if a man receives the promises contained here, and offers himself to God to serve Him, yet His obedience is always imperfect and deserves to be cast off. And why so? Because, as I have said, we are not to be hirelings, but our yielding of ourselves to God must be because we are His, and because He is worthy to have our lives employed in His obedience, and especially because He is our Father. He begins with promises because of our infirmity, to get us going, and when He has brought us on so far, then He manifests to us a greater perfection.

To summarize the matter, we have to note that there are three kinds of people who keep the law of God in outward show. One sort does it out of compulsion, with gnashing of teeth, though they do discharge its commands after a fashion. And why? Because they know well that they cannot escape the hand of God; they fear His anger and His vengeance; and therefore they do serve Him, but only by compulsion. But as I have said, all this is rejected.

A second sort takes the middle way; for they know that God is faithful, and that such as serve Him will not lose their labor.

---

2. Calvin pits the ultimate motive (love of God) against proximate motives (promises and threats) at this point, in order to bring out the fact that only the regenerate heart can properly relate to any of God's covenant words. Later on, Calvin will declare that proximate motives are proper extensions of the ultimate motive, since the God we love is a merciful Father who deals with us in terms of rewards and chastisements. Calvin is mainly concerned that we do not get the cart before the horse.

These hearken to the promises that are expressed in Holy Scripture. And so, a great many do yield themselves to serve God, because He lures them thereto by promising them reward, as we have seen before.

[And now, moving to the third sort, Calvin says:] But, as I said, we may not stay there, but we must rather consider that since God has made and fashioned us, redeemed us, and is our Father, these things ought to suffice us apart from what He has promised us. And since He has gone before us with His mercy and shows Himself so bountiful towards us, we should be inflamed with ardent affection to serve Him. This is one of the principal points of our life.

But as I said before, our Lord in His law has respect for our imperfection and therefore He promises to reward us so that we should have a better courage. And indeed, though we serve God with a pure and free affection, yet we must always wait for what is promised us and stay our minds on it. We must, I say, hope for His blessing when we have served Him with a good courage, but we must do it to that end; we must not be drawn by this respect [rewards] only. For, as I have said, we must be His children, and honor Him as our Father. And since it is He that upholds us, so we must assure ourselves that it is not for us to imagine any merit in ourselves, but that He accepts us out of His own unique infinite goodness, and therefore that we for our part must seek nothing but to vow and dedicate ourselves wholly unto Him.

But setting that aside, what we must learn here is that when God has set out His promises before us, He must also proceed to spur us forward [by means of threats – ed.]. Why? Because our nature is full of rebellion against Him. We are not only slow, but also there is in us an inclination to draw away from what God commands us. If there were nothing more than slothfulness, yet that certainly is a vice that needs correcting, and therefore we would have need of the threats mentioned here. But seeing we are so rebellious, and are always kicking, so that God cannot reclaim us or place us under His yoke, it appears that the manacles are doubly necessary.

We see in this the justice of our condemnation, since God cannot win us to love Him, but finds it needful to show Himself dreadful to make us afraid, without which we should fall asleep. Seeing then that God prevails so little with us when He trains us gently, seeking nothing but to make us follow Him with a willing heart, let us acknowledge our rebellion and condemn ourselves. And along with that let us also confess the fatherly care that God has concerning our salvation, seeing He uses all the means that He knows are fitting for us. For it is all the same as if He would, you might say, transfigure Himself. His only aim is to reclaim us. At one time He smiles on us; at another He frowns at us; but all this tends to the end that we may be drawn to Him to give ourselves over to His service.

Threats as Motives

Now someone will say, "Look, since our lives displease God and He reproves them when we serve Him out of compulsion, if the threats only leave us there, what good are they? It would be better for God to leave them off altogether." But let us note that He trains us by degrees, according to His knowledge of how necessary it is for us. It is certain that if nothing but fear will bring us to serve God, it is worth nothing. It is, however, a good preparation, and it leads us further on after we have begun with it. For example, before God has made us meek, we are full of pride and our flesh is wholly rebellious, and in brief we are as colts that have never been saddled or ever tasted the bit. God must take pains to prepare us and to bring us into order, and He uses threats to do so. But this, as I have said, would accomplish nothing at all unless He bonded us to a voluntary obedience and subjection afterwards. And when we have that tendency, then we have greatly profited in that this pride of ours is beaten down, and we are no longer wild-headed, but we know that there is a Judge before whom we must make an account; and we profit in that the same consideration restrains us from using such looseness any longer, and from being so heady in doing evil as we have previously been.

This is a beginning, and indeed it is only a beginning, insomuch that if we should remain there, we would not yet be plucked out of the mire. But when we have thus begun, then does the Lord match His threats with a taste of His goodness in such a way that we are drawn to Him. And in so doing, He shows Himself to be our Father. Now when we understand that God indeed is ready to reward us when we have served Him, even though we are not able to merit anything but rather only provoke His wrath, then we must have our refuge in His mere mercy to obtain remission of our sins as it is offered to us in our Lord Jesus Christ and as He has purchased it for us by His death and passion. When we are thus reformed, and are rid of all trust in our own works, then we ought to offer up ourselves willingly in sacrifice to God, as St. Paul also exhorts us in Romans 12:1. He sets forth no reward, but says, "I beseech you, brethren, by the mercy and compassion that God has shown towards you, that every one of you renounce this world and also himself, that you become living sacrifices to God, for that is your reasonable service."

Promises Come Before Threats

But yet, somebody is sure to raise a second objection, and say, "If threats make us ready for the promises of God, it seems that they should be placed in the first rank, and that the promises should follow them." But the answer to this doubt is this: that God will hold us more convicted before Him when He begins with us by means of His promises. For we shall have to admit that there is a shameful thanklessness in us, seeing that while our Lord seeks only to win us by love, we still deal rebelliously with Him and draw backward when He comes so lovingly toward us. You see then why promises are set before us first of all: that we might be the more reproved for our rebelliousness.

Then God moves on to show us that His goodness will not avail us unless He threatens us. In doing so, He uses rigor, and the same rigor is profitable to us, since when we are touched with it our hearts are daunted. Not everyone, of course, for there are many that take the bridle in their teeth to strive against God; but I mean the faithful. They are the ones who are prepared for the promises of God through His threats. Afterwards, God turns yet again and allures them afresh with His goodness, as I have said before, insomuch that when He has stung them with His threats to tame the stubbornness of their flesh (and surely it is requisite that God should show some sign of His wrath), thereupon He sets before us His mercy, which is the accomplishment of all, to the end (as I have said) that we should learn to yield ourselves wholly to Him with a free-disposed affection.

To Whom Much Is Given. . . .

Now let us come to the words set down here: "If you will not hearken to the voice of the LORD your God, to observe to do all His commandments and statutes that I set before you this day, then all these curses shall come upon you, and overtake you" (v. 15). Here Moses speaks expressly to those who have been trained in the Word of God. It is true that those who offend without the law shall perish all the same, as St. Paul says in Romans 2:12. And we ourselves see that the ignorant and blind do not escape punishment at God's hand. Even though they might plead that they were not taught, yet they are plenty at fault. But let us note that here our Lord doubles His curse upon those to whom He has showed such favor as to manifest His will to them, for He has shown them the way to saving health, had they obeyed Him and yielded themselves unto His teaching. This, then, is not general to all men.

Now first of all God shows that when He has given His law, and published it abroad, the fault lies in the people when they do not understand it. This is the reason why Moses expressly says: "the commandments and statutes that I set before you this day." When he says, "commandments and statutes," it serves to show that they contain a sufficient instruction, just as we have told you here before that God has not spoken by halves, but that He has taught His people. Thus, they cannot reply and say, "We don't know what these things mean." Moses says, "Behold, the statutes and commandments that I set before you. If you apply your endeavor to them, you cannot go amiss."

And therefore let us bear well in mind that according as God has delivered to us His Word, our ungodliness is doubled before Him and our punishment must be so much the more severe if we are not willing to do good, yea and also profit therein, and from day to day be established in His obedience. That is what we have to consider upon this text.

Moreover, when he says, "if you will obey the voice of the LORD your God," it serves to touch us thoroughly to the quick. For seeing that God vouchsafes to speak to us, is it not fitting that we should at least pay attention to Him? And if we act deaf, is this not contrary to nature? For if we refused to hear someone who is our equal, surely he would take offense at it; how much more would one who is our superior? And since God has all sovereign dominion over us, and has done us the favor of delivering to us His Word, and has familiarly acquainted Himself with us, if He finds us stubborn against Him, disdaining to hear Him, is it not fitting for Him to avenge Himself of such contempt? Especially when He sees such a villainous stateliness in us, who are but worms of the earth. So then, what we have to bear in mind from this text is that here Moses intends to condemn the ungodliness of men that continue in hardheartedness after God has given them the means to return by setting His Word before them.

Encompassed With Curses

Now, when he says that these curses shall take hold of us [encompass us], it behooves us to remember what was spoken earlier. For in speaking of the blessings of God, he said (v. 2): "You shall be compassed round about," and now in like manner he joins the curses in the same way, so that we may not think we can escape the hand of God. No matter how sly we are, we shall always be entrapped. It will do us no good to seek places to hide, according to what He has said by His prophet, "If you go into your house, and shut your door and double-bar it, yet shall the serpent come in and sting you there; if you go into the field and seek a way to escape, you shall meet a lion on the way; if you slip aside from the lion, a bear will meet you" (Amos 5:19; cf. 9:1-4); and to be short, whatsoever men do, when God is against them and has become as it were their enemy, they must come to find that they are discovered, caught, and entrapped, for they are environed round about with these curses, with no hope to get out. Therefore, let us not deceive ourselves in seeking worldly means to save us, for if the hand of God is lifted up against us (as we shall see in the song here at hand – Dt. 32:23), He has His storehouses full of arrows, and not of three or four sorts only, but of infinite. And if we suppose that we have escaped when we have overcome some evil, then we deceive ourselves, for God has laid by one hundred more. Let us then look for all manner of woe if we disobey God's law.

But it would be a miserable appeal if we should come unto God by compulsion, solely for fear of His punishments. What must we do, then? We must submit ourselves willingly unto Him, praying Him to keep us from His wrath, and from warring against Him, and from forcing Him to come to destroy us. That would be as if some petty lord should attempt war against a great prince, having neither strong town, nor munitions, nor anything else, and yet should presume to defy one that is able to swallow him if he but lifts his finger against him. Wouldn't that be insane? Likewise, when we provoke our God by setting ourselves against Him knowingly, He must war against us and put us in prison.

So then, let us pray Him not to allow us to be so far gone as to fall into the practice of defying Him, but rather to enable us simply to obey Him so that we may be crowned and encompassed with His blessings, as it is said in Psalm 32:10, "He that puts His trust in God shall be crowned with His benefits," which is to say that God will make him to possess His blessings round about him, and he will be so thoroughly fenced on all sides with His safeguarding that he will have no need to fear. Although we are laid open to many dangers, yet shall we be preserved through His goodness. Now, as touching what he adds, we have expounded here before.

God, the Bringer of Evil

Now concerning the curses, he says, "You shall be cursed in the town; you shall be cursed in the field; your coming in shall be cursed; your going forth shall be cursed; the fruit of your womb shall be cursed; and the fruit of your cattle and of all your flocks" (vv. 16-18). From this we again understand that all the evil we see in this world proceeds from the hand of God. By the word "evils" I understand all the punishments, and all the wretchedness to which we are subject. This is what is said in the prophet Isaiah, where God says (45:7), "I am the LORD who made light and darkness; I have in My power both life and death; and I do both good and evil." He uses this kind of language purposefully; not that such evil as is our fault proceeds from God or that it ought to be imputed to Him; not so. Rather, he means that all the miseries and calamities we suffer in this world are as it were so many chastisements. We may not attribute them to chance, as we shall explain more fully later on, where God says, "If you walk contrary to Me, I will walk contrary to you" (Lev. 26:23-24).[3] Those are His words.

And why? Because men put mist before their own eyes and say, "Lo, what misfortune has befallen me!" When they come to be afflicted in some way or other, they cast up spiteful words against God and go beyond their places, not considering that God is a judge and governs the world by His providence. They are not able to perceive that, so dull and senseless are they. And that is why Moses uses this kind of declaration, enlarging it so much in this text.

And it serves to bring us to what I just cited from the prophet Isaiah, where God shows that He made both light and darkness, and does both the good and the evil. We are not allowed to conceive vain thoughts, saying, "Whence does this come upon me? It is a misfortune. Would to God it were not so." Rather,

---

3. Calvin says we shall come to this verse as we go on in Deuteronomy 28, but the verse he quotes is actually in Leviticus 26. Anyone familiar with these two passages can see how Calvin could easily have made this mistake as he quoted from memory during an extemporaneous exposition.

we must acknowledge the hand that smites us, for in that is great wisdom. And for the same reason God complains thus by His prophet, "This people has not regarded the hand that smote them" (Is. 9:13).

You see then how we must understand that all the afflictions and miseries we endure in this world are indeed strokes from God's own hand. And along these lines it is said by the prophet Amos, "Is there any, evil in the city that God has not done?" (Amos 3:6). That is to say, "Can there happen either war or pestilence or famine or disease or poverty or any other calamity whatsoever, that does not come to you from God? Wretched people, are you so foolish and beastish as to imagine that God, who created the world, has left it at random and has no care to watch over His creatures, or to bestow on them what He thinks fitting for them? Does He not sometimes show His goodness and sometimes make them feel Him as judge, punishing the sins of men, and making men know what His office is? Do you think that He lives idle in heaven, and that He does not set forth His power, or that the world is not guided and governed by His providence?"

So then just as God earlier has showed that we cannot prosper except by His grace and love, which He extends to us, in that He has chosen us as His children and will also accept our service (Dt. 8:18; and earlier sermons on Dt. 28), so now He shows in the same way that if there is any affliction, poverty, or other misery, they come not by chance, but are the very punishments of God, sent by Him. And therefore when things do not fall out after our liking, we must fall to considering and examining our sins. If we are grieved in any manner of thing, so that one is troubled with his household, another with the loss of his goods, another with some disease, another with some vexation of mind, and another with the loss of something he loved, let us acknowledge it, saying "Lo, it is our God who has lifted up His hand, and holds it up still. And why? Because we have offended Him." The first point, then, is that men may not deceive themselves when God visits them, but they must know that by this means they are made to understand their offenses, to the end that they might humble themselves and bewail their sins. So much for one point.

No Escape From God

The second point is that we must not think we can escape the scourges of God, no matter how sly we are. We shall always be caught by the back of the neck if God is against us. And if we make shields and ramparts, and do whatever we can, yet our Lord will not fail to find us. He only needs to blow upon our defenses by which we imagine we can protect ourselves from Him. It is not like dealing with mere creatures; against such we might fortify ourselves both behind and before. But God will slap us down from heaven. We can erect neither shield nor rampart against Him, hoping thereby to stop His hand from touching us when it pleases Him to punish us.

Again, what is the end of all the fortifications that we are able to build against Him, except the overthrow of ourselves? Let us therefore understand that anything men try to do against God will simply turn to their own confusion and overthrow. That is what Moses meant when he said that we shall be cursed in the town and in the field, in our going forth and in our coming in, if we do not obey the voice of our God. And just as he earlier said that God will open His good treasure from heaven to give us rain in due season, so now he says that God will make our heaven as brass, and our earth as iron, and that instead of rain He will send frost; He will send us dust and ashes, and there will be nothing but barrenness among us.

Here we must call again to mind the lesson that has been laid out briefly before, which is that just as every one of us is visited by the hand of God, we should benefit ourselves thereby and every man should apply to his own use what is here mentioned. For God uses many ways to chastise us. One is punished in his own person with diseases, reproach, and I know not what else; another has some secret heartache, so that though he is whole in body, he is continually in torment in mind; another is plagued with his wife or with his children; and another is troubled with his substance. According, therefore, as every man finds himself afflicted, so let him resort to what is here told us, saying, "Alas, I see how my God calls me to Himself. I must not provoke Him, for what shall I win by using many crafty devices as worldlings do, who desire to fall asleep in their miseries. The only comfort they feel is to have no regard for God." Now if we do so, then must what is spoken of in Psalm 32:9 be done to us, which is that God will deal with stiff-necked and hardhearted people as with restive horses and mad mules. We shall see more of this at length.

So then, we must come to the point of feeling God's hand, everyone according to his affliction, first on his own behalf, and also in common. When we see a drought, let us not accuse the heaven or yet the air, saying it was the disposition of them. Let us not do as fanatics do, who look no higher than the stars, but let us think about the hand of God, so that as many afflictions as fall upon us may be to us as visible signs and marks that God executes the office of a judge toward us, and that although He condemns us as often as He punishes us, yet this is not a condemnation to death but our summons to appear before Him, there to frame new process against us. We should mark this point well.

Therefore, when we feel any evil or grief, let us understand that we have offended God, but let us think at the same time that God nevertheless does not mean to execute a final sentence upon us when He thus calls us again unto Himself. What, then, is the purpose? Is it to condemn us without mercy? No; rather He does us this favor, that we might be our own judges (1 Cor. 11:31). When He summons us, it is to the end that every one should plead guilty of his own free will, and thereupon ask His forgiveness and flee for refuge to His mercy. Behold here is an inestimable privilege!

And so let us benefit ourselves both privately and publicly by the things that are told us here; that when we see the heavens burning hot, and we ask rain and yet go without it so that the fruits of the earth fail and the heat dries up all things, let us understand that it is the hand of God that visits us, and let us confess our sins with one common accord. And if any man feels any household vexation, let him confess, "Well, God is wakening me by this visitation, because I have offended Him."

Thus, the main thing God would have the faithful exercise themselves about is the examining of their sins after this manner. As a result it will come to pass that, as Solomon says, blessed is the man who troubles himself and awakens himself; not that we must so trouble ourselves as to fall into immeasurable despair, but we must quicken up ourselves with fear, because the Devil seeks nothing else except to make us dull and dense, so that we should offend God and razz at Him with our tongues, as we see certain despisers do who set themselves against Him, dashing at Him with their horns and vomiting out their blasphemies. Therefore, so that we do not come to that pass, we must arouse ourselves with fear and trembling, which cannot be done unless we profit under the correction of our own indictments, and not tarry until that final laying of His hand upon us, but go before Him, just as St. Paul says that those who judge themselves will not be judged by Him (1 Cor. 11:31).

God Actively Runs His Creation

Now finally it is here declared to us that the course of nature, as we call it, is nothing but the disposition of the will of God, and that He bears such rule over both heaven and earth and over rain and fair weather, that He changes them at His own pleasure, and yet does not send either without cause. If there were a permanent order in nature, it would seem unto us that God never meddled with it; we would grant that He made the world, but we would then say that He does not govern it. We would think thus: "What? When the springtime comes, we see that the rest of the year goes on in the same course as did the year before. It is always the same." But in fact we see one winter is longer, and another winter later, and another earlier yet longer; we see one winter rainy, and another dry; we see abundance of snow in one year, and another year none at all; one year is hot, another cold. Now, does not such inequality make it manifest that God is at work? For the sun performs his office in one year as well as in the next, and always keeps his just course better than the best clocks in the world. How, then, do we get such variety of weather? It is God's doing, to call us to Himself.

Truly the philosophers (and scientists) do seek out causes as they term them. There is such a meeting of stars (say they), and this proceeds of such and such a conjunction. But where does all this come from, if not from the hand of God? We must always resort to the first cause. And indeed, such men are nothing more than beasts if they will not admit that!

Yet it is not sufficient to know that God guides all His creatures, and that He holds them bridled in order to make them bow, just as a horseman makes his horse to turn on this hand and on that, to stop, and to run. It is not enough to know that God looses and binds and sends such changes as He likes; rather, we must also understand that God does nothing without reasons. For if we say that God governs the world and do not know why He plagues us, we shall quickly be inclined to murmur against Him. And meanwhile we shall not profit under His chastisements and corrections, but continue dulled in our sins. So then, let us mark that in shutting up the heavens that it yields no rain, and in drying up the earth as if it were iron, He is showing us our sins and that He is our judge. This is what we have to bear in mind concerning the course of nature, as it is here declared to us.

Nor is God content simply to say that the heaven will be as brass, but He goes on to say that He will send us ashes and gravel or sand instead of rain. Just as we see caterpillars that eat, mar, and destroy all that is on the earth, so it only takes one blasting or mildew to eat the corn and consume it wholly. It is worse than if God should sow salt. And these blastings and mildews are of the same substance as the rain. God only needs to make little changes. He can send a little sharp cold and that same cold will make a clean riddance of everything. When we see such things, then, let us always take warning from this teaching and let us be no longer entangled in our follies. Let us never say, "Ah, evil fortune, evil fortune." But let us understand that our Lord is calling us back to Him, and has His Hand stretched out; and let us know that it is He that smites, as if He should say, "I have gone about to draw you to Myself by fair means, but you have not humbled yourselves before Me. Seeing then that you will not be brought to it willingly, I shall now compel you, as if I drew you by the hair on your heads." Let us, I say, be admonished by this teaching, here mentioned, to prevent the wrath and vengeance of God, as often as He gives advertisement of the same.

Again, when God makes the earth fruitful, let us acknowledge it to be His work, and that there does not spring up a blade of grass except He has put His Hand upon it. Let us then take our daily food from Him, not cramming ourselves like brute beasts, which fill their bellies not knowing whether there be a Creator that causes the earth to bring them forth food; but let us understand that God blesses the earth and causes it to yield fruit for our nourishment and sustenance. Let us bear it in mind, that in affliction as well as in prosperity we may turn our eyes ever more unto God.

The Curses Cling to the Sinner

And it is expressly said further that God will make pestilence cleave unto us and that He will send other diseases and that they shall continue upon us until we are consumed by them. This should waken us even better, seeing that God does not strike as it were a single blow and then quit, but that His curses shall follow us and cling to us unless we forsake our sins and wickedness.

Finally, let us learn that those who stay away from God and hide from Him day after day, only deceive themselves. For example, we see many who, when God sends them some affliction, take some notice of it, but soon they forget it. They shake their ears and think it is over, and like a dog that has been stuck with a whip they turn their backs and run away, thinking that they may appease God by some means. Thus deals the world. But let us beware of such stupidity, for we see what is said expressly in this place.

After God has spoken of His curses, and added that they shall hem us in on every side, He concludes that they shall cling to us. And why? Because if we cling to our iniquities, so that they reign in our bones and in our marrow, and are fixed in our hearts and minds, then must God's curses follow us similarly. When a man will not do away with his evil affections, but is delighted in them and continues to soak in them, God for His part must then shut him up in them. And when we so do, then He must send up His curses to stick fast to us like a leprosy that they may consume us utterly, so that they do not respond to medical plasters, being so deeply rooted within us and in a way, incurable. Therefore, let us be afraid at the hearing of these things.

And so we see now to what purpose Moses adds that the curses of God shall cling to us, namely to warn us that if the mischief has taken root, we must strain ourselves the more in praying to God to show us the favor of the cleansing of His Holy Spirit, whose property it is to search the bottom of our secret affections; that it may please Him to reprove us in such a way that this fear may cause in us a marvelous purgation, expelling our sins from us that we may no longer be wedded to them.

And therewithal let us realize that when diseases begin to reign, or any other afflictions, we may not hope for any end thereof unless we cease to offend our God. It is said in a common proverb that diseases come on horseback (that is to say, very rapidly), and that they return on foot (that is to say, quite slowly). But even though the reason for this is readily apparent, we consider it not. And as I have said before, it is because we do not look to the hand that smites us. Nor can God win us to Himself by the first stroke, when He punishes us. Sure, we are full of fine words: When a man is sick he will protest that his whole desire is to serve God, and that if he may only recover his health, the world will see him a new man. But all is quickly forgotten.

Therefore, it is no wonder that instead of lessening our punishments God at various times increases them and allows us to languish in our adversities. It is because He sees that our diseases are so deeply rooted that He must come again more often than only once or twice to purge us of them. And therefore let us learn to pray to Him to vouchsafe to cure our faults in such a way that they may not proceed to the extremity here expressed, but that as soon as we feel a little stroke of the rod of His hand, the same may be sufficient to bring us again to Him; indeed, to Him with the kind of repentance that will show that we are honest, acting in simple truth, and that we continue therein to the end.

Prayer

Now let us fall down in the sight of our good God, accusing our whole life of the malice and rebellion that is therein, beseeching Him to vouchsafe to chastise us with gentleness and to spare us in such a fashion that we are not cast down into despair but rather are brought home again to Him. And therewithal, since we cease not to offend Him and it is also necessary that He should daily call upon us and awaken us that we may fare the better by His corrections, let us continue to lament and mourn until that time when He has rid us from all the corruptions of our flesh and has brought us to the perfection of righteousness wherein lies our true rest, which is the heavenly blessedness we hope and long for. And since we cannot obtain any such matter except by means of our Lord Jesus Christ, may it please Him to reconcile us to God His Father by His death and passion and in the meantime so to mortify our old Adam that His own Image may be restored in us, and His glory shine forth in us. That it may please Him to grant this grace not only to us but also to all people and nations upon earth; etc.

9

GOD'S PLAGUES

Sermon 157. Wednesday, 18 March 1556.
Deuteronomy 28:25-29.

25. The LORD shall cause you to be smitten down before your enemies; you shall go out one way against them, and you shall flee before them seven ways, and you shall be removed into all the kingdoms of the earth;

26. And your carcass shall be food for all birds· of the heavens and for the beasts of the earth, and no man shall frighten them away.

27. The LORD shall smite you with the boils of Egypt and with hemorrhoids and with the scab and with the itch, from which you cannot be healed.

28. The LORD shall smite you with madness and with blindness and with bewilderment of heart;

29. And you shall be groping about at noon, as the blind man gropes in darkness, and you shall not prosper in your ways; but you shall only be oppressed and robbed continually, with none to save you.

If we were threatened by a mortal man in the way that God threatens us in His law, surely we would be moved to fear, even if such a man had no great power over us. From this we see our ungodliness, so much so that even though we try to hide it, yet it betrays itself in that we attribute more power to mortal creatures than we do to the living God.

By these words God intends to test the honor and obedience that we bear Him, in this way: that He assures us of His love, and we should rest everything wholly thereon and keep ourselves contented therewith. And likewise on the other side, when He gives us any certain token of His anger, we should quake at it. Let us take good heed therefore of what is here mentioned, namely that we not be so blockish as to scorn God's wrath.

But let us return to what has been said already, which is that His hand must be against us if we do not live according to His law. It is certain that men will naturally give liberty to their lusts, to do whatsoever God has forbidden them. They will not admit to it, but their actions show it to be so. And when we on our part have defied Him and assaulted Him, is this not a good reason for Him to arm Himself against us? It is true that as long as we live in this present world, the infirmity of our flesh is such that we are not able in all respects to satisfy the law of God. Nevertheless, when men pass their bounds so far that good and evil is all the same to them, and when they do not strive at all against their lusts, they show themselves open enemies of God. And to that end also is Moses speaking.

Even though we do our utmost to resist evil, and do it in the fear of God that restrains us, yet we do not cease to deserve to be chastised by Him. We see, thus, that the faithful are not exempt from many afflictions and that God acts to reclaim them much more than He does the despisers of His majesty. For since they are His children, so He has the greater care for them, and therefore He chastises them the more earnestly. Howbeit, Moses in this place does not speak of them, but of such as harden themselves in stubbornness, flinging out of course in such a way that they make no conscience about evil-doing. They never think that there is a Judge in heaven until He makes them feel His hand.

And therefore Moses does not say, "God shall chastise you as a father does his children," but "God shall strike you fiercely; and you shall feel His hand so roughly and strongly that you shall not be able to abide it, and that not for one day, but continually until you are consumed and perish." Seeing then that we hear such threats, let us understand that they are prepared for such as are hardened in evil and are not restrained by any fear that might make them resist when they feel temptation within themselves; rather they go on, taking the bridle in their teeth and mocking God.

And what will follow from that? Over and besides the things we have seen before, Moses adds that God shall smite such despisers with various plagues. First, He shall send them enemies, and give them power to destroy and to consume them, insomuch that they shall persecute them even in their dead carcasses, so that when they are overthrown He shall not do them the honor of permitting them to be buried, but shall leave them as food for the crows and for the beasts of the earth. And moreover, He has various other means of plaguing them in their bodies: by sending them various diseases, such as cankers and other boils and scabs whereby they shall be brought to such a pass that they no longer have any understanding, but are utterly out of their minds so that they grope at noonday, as the blind do in the dark. And surely the sorest point of God's vengeance is when men are so overthrown that they have no more heart to return to Him, nor are able to recover themselves to acknowledge their faults and to perceive that when the hand of God destroys them there is no help unless they flee to Him for mercy; rather they remain bewildered as men beside themselves. By this, God shows Himself to be their mortal enemy.

Wars

Now concerning what Moses says here about enemies: We see again how God holds the hearts of men in His hands, so that if we are in peace and suddenly war is made against us, and we did not know it was coming, it is because God is angry at us (as I have shown before). Because we have despised Him, He must also war against us. He has soldiers enough — as soon as He makes any sign (as Is. 5:26 shows) all the earth is moved, even though only a little while before no man thought to have stirred himself up. Let us therefore understand that when wars occur in the world, God shows tokens of His wrath.

It is certain, as we have already noted, that even though we serve God faithfully and stand in His protection, yet we shall not cease to have enemies. For it is His will to exercise us by that means. Such is the present state of the Church, and such it has always been. But this good comes from it, that God will maintain us against our enemies. When they have devised evil against us, yet they will not bring their purpose to pass. They will be disappointed. And though they are as fierce as lions, and full of desperate rage, yet will God tame them at the last; and though they continue in their purpose to devour us, yet they will not have the power to do it. As has been said before (Dt. 28:7), if they come against us one way, they will flee seven ways.

But now it is said contrariwise that even though we are more powerful than our enemies, and attack them in good order so that the victory may seem to be already gained on our side (as we see how the wicked are inflamed with pride and presumption), yet when we think ourselves to have attained the goal, God will touch us with such a fear that we shall not know which way to run fast enough, but every one of us will be at his wit's end. Let us understand from this that when God stirs up wars to chastise us, though we are fully equipped and have all the means possible for fighting, yet we must perish if God is against us. For victory is not obtained by the force and valor of men, but by the Lord of hosts. And there is no other help for us but to be at peace with God, that He may choose to guard us under His wings — according to His use of the same similitude, that He will play the part of a hen towards her chickens (Matt. 23:37). For then we shall be safe, though all the world conspire for our destruction.

And even though our enemies be exceedingly mighty and strong, and fully determined in their malice to destroy us utterly, yet is it sufficient that God protects us, and that even though we have no succor from men, yet we are sufficiently fortified by His power alone. But if we proceed to offend Him, and He sees that after He has spared us and recovered us to Himself, we depart and become His adversaries and continue in our rebellion, then after He has put up with us long enough, He must perforce bring us to this point of being consumed by the hands of our enemies.

And although others seem as wicked as we are, and it seems that God is prospering them no more than He is us, let that not deceive us. For God will sometimes give victory to the wicked, which are no better than we are, but even worse; yet He will not refuse to destroy us at their hands, though their turn will come as well. Meanwhile, we must not think that this threat is uttered in vain. Therefore, let us not compare ourselves with others, saying, "Well, aren't they just as bad offenders as we are? And doesn't God have just as good reason to punish them?" Yes, He does; but He knows the proper time and season, and He can use them as seems good to Himself. But let us prepare ourselves to abide His blows if we stop up our ears against His threats and sleep when He would awaken us. For if we give no heed to His threats we must feel by experience that He who pronounces them has power to put them into execution, and that He does not speak, as they say, just to frighten little children!

It is certain that God will threaten often before He finally comes to execute judgment. Let us therefore consider His long patience in tarrying for us (Ps. 86:15; Rom. 2:4). For if we abuse the same, it will result in nothing other than a heaping up and doubling of God's wrath toward us, so much so that it would have been better for us if He had rooted us out the first day than to have borne with us so long. Let scoffers say that respite is worth gold. There is no respite that we would not redeem with a hundred deaths, were it but possible, when we have been so stubborn against our God and so disobedient to His Word that we have made into a laughing matter His giving us some token of His anger.

Let us therefore consider that as long as God is sparing us He is giving us leisure to return to Him, and that if our enemies have left us alone, it shows His favor to us, that we might act to prevent His wrath. But if we will neither hear Him when He speaks nor receive His warnings, then we will need to give ear to these His threats here set forth, and it becomes necessary for Him to send us off to another school. It is of the wonderful goodness of our God that when we have thus provoked Him (as we see we do), yet He forbears us and does all to recover us to Himself, not by forcing us with many strokes, but by attracting us after a loving fashion, being ready to receive us to His mercy, not standing as a judge to vex and to condemn us.

But what? When we have shown contempt for all this, it must come to pass in the end (as I have said before) that our Lord will stir up against us other masters, so that the wicked will rise up against us and seek to make a slaughter of us by butchering and murdering us, being in very deed the executors of God's vengeance – of which we were warned long beforehand, though we chose to laugh at it, continuing in our sins and wickedness. That is why I said that as long as God speaks to us, and we condemn ourselves and acknowledge our sins and seek atonement with our God that we may live in peace in this world, then even if it is God's will that we should have enemies and be kept occupied with wars, yet notwithstanding He holds us still in His keeping, and we are maintained and defended by His power and goodness.

The Privilege of Burial

Now let us turn to the next verse (v. 26), where Moses says that their dead carcasses shall be food for all birds of the heavens and for the beasts of the earth, and no man shall frighten them away. This seems an empty threat, for what difference does it make whether or not a man is buried when he is dead? What is he the better or worse for it? It seems then, at first glance, that this threat should not be highly regarded. But God intended to show that He will make His wrath felt even in the bodies of those that are dead. And indeed, burial is a privilege that God has given to mankind as a warrant of the resurrection.

Let us not think that burying the dead proceeds from a foolish superstition, or that men devised it themselves. It is true that the heathen have used it, and it will be a witness against them at the last day when they will be convicted by their employment of that ceremony, which should have taught them to look for the last resurrection; their failure to consider it so is inexcusable. For our burial ought to be for us an impressive mirror or portrait to show us that we are not created to decline into corruption, as if there were not another life and as if we should not be restored into a new state. And it serves always for a larger declaration, which is that mankind perishes but for a time, and that their bodies will be renewed.

Now, since burial is a memorial of the resurrection, as I said before, therefore it is given to men as a privilege to be buried. In this respect there is an honest virtue in it, so that we who remain are taught as it were by eyesight to look continually for a second life. For the dead man also bears a certain mark in his body, that he is as it were laid up in safekeeping until the day comes that God will raise the dead again.

Now on the other hand, when it said that men shall not be buried, but that they shall be eaten by beasts and fowls, it is as much as if God meant to deprive them of the common benefit that He had granted to all mankind, and as if He had showed openly that both in life and in death they were accursed of Him. And that is why it is said, "You shall be buried with the burial of an ass" (Jer. 22:19). This was spoken by the prophet to a king, even the king of Judah. And because he would not be corrected in his sin, and because God had given him the honor to bear in his lifetime the figure of Jesus Christ, and notwithstanding he had abused the same privilege and given himself over to all kinds of ungodliness, then "you shall be buried with the burial of an ass," says the prophet.

Hereby we are warned to have very great regard of all the corrections that God sends us, even of the very least, that we may always be stirred up to fear. For why do we pass over so many chastisements of God without profiting from them? It is because we shut our eyes willfully, and unless we are compelled by sheer force and necessity, we are content to think that it is not God who chastises us and, as we shall see hereafter, we fall to such stupidity that we attribute everything to chance. Let us therefore be admonished to mark all the corrections God sends us, both upon ourselves and upon our neighbors, that we may receive a warning by them.

It seems to be only a small matter not to be buried, indeed, but God wants to have it noted and to be understood that it is His hand that is in it, and that He shows Himself a judge against such as have offended Him. Seeing that God will have His judgments known in such small matters, let us be advised to have more wit and discretion. And as often as God gives us, as we say, a mere flick of the finger, let us be moved to think on Him and not tarry until He draws His sword or bends His bow to hit us with a mortal wound, but let us by all means humble ourselves under His hand.

Moreover, we have here a testimony of the life everlasting. It is true that this point was not so plainly declared in the law as it is in the gospel: neither the doctrine that we should rise again to the heavenly glory, nor that we should live with God after our death. But yet for all that, the ancient fathers did not live the life of beasts, nor did God leave them in such ignorance that their faith was closed up to this present world and to this transitory life. Here we have record that when we have finished the course of this life there is yet a greater judgment prepared for all men. And if God forbears with us here, so that we escape all the curses mentioned in the law even to the end, yet we must come to a greater reckoning. For it would be needless for God to speak of depriving men of their burial if, as I said even now, He had no further meaning in it.

Therefore, let us so use this doctrine that we may be provoked to have an eye to the life that is yet hidden from us, for which we look by faith. And let us not think it will greatly avail us when God does not punish us in this world. For it is far better for us to linger here below and be continually in misery, than to enjoy our ease and delights if in the meanwhile God is but tarrying with us in order eventually to thunder upon us when He has taken us out of this world. Thus you see what this text of Moses serves for us, where he says that the birds and the beasts shall eat our carcasses, and that no man shall drive them away.

Now, if God gives such tokens of His wrath to our bodies, which have no motive in themselves, what will become of our souls, in which is the very seat of evil and the kingdom of Satan? For our hands, our feet, our eyes, and our ears do not offend of their own proper motion, but by the direction and provocation of our wicked thoughts and affections. And where do all those things lie and whence do they proceed, but from our souls? Seeing then that the bodies, which were but instruments, do feel the wrath of God and do answer to the same, as we see, let us not suppose that the souls will escape. Let us therefore always look higher than this transitory life in order to wake ourselves up, and let us walk in such obedience that, first, after we have fought against sin and Satan and have been exercised in patience and in various afflictions in this world, having done our endeavor to serve God with all diligence, our souls may be taken up to rest, and that, second, our Lord in like manner may show the same favor to our dead bodies.

Notwithstanding, this favor and blessing of having their bodies buried does not always happen to the faithful, and it falls out that many of the wicked are very honorably buried, even though it is nothing to them and their state is not improved in the least thereby. We see what is said in Psalm 79:3 concerning those that have faithfully served God, namely that their bodies were laid out as a prey to the fowls and the beasts; and yet they were the children of God. And although this is a testimony of God's wrath upon the wicked, yet it may oftentimes come to pass that our Lord will use the same manner of chastisements upon His own people, and yet it shall not harm them.

It is true that we must always humble ourselves when such a thing happens, and we must understand that such things are as it were marks of Adam's sin and of the corruption that is in us, and also of the offenses we have committed. And yet when He permits the faithful to be deprived of burial our Lord turns this

evil to good. We see what is said of the rich man and of Lazarus
(Luke 16:22). It is said that the rich man died and was buried.
Behold how the world's pomp is bestowed on the reprobate. It
seems that his soul should have been received into paradise when
his body was sumptuously carried and treated with great ceremonies. And what of Lazarus? He died, too. But what mention is
there of his burial? None at all. By this our Lord Jesus intends
us to understand (for it is He who speaks) that we must not rely
altogether upon visible things. But yet this threat, however the
case stands, is not in vain. What are we to understand, then? Let
us gather generally (as we have said) that burial serves to lead
us to the hope of the heavenly life, and of the resurrection we
must hope for. So much concerning that point.

When we bury the dead, let it serve always to provoke and
to stir us to understand that we are not created to live in this
world only, but that there is another better life prepared for us.
And again when we see that our Lord deprives anyone of burial,
let us understand that thereby He shows His wrath. Nevertheless,
it is better sometimes for a man to be devoured of beasts and
birds, and to be chastised by God after that sort in his body for
the sparing of his soul and to have a temporal condemnation,
than to perish forevermore. It is better sometimes for a wicked
man to be hanged than to die in his bed. For how many do we
see who gnash their teeth against God when He has patiently
tarried for them and given them so many plain and apparent
tokens of His wrath for their behavior, and yet nevertheless they
made a mock at Him and still continue obstinate in their rebellion!

When a wretched evildoer is condemned by men, he is ashamed
of it and cast down in himself, and acknowledges and bewails his
sins. This condemnation, then, that he bears in his body, even
though it is an execution of what is here spoken of by Moses,
does serve to his salvation; and therefore let us keep these things
in mind. Moreover, when the faithful, even the very martyrs, are
burned and their bodies are reduced to ashes so that they do not
have what should be common to all mankind, let us understand

that God converts the same to their welfare and their glory is
thereby doubled. How do we know this, for it is certain that it is
a threat of God, as are also all diseases? But when our Lord says
so, He means that these are the ordinary means He uses to correct
our sins. Nevertheless, He does chastise those who have not offended Him, and whom He does not intend to pursue with rigor,
and that in such manner and with His own hand. This is in sum
what we have to bear in mind concerning this text.

Disease

Now let us come to what Moses says next, that God shall
strike the despisers of His law with many diseases (v. 27). He has
spoken earlier (v. 22) of fevers and of inflammations and of the
yellow jaundice, as well as of others. Now he speaks of the itch
and canker and of other worms and scabs. Mention also is made
of hemorrhoids, as some understand it. All these things are the
weapons of God to punish the offenders of His law. In brief, they
are His men of war to fight against us, when He sees that we take
courage against Him. And indeed, when we favor our own lusts
and violate His righteousness, breaking the order He has established among us, and when He sees our lusts to be so inordinate
as to be thieves and robbers, then He arms His people and
substitutes, which are the diseases that are here spoken of and
other sorts as well.[1]

Let us therefore learn that whatever diseases we suffer in our
bodies, they are all messages from God to make us feel His wrath
because we have offended Him. The extraordinary diseases are
especially so, however, as when God sends upon us such sicknesses as are not common among men, and of which the cures are
unknown or very difficult to discover. By these God means to
make us feel His anger toward us doubly, and to show us that
we have provoked Him too much.

But we think little of this. Concerning the ordinary diseases,

---

1. That is, He arms His people (our enemies) to make war on us, or else He
sends substitute warriors (diseases).

their very commonness makes us think that they do not proceed from God. We say, "There is a man who has a fever; there is another who has a bad problem with catarrh or a head cold, or some other such disease." We tend to be hardened in these things. How? By custom. And must God, therefore, let go the possession of His right? If He continues to show Himself a judge towards us, in chastising us, is that any reason why we should forget Him and have no regard of His hand? All the same, such is our bullheadedness. I would to God that the examples of such were not as notorious as they are! But let every man look to himself and see if the ordinariness of sicknesses does not cause us to turn our backs upon God, and to have less regards of His judgments and of our own sins, so that none of us finds any faults with himself. So much concerning the common and usual sicknesses.

And as for the extraordinary diseases, we see how men are hardened by them as well. I pray you, have we not seen that God within these fifty years has brought up new diseases against harlotry?[2] Whence comes syphilis and all these other filthy diseases, which cannot be counted at this time? Where do these come from except from God, who utters such vengeance as formerly was never seen? The world wondered at it, and for a time men were greatly afraid of it; but yet in all this they have had no consideration for the hand of God. And at this day it has become so ordinary a matter that the despisers of God (I mean the lecherous sort and the whoremongers, who give themselves to all sorts of lewdness) do but wring their groins at it.[3] Though God smites them with such a leprosy (for it is a kind of leprosy indeed), so that they are eaten up with fretting and with other filthiness, yet they do not cease following their practices and only mock at the illness.

Truly it is a strange thing that such a punishment of God should be scoffed at! How they jest about their bawdiness, at the same time they are being punished by God! It is amazing: They

_____
2. Syphilis appeared in Europe around 1495.
3. An expression of contempt.

jest and scoff at it, as it were in spite of God, and while He calls
them to humble themselves in sackcloth and ashes, they razz at
Him with their tongues and are so far from being ashamed of
their deeds that, even as it were in spite, they make a sport of
their own filthiness and miseries. We see, then, how perverse men
can be, seeing that they can make no better profit in God's school.
I don't mean in the school of His teaching, where He speaks to
them, but in the school of His smiting them with heavy strokes,
and raising up wars and troubles, which ought to make men
beside themselves with fear. All the same, Moses did not write
this in vain.

Let us, therefore, be the better advised, and when God sends
us any strange diseases, let us understand that our sins are multi-
plied, and that God must on that account be more moved than
He was before. For this reason, let it bring us to repentance, and
let us not double our iniquities; for in the end we shall find out
from experience what we have seen even now, namely that such
evil will stick with us, even in our marrow and bones, until we are
utterly consumed. Besides this, God has other means to punish
us, and when He perceives that the usual methods do not prevail,
He has other rods laid up in His storehouses, as it is said in the
Song [of Moses; Dt. 32:34].

Indeed, we shall see what it means to walk recklessly against
Him; namely that in the end He will overtake those perverse and
crooked persons, who pretend to be innocent fools and do nothing
but scoff and shake their heads when He has punished them one
way or another. Let us not, therefore, tarry until God must use
such extreme measures toward us, but being warned beforehand
by what is here mentioned, let us look to it and consider that
however many diseases He sends us, they are so many witnesses
He sends to prove that we have sinned against Him, that we
might think on it and turn to Him with all lowliness.

Forsaken of God

I said earlier that the very worst of all is what Moses adds
here at the end, that God shall smite us with all astonishment,

so that we will be groping blindly at full midday as do the blind in their darkness, and that our hearts shall be bewildered (vv. 28-29). Hitherto we have seen that God shows a singular favor towards men, in afflicting them in their bodies while their minds remain at quiet, that they may be patient. Thus they feel their sins and bewail them, and cease not to call upon Him who chastises them. And in truth it is sometimes seen that the grace of God is much more manifested towards such people than if they had no such great afflictions. For example, if God spares a man, and he comes to serve God, we see that God blesses him. When we see a sound and holy life in one, we say, "Here is a man who serves God, and God also shows Himself gracious towards him." Again we see another that is visited with great diseases, so that every man has pity and compassion on him; he pines continually and has vehement pains; he is vexed with various maladies, and the very remedies that are given him prove so grievous that nothing can be done; yet notwithstanding this man does not cease to hold himself in quiet, confessing his sins and craving pardon from God. In such a man we see such patience as moves us to glorify God, and the man himself continues in prayers and supplications. When a man is thus mortified, and God holds his heart in awe so that he continues in patience under His hand, then we perceive a great grace of God in the midst of these chastisements. But when we are without reason in our sickness, and act madly and in bedlam, and stand chewing on the bridle without knowing which way to turn, all the while never making any attempt to flee to God for relief, then we are in the full measure of all misery.

Therefore it is with good reason that Moses, having spoken of the sicknesses and griefs that God sends upon men's bodies and also of extraordinary chastisements that constrain men in spite of their pride to feel their sins, adds here that God shall strike with blindness, and He shall so strike that our minds shall be amazed; we will grope at noonday as in the dark, we will have no more sense of feeling in our hearts, and we will be altogether blockish. Here we are warned again that the chastisements that happen to us in our minds should be more dreadful to us than anything we can endure in our bodies. It is true that our nature draws us clean contrary, for we are so tender and nice to our bodies that as soon as we feel any grief, by and by we cry out and lose our patience, and therein we see a part of our brutishness. For if we had even a drop of firm understanding, we would be a hundred times more afraid of the chastisements that God threatens to our souls than of all the evil we can endure in our bodies. In what case is a man, when he is forsaken by God so that he seeks Him no longer, but endeavors by any means to hide himself from His presence? Surely when we come to that point, if we could pluck God out of His seat, we would gladly do it. He that seeks such hiding holes to evade coming to God, is doing whatever he can to rob Him of His majesty, for he is loathe to come before such a judge.

And truly, although a man suffers no further harm than this blockishness, so that he does not feel his own misery, is it not a token that God has already given him over to a reprobate mind? Yes, for there is not a more evident sign of reprobation than to be without remorse or scruple of conscience. Moreover, when a man is frightened and out of his right wits, so that he does not know which way to turn and has no more taste or feeling of God, and has no skill to lament for his sins or to ask forgiveness of them and to repent of them, but gnashes his teeth and bites the bridle like a mule – is such not a dreadful thing? When we behold such mirrors, our hairs stand upright on our heads, and even nature forces us to it. And yet for all that, if we do not think upon it, that we may stand in awe and walk in fear and humility, is it not a tempting of God?

Let us therefore learn not to harden ourselves in such a way that God is forced to fall to this rigor, wherewith He here threatens us, namely that He shall make us grope as the blind in the dark, and that we will have neither understanding nor discretion, so that we fall into such a fearful state that we do not know whether we are living creatures or not, nor will we perceive whether or not there is a God that will receive us to mercy and whether or not we will prevail in calling upon His name. Let us not tarry till such evil comes upon us. For it is a deep pit from which very few can get out.

Indeed, God will sometimes bring His people to that point, so that they do not know where they are and are so greatly afraid and so troubled with it all that they become dull and blockish; this is well seen. But He lifts them up again after He has brought them low. Since, however, this example is very rare, let us not tempt our God, but when He afflicts us in our bodies let us understand that He spares us greatly and that He mitigates the rigor of His wrath, and let us be no longer as impatient as we have been prone to be. Although the grief be hard and bitter to us, yet let us confess, "And yet God has not touched me in my soul." Let this come always to our remembrance so that we, acknowledging the goodness of our God in that He forbears us, may return to Him and not doubt but that He is ready to take pity upon us when we seek Him unfeignedly. Let that serve for one point that we have to remember in this lesson, where mention is made of the said blockishness.

Now Moses says expressly that the transgressors of God's law shall grope at noonday. It is as if he should say: Notwithstanding that God gives them many occasions to rejoice, yet they shall be frightened in such a way that they shall not take hold of any grace but be as blind wretches. Seeing it is so, let us mark further that although God mitigates our griefs and comforts us, yet that serves no profit if He does not give us the wisdom to understand that we are not able to enjoy the good that God offers to us when we are destitute of His Holy Spirit. And this is one execution of the threat here uttered. It is true that we should always return to this point, that our Lord does not desire the utter confusion of sinners, but that since such miseries do happen oftentimes, we should not tarry till they light upon our heads but rather seek the remedy, to the end that God not have occasion to withdraw Himself from us.

But whatever the case may be, let us first of all mark that God directs His teaching to such as have been trained in His word, as we have already said. It is certain that He is judge of the world, yet we deserve to be well chastised after a more severe

fashion when we have been taught by His mouth and have rejected His will and are so far corrupted that we make but a jest
of His word; and that whereas He sought to retain us as His
people, we have despised Him. It is very proper therefore that
we should be grievously punished; and therefore let us think that
since God does us the favor of letting us have the pure doctrine
of the Holy Scripture, the same serves to remove from us all
excuses and also to quicken us up to walk so much the more in
fear.

But with all this let us mark further that God not only uses
threats towards us, but also daily exhorts and allures us to Himself to reconcile us to Him, showing that on His part He is ready
to come to reconciliation if we condemn our sins and return to
His mercy. What else is the gospel that we hear everyday, except
a message of reconciliation, as St. Paul calls it in 2 Corinthians
(2 Cor. 5:18)? Seeing then that God sends us a herald to declare
peace unto us, and to show that He is ready to do away all our
offenses, let us take heed that we use this time of our salvation to
receive the grace that is offered to us in due season, as the prophet
Isaiah tells us and as St. Paul says, using the same testimony (Is.
49:8; 2 Cor. 6:2). Again, when we have been overly hard, and
God has patiently waited for us, and we still continue in our sins,
let us not think that He in the end has either given over or
forgotten His office. We must yield an account of such unthankfulness. When we forsake the salvation to which He has called us
and despise Him out of measure, such willful stubbornness must
of necessity come to reckoning.

Then let us stand in fear, and as often as we hear words of
the grace of God that is offered to us in our Lord Jesus Christ, let
our hearts be inclined to receive it; and let us give way to God to
come in. And when we go to Him, let it be done with bewailing
of our sins and with admission of our guilt, not only in word of
mouth but also with such grief of heart as may prove that the evil
displeases us. And when we thus come to dislike ourselves, let us
not abide until our Lord puts into execution the threats He sets
forth here, but let us turn them to our use. And when we hear the

promises of the gospel, let us remember the threats also, that we may be so much the more provoked, and every man make haste to receive the good that is offered to us to enjoy and to possess, unless the fault be in ourselves.

Prayer

Now let us cast ourselves down before the majesty of our good God, with acknowledgement of our sins, beseeching Him to make us to feel them yet better until we are utterly beaten down in ourselves and seek for the remedy to which He calls us, namely that being guided by His Holy Spirit we may increase and profit more and more in all holiness and righteousness, and that we may endeavor so to glorify Him in all our whole life, that in the end we may attain to that same everlasting glory unto which He calls us. And so let us all say, "Almighty God, heavenly Father, etc."

10

GOD'S ANGER

Sermon 158. Monday, 23 March 1556.
Deuteronomy 28:29b-35.

29b. You shall be only oppressed and robbed continually, with none to save you.

30. You shall betroth a wife, but another man shall violate her; you shall build a house, but you shall not dwell in it; you shall plant a vineyard, but you shall not begin to use its fruit;

31. Your ox shall be slaughtered before your eyes, but you shall not eat of it; your donkey shall be torn away from you, and shall not be restored to you; your sheep shall be given to your enemies, and you shall have no one to rescue them.

32. Your sons and your daughters shall be given to another people, while your eyes shall look on and yearn for them continually, and there shall be nothing you can do [lit.: nothing in the power of your hand].

33. A people whom you do not know shall eat up the produce of your ground and all your labors, and you shall never be anything but oppressed and crushed continually.

34. And you shall be driven mad by the sight of the things your eyes shall behold.

35. The LORD shall smite you on the knees and legs with sore boils, from which you cannot be healed, from the sole of your foot to the crown of your head.

We ought to remember Moses' intention, of which we have spoken before; that is, the reason why he continues to utter so many curses. It is because we are so slow to be moved. When our Lord threatens us, we make a game of it; and although we confess that we should meditate upon it, yet it escapes our minds. Moreover, we suppose that we shall always find places to hide, so that if God follows after us one way, we shall be able to avoid His blows by fleeing another. Thus do men deceive themselves, and for this reason they become hardhearted.

Now Moses (or rather, the Spirit of God, speaking by his mouth), perceiving that men are thus careless, and that they do not cringe as they did when God's judgments were first set before them, continues further and adds threats upon threats. Again, perceiving also that men seek hiding places, and thereby deceive themselves, thinking that they can save themselves by flinging over the fenne (as they say),[1] he shows that God has infinite means to punish us with: both above and beneath, both before and behind, both on the right hand and on the left, so that we are so hemmed in on all sides that it is not possible for us to escape.

Delivered Unto Oppression

Now after the threats we have seen already, he adds that those who so resist God shall be afflicted and tormented, so that men shall spoil them and they shall be laid open to all sorts of violence forever, and no man shall deliver them (v. 29). We see here that God uses the wicked for His own purposes, and that although their own intent is not His, yet He applies them to a good use when He inclines to punish us. In that there exist thieves and robbers, although they are given over to Satan, yet they do not fail to serve God's purpose. Indeed, for we see in this text that our Lord does not leave them at random to rob and to spoil whether He wishes it or not, but He threatens His people, saying "They who disobey Me shall be vexed and robbed." And where

---

1. If the word "fenne" here is "fen" or marsh, this might mean "escaping to the other side of the marsh."

does it come from, except from Him?

Now although God permits oppressions, robberies, and violence to be done, He is very properly also able to condemn them according to His righteousness, for He must hate injustice. Yet notwithstanding, by His wonderful wisdom, which to us is incomprehensible, He turns such things to His own service. Thus, when we have offended Him, He must needs punish us by the hand of the most wicked. This is the more to our reproach; for if He Himself should have punished us, and we saw before our eyes that He revenges His honor because of our iniquities, we would well say, seeing that we have offended Him, that it is with good reason that we should come to account for it. But when He stirs up evil people, who despise His majesty, such as are given to all wickedness, and makes them our judges, it is to make us so much the more ashamed.

Let us therefore consider that wherever the evil comes from, we always ultimately have to deal with God, and we must keep in mind that there is nothing done in this world except by His direction. And on that basis let us enter into the examination of our faults. For it is not enough to know that God rules all things; every one of us must indict himself, and consider that all afflictions and adversities are tokens of God's wrath. Now, when we speak of His wrath, we must in like manner remember His justice, and conclude from it all that we very well deserve to be punished. All the same, He threatens us before He strikes, so that we should not stand idly by until His threats come to pass, but rather prevent them beforehand, as St. Paul also admonishes us (1 Cor. 11:32). As long as God spares us, let us be advised so to walk in His fear that we do not provoke Him to stir up thieves to torment and vex us, but that rather (if men attempt such injuries against us) we may stand in His protection, even as He promises to uphold all those who walk in His obedience.

So then, let us see that we do so, and let us remember what is spoken by the prophet Isaiah, which is that they who have robbed must be served with the same sauce (Is. 33:1). And that is the reason why violence and extortions do so continue in the world. Men marvel that evils grow worse and worse, but they should note the cause thereof. For those who bear chief sway and preeminence do not restrain themselves, and seek nothing except to enrich themselves by swallowing up other men's substance. And if they have robbed, then God must send an overturning, so that other robbers will come and bereave these of their booty, and afterward a third group must step in to spoil them again. So, there is never any end. And why? Because the world never ceases to provoke the wrath of God. And since we are headstrong, it is reasonable that our Lord should continue to show Himself our judge.

But, as I said even now, let us be well content to walk in such a manner that innocent blood not cry out for vengeance against us. Let us not do injury or outrage to any person, that our Lord may bless us for so doing, and not pay us with like measure, just as we see how our Lord Jesus Christ says that it will come so to pass (Matt. 7:2). Let every one of us therefore rein himself in, in such a way that this curse not come upon us — that is, being robbed as punishment for using robbery and extortion against innocents. But since men imagine that their adversity will be short, and that they will soon be rid of it, Moses adds that it will be continual, and that when the hand of God is against us, no man will be able to save us.

It is sure that just as God is slow to anger, so He is soon pacified, as far as the faithful are concerned. As for the wicked, He is unrelenting with them, and they feel their burden every day heavier than before. And why? Because just as they harden their hearts against God, so they must likewise feel Him the harder against them. And although this is not always the way it is, yet do we see it often come to pass. God will sometimes withdraw His hand after He has menaced the wicked, or else when He has given them some stripes with His rod He will let them go again. And that is, as it were, a respite, that they may have leisure to turn to repentance. Notwithstanding, when He sees them to be unreformable, His dealings must of necessity be turned to their sorer condemnation.

If God, then, spares the despisers of His law and those that are obstinate in malice, it does not therefore follow that they will be saved. Rather, it is to the end that the plague will come double upon their heads for their abuse of His patience after such a fashion. For when He has waited for them and they continue to proceed from evil to evil, He must put forth His hand at last.

No End and No Deliverer

However the case stands, it is not in vain that Moses tells us here that when God is our enemy, our life shall not be miserable only for a day or yet for a little while. We must not think to limit ourselves to any term in this matter, but we must look for one evil to draw another, until He has laid us quite under His feet, unless we turn to Him to obtain mercy. So then, let us weigh well this word that Moses adds, where he says that if God begins to smite us for despising His justice, it shall not continue only for a little while but we must be miserable forever. And why? Because inasmuch as the majesty of God is everlasting, He must take endless vengeance of those who despise His justice. Therefore, as soon as we see the blows come near us, let us be afraid, and let every one of us make haste to return to Him whom we have offended — that is, our God — to obtain forgiveness of our trespasses. That is the only remedy, without which there will be neither end nor limit to our afflictions, except we take care to reconcile ourselves to our God.

Now in that he alleges that none shall save them, it is to cut off all the vain hopes that men do forge for themselves in their own brains when He punishes them. They look here and there, and if they find any comfort in this world, it seems to them that they can hold God off. Of course, they will not say so, for it would be a blasphemy that all of us would hold accursed. But yet we are so sinful that we hope to turn away the hand of God when we find any help here, insomuch that if men show us any favor and we are supported in anything, we arm ourselves therewith against God.

But Moses tells us here that it is in vain for men to seek

various succors after that fashion, when God wars upon them. And why? Because all creatures are in His hands and without Him they can do nothing. Moreover, what is (apparently) for our benefit will become our curse and all things will redound to our confusion. Let us not, therefore, look to be saved by any means that come to hand when our Lord opposes us, but let us return to Him, seeing that there is no other remedy but that, and let us rid ourselves of all such things as may hinder us to come to repentance.

Let us then be quickened up by these two sayings of Moses, that we sleep no more in our vain fantasies as we have been accustomed too often to do. But what shall we say? There are very few who think about that. For every man torments himself, if his griefs continue and he finds no help in men. In all our afflictions we can complain well enough, but we do not consider that God withholds the help of men from us when He intends to punish us in such a way that we shall, after a fashion, be utterly overwhelmed. And again, if our sorrow continues, it is because we have persisted too much in our stubbornness. We don't think a whit about all this. But all the same, these things are not written in vain. And therefore let us learn to profit better from them than we have done in times past.

Multiplied Chastisements

Finally, Moses sets forth by these threats, *how* we shall be vexed and robbed, if we offend against the law of God. He says, "You shall marry a wife, and not lie with her. You shall build a house, and not dwell in it. You shall plant a vineyard, and not gather its fruits. Indeed, they shall take your cattle and your sheep and kill them, while you stand by starving. And not only shall your cattle be made a prey and a booty, but your children also shall be delivered into the hands of your enemies, and you shall yearn for them and your eyes shall be dazzled due to grief and sorrow, and meanwhile your hand shall be without strength or power to recover them" (vv. 30-34).

It would have been enough to have said, in a few words, "You shall suffer robberies, extortions, and wrongs." But because men are slow, it is good for them to be so much the better touched and to behold the thing as it were before their eyes. That is the reason why Moses speaks here of houses and vineyards, of wives and children, and of cattle. It is as if he should say, "Some shall bewail the robbery of their houses that they had built; some their being separated from their vineyards and other possessions; some the spoiling of their goods and the driving away of their cattle. And others shall bewail the wrong that is done to them in their children, and in their wives." But we are to consider that all these things are the scourges of God, with which He punishes us for our sins.

It is certain (as I have said already) that God sometimes, in order to exercise the faithful in patience, sends them the very chastisements here mentioned, and yet He is not punishing them for their offenses. For Job was not punished for his sins; not that God did not have just cause to do so, but in that He had no respect to it.[2] However the case stands, it is something we see every day.

Indeed, we may find many examples of men that are tormented and vexed by the wicked, so that they are driven from pillar to post and robbed of their goods. Such things happen every day, but this does not prove this doctrine invalid, or that it is not true as an ordinary rule that God punishes men's sins by such means.

Now when we have walked in the fear of God and endeavored to serve Him, and yet notwithstanding our substance is taken away and robbers possess it, let us consider that if this is not done for our sins, our Lord is giving us a great preeminence. For first of all, if we have not offended Him, to whom does the credit [for our faithfulness] belong? We were preserved by His Holy Spirit. And moreover [secondly], notwithstanding any good affection and zeal that we have had to live uprightly and uncorruptly, yet we

---

2. That is, Job's punishment did not have reference to his sins, though he was, as are all men, a sinner.

do not cease to be guilty before God. But what of that? He spares us, and yet He intends to try our patience, to humble us. When it is His will that we bear these miseries, which are punishments for them that despise His law, and that we feel them, well then we must bow to them. And thereby He tests how pliable we are under His hand to yield to His governing, according to His good pleasure.

Moreover, this always takes place, as we have said before, that our Lord punishes the offenses and transgressions of His law by the things that are specified here. So then, when a man builds, let him take heed that he does not build with extortion, pillaging, cheating, and robbery, unless he intends to have his house taken from him, as it is said by the prophet Habakkuk (2:12). For the prophet shows us the walls singing and answering one another.[3] For since men's houses and palaces are often built with blood, robbery, extortion, and wicked practices, so that the very walls themselves cry out that they were built with pillaging and cheating, it must wake up God's wrath and vengeance against such builders. Do we desire, then, to live in peace? Let us look that we build without doing wrong to anybody, whoever he is.

And moreover, let every one of us in his dwellings dedicate himself in such a way to God that He may dwell with us. For they that are driven out of their dwellings have commonly driven God out before. That is to say, they have followed some evil practice, so that God has not reigned there. Is it then any wonder, if they are driven out in the end? No. And why? Will God be thrust from His right, and we in the meantime possess every man his dwelling in peace? Is that reasonable? Therefore, when we see such changes happening as are seen in this world, let us understand that God drives them out who earlier would give Him no lodging. And let such examples admonish us to stand in fear of the threats here specified. And let us not tarry till our Lord banishes us from the place where we are harbored, but let us

---

3. "Surely the stone will cry out from the wall, and the rafter will answer it from the framework" (Hab. 2:11).

rather endeavor to serve Him so that He may continue always with us to maintain us.

And if it comes to pass that we are driven out, let us understand that it is for our sins; for it is better late than never. Moreover, if we are driven out for any other reason, as at this day we see many poor faithful people who are like birds on a bough, as though the earth could not bear them, as St. Paul says of his time (1 Cor. 4:13); and as it is seen at this present time that the children of God are as vagabonds, having not a hole to hide themselves in — when we behold these things, let us understand that since our Lord leads us this way, He does us a great favor; that this is not because of our sins, but for His name's sake and for our better establishment in the hope of the heavenly inheritance, seeing that there is nothing sure or stable in this present world, but that we must always aspire to the eternal life, and to the rest that is prepared for us on high. Let us then acknowledge the good that He does to us in this matter. But in any case, let us take good heed that we do not provoke His wrath against us in such a way as I have spoken of before.

Concerning Marriage

Now, when it is said, "You shall betroth a wife, but another man shall violate her" (v. 30a), let every man take heed to walk in such chastity that he draw not upon himself this curse of God, so that he is deprived of the wife he desires, and the wife in like case of her husband. We see how men are given over to all unchastity, and God has to give them their reward accordingly. David himself was not spared in this case. We hear how it was said to him, "You have done this in secret, but I shall do it to you publicly" (2 Sam. 12:12). He was forced to suffer reproach before all the world, in having his wives ravished openly. Since it is so, let us be careful to walk in such chastity that when men take wives, they may so live together that they may feel the blessing of God, and that their marriages not be broken, through the committing of any offense.

For, as I have said, it is no wonder that there is so much

trouble in the world at this time, because men are more and more kindling the wrath and vengeance of God. Similarly, concerning adultery: For what is the reason that men are so riotous, and have come, as we would say, to their full pride? It is because wedlock is so little regarded and there is no fear of God. There is neither faith nor truth, and therefore men plunge themselves into all misfortune so that in the end there will be nothing but disorder. So much the more, therefore, ought we to take warning to walk in all cleanness of life, that every one may keep him to his own wife, and the Lord bless his marriage and maintain him in quietness.

Moreover, seeing that God is matched with us in the Person of His only Son, and would have us to keep fast the faith of wedlock towards Him, according to the simplicity of His gospel, let us cleave thoroughly to what He has commanded us; and in brief let us be hallowed unto Him and follow His holy calling. For if we do so, our Lord will grant unto husbands the grace to live quietly with their wives and households, and unto the wives to learn to live in good agreement with their husbands. For we must mark that if a man and wife do not join in one mind, there must be discord in the whole house, and they will bite and snatch one another like dogs and cats, and the one will wish the other a hundred feet under ground, so that they will live in continual misery and disquietness. And why? Because neither the one nor the other has any regard to God, to yield himself to His direction. Therefore, let us learn to stop provoking the vengeance of God in this matter.

Concerning Lands and Possessions

Concerning lands and possessions, he says that the transgressors of the law of God will plant vines, but they shall never gather the fruit of them (v. 30b). We have seen that those who have thus offended God are of the strongest and boldest sort, believing that no harm can come near them. And that is why we see that those who acquire the most, and engage in the greatest enterprises, are those who willfully give themselves to pillaging and robbing by hook and by crook, having no concern what robbing and extortion they commit, and offending both God and man without end or measure. Such persons as these must afterwards give an account. They think that when they have planted vineyards, they will enjoy them without controversy, and that when they have built houses, they will dwell in them without further effort. Thus do men harden themselves against God.

But Moses declares to the contrary, that when they have planted vines, other men shall gather the fruit thereof. And indeed, when we see at this time so much thievery in the world, let us understand that it is because there are so few that have clean hands, and because so few are able to protest that they have not encroached upon the goods of other men by unjust means. Indeed, there is such unmeasurable disorder these days that the children of God are fleeced, though they abstain from wrongdoing. We must, however, always bear in mind the ordinary course of things, of which I have spoken, which is that our Lord shall not fail to punish the sins that break out in this area like a waterspout. And as for those who have lands and possessions: They will not go around and steal other folk's goods or pick a few grapes. They will not go filchingly to cut down a patch of meadow. It is for beggars to do so, and we see in these days that for the most part it is poor folks who are the pilferers, filching and stealing anything they can finger. But yet they that have lands and possessions are the greatest thieves, for the things they possess they get by unlawful means.[4] It is no wonder then, if God requites them with the same, and that they come to be vexed in their goods and possessions.

God, therefore, shows us by experience that His uttering of such speeches is not in vain; but we ignore it. Men are well able to complain, as I have said before, but they have no regard to the principal point, which is that God is putting into execution those

---

4. One almost gets the impression here that Calvin is against all wealthy men, and believes that wealth can only be acquired through sin. Not so. For a full treatment, see Gary North, "The Economic Thought of Luther and Calvin," in *The Journal of Christian Reconstruction* II:1 (Symposium on Economics).

things that He spoke by the mouth of Moses. Let us therefore consider these things, and when we see so much stealing of vines, of grain, and of such other things, let us understand that our Lord punishes the ravenousness and extortion that is committed both in merchandizing and in all other trades of occupation. And let us not tarry until God punishes us, but let us walk uprightly, if we wish for Him to be our Defender. For although all places are full of thieves, yet our Lord will keep our goods in safety if we walk in His fear and abstain from all manner of evil-doing. That is what we must have our recourse to, and we must not think to escape evil by evil-doing, but we must use the remedy that our Lord sets forth in this text.

The same thing is said of our cattle and our children (vv. 31-32). Indeed, Moses continues to enlarge on the matter, to the end that men should so much the better perceive what is the effect of this speech that he employs, namely "this shall be forever [continual]." It is as if he should say that the hand of God shall always wax heavier and heavier. So much so that if a man is driven from his [city] dwelling and thinks to remove to his possessions and to his lands, God shall persecute him even there. And if he thinks to cheer himself with his wife, she shall be taken from him by force. And if he thinks to find some comfort in his children, they shall be delivered into the hands of his enemies. And if he thinks to have any recourse to his cattle, they shall be all stolen or taken away by force. Moses therefore besets us here on all sides, to the end that we should learn to resort unto God, since it is in vain for us to labor to escape any other way. This is the matter in effect that we have to bear in mind from this text.

Concerning Invasions

Now he adds, moreover, to increase the evil, that the fruits of the earth and the labor of our hands shall be eaten by a people that we have not known, and that we ourselves will be distracted by the miseries that will thus light upon us (vv. 33-34). That is to say, we shall be out of our minds, beholding the horrors before our eyes. And being bewildered at it, we shall be forced to admit

that the hand of God is against us. That is in effect the matter
that is intended in this text.

Now I have mentioned before that the misery is all the more
grievous to bear when an unknown people come to pillage and
ransack. It is hard to bear when we are robbed by our neighbors,
by those who should be at amity with us. But if there comes a
strange people, there is less mercy. For when men are separated
one from another and have no intermingling at all, there is less
likelihood of any means of safety. And we see how this is often
repeated in the prophets, so that it is said sometimes that the
people who will persecute us will be a barbarous people without
language comprehensible to us (Is. 33:19); so that when we ask
them for mercy and cry alas, it will seem to them that we curse
them and they will increase their cruelty. So then, let us mark
that his speaking thus of a strange people is to make us understand that God will send us such chastisers as will have no pity
or compassion towards us, who will thoroughly root us out.

And now be warned, that although the plague has not yet
come near us, we must not therefore fall asleep. For we always
measure God's threats by our own conception of them and by the
things that offer themselves to our eyes. When men speak of war
and threaten us with the Turk, we reply, "But how can he come
at us? He is too far off." Again, "Can such a prince invade us?
Impossible! He will be prevented by such and such a means."
And, "The plague cannot come that way, because of such and
such a reason. It may be dealt with by all such means. It cannot
be." When we use such kinds of shifting thoughts to comfort
ourselves, we are despising God, not in word but in deed, for we
continue unreformable and proud and do not fear that the plague
can come at us. Therefore God says that He shall stir up strange
people against us, even people of far countries. When men think
least about it, then they will wonder to see how God will come in
upon them on that side that they never thought of, and bring
them enemies to spoil them.

Let us then mark by this text that God's scourges lie sometimes hidden and break out suddenly, so that men are taken

asleep by them, according to the saying that they are like to a woman that is childbearing. For a woman that is with child is utterly undone when her hour is come. Even so it fares with them that are puffed up with their iniquities, and delight therein. They do not see that the hand of God is near them. It comes upon them like a tempest. While they are saying "Peace and safety," then their ruin and utter destruction comes (1 Thess. 5:3). Therefore, since we are told of strange people, let us learn to look far before us when God threatens us, for just as faith must look above the world in order to take hold of God's promises, that it may rest wholly upon them, so likewise when God threatens us our faith must look further off than we can see with our eyes. We must not trust what we see.

We can take Noah as an example: He did not tarry until the Flood broke out or until God unlocked the rain of heaven and opened the fountains of the earth, but as soon as he heard the word, he did nothing but think about the vengeance of God (Gen. 6:22). And by virtue of that word, he beheld the flood as if it had been present, and he lived in such fear and carefulness as if he had seen the rain both evening and morning destroying all things before his eyes. Even so should we. And we should be warned thereof by this saying, where God speaks of distant lands.

Moreover, we are warned to live in peace and concord. For seeing that God has formed a society of us and we are intermingled together, we must learn to live in such unity that our Lord will not need to bring strange enemies to chastise our churlishness, when we resemble dogs and cats. For when men who ought to agree together start vexing one another, it causes God to stir up foreigners to be their enemies, because the closer God comes to us, the more He will have us given to doing good one to another. And if we do contrary, then must God stir up a people to come to spoil us, because we have not lived in peace like brethren, nor have we knitted ourselves together like fingers of one hand. This is what we have to bear in mind touching this text.

Concerning Distraction

Now, where he says, "and you shall be amazed at the sights

you shall see" (v. 34), it is just as what we saw in verse 29 above, namely that men should be distracted and grope at noon like the blind in the dark. For if we are held up, so that we gather our spirits to call upon God and are enabled to be patient in our afflictions, that is a great grace, and such a one as cannot be sufficiently esteemed. But if our Lord does not encourage us to repentance or give us wherewith to assuage and diminish our sorrows, but all hope is taken away and we are totally forlorn so that we see the naked sword continually before us, having no means to remedy or succor at all, that is a dreadful threat. Nevertheless, it is not sent without cause, considering the hardness of heart that can be seen in all men.

For until God has brought us to this condition, we are wholly blockish. We are contrary. We are certain to complain when anything troubles us. Indeed, sometimes we lie as beaten down, but that does not make us to come again to God. For we see how every man takes the bridle in his teeth, so that they shake off all fear and never think upon what is set down here. And so we see how men become blockish. Now our Lord would fain draw them to remembrance, if they are teachable; that is to say, if they are not willfully stubborn. For He tries all manner of ways to draw us to Him. This is the reason why He corrects us gently, and as it were with His little finger. But when He sees that such will not prevail, then must He bring us to this kind of shock. For until He has left us as men distracted, we shall never have our minds peaceable and obedient; we shall never be won.

Therefore, let us mark well that this threat is directed to such as do not bow under the first blow God gives them, but go from evil to worse; for then must they of necessity come to this place. Now, He speaks expressly of the sight of the eyes. For men blind themselves, as I have said before, persuading themselves that they can escape by some means. Even though we see the evil at hand, yet we may wonder to behold how we hold on to our course and pay no heed to it. It is just as the prophet Isaiah says, speaking of the wicked, that when the scourge passes over the whole earth and the storm overtakes them all, they are not one bit moved by it all (Is. 28:15). In such a way do the despisers of God speak, and there are an infinite number of them.

So then, men do indeed thus blind their eyes, and have no respect at all for the plagues to which they are subject; but notwithstanding they may fall into an infinity of troubles, out of which they cannot get again. Yet they hold on still, since they are so rebellious. Moses says expressly in this text, therefore, that they shall have a sight set before their eyes.[5] That is to say, after you have been hardened for a long while in your vain fantasies and have flattered yourselves in your sins, imagining that God should spare you and that you are (as it were) His buddies, and have made a pact with death and with the grave, as the prophet speaks of it (Is. 28:15); when you have been thus a long while untouched with any fear and have deceived yourselves, assuring yourselves that your plague will not last — then will come a sight that shall make your eyes dazzle in beholding the infinite horrors you must endure. And whichever way you turn your eyes, whether upward or downward, forward or backward, you shall see the hand of God continually pursuing you, by reason of which you shall be driven to madness.

Let us learn, therefore, to convert this text to our benefit; and while God forbears with us, or at least so moderates His plagues that we are not thereby altogether overthrown, let us fear Him. And let us consider how many ways we have offended God, insomuch that if He inclined to deal rigorously with us, we should then perish every minute of the hour. And with all of this, let us not tarry till He thunder down upon us and pour out His curses upon us in such a manner that they sink into our very bones, but let us return to Him and to His goodness.

And above all things, when He gives us the grace to foresee His plagues afar off, so that we may say that others are punished for our instruction, let us take warning from their example. By

---

5. Calvin has a way of taking his time in getting to his point. The analogy of blindness and sight is strikingly used here, however. God deals men a severe blow in order to dazzle open their sin-blinded eyes. Thus, His severest chastisements are still merciful, if men will only open their eyes and benefit from them.

faith let us receive God's corrections wherewith He threatens us, so that we may be preserved from that sight of which Moses here speaks, so that our Lord does not strike us with such fear that we cannot in any way think to receive any manifestation of His goodness because of our sins. No, rather let us put this lesson of obeying Him and of submitting ourselves to Him to good use, so that we may escape the aforesaid dazzling of the eyes, and be not so oppressed that we should become like people who are out of their minds. Let us not come to such an extremity; neither let us compel God to execute such threats against us.

Prayer

Now let us fall down before the majesty of our good God, with acknowledgement of our sins, beseeching Him to vouchsafe to make us so to understand them, that every one of us may be his own judge and turn to Him before we are constrained thereto; and that having willingly condemned ourselves and bewailed our sins, we may seek to return to His obedience in such a way that the same may serve to dedicate us wholly to Him. And that in the meantime it may please Him that, just as He has sent us the message of reconciliation in His gospel, He will also give us that grace to obtain mercy from Him and forgiveness of all our sins in the name of our Lord Jesus Christ; and that resting thereon, we not fail to walk always in His fear; and that His bearing with us through His fatherly goodness may not cause us to sleep in our sins, and to flatter ourselves in them, but that every one of us may quicken himself up, until we are quite clean rid of them. And that since we are to pass through so much filth in this world, we may be taught to amend our misdoings continually until we are thoroughly rid of them, for the full uniting of ourselves with Him, making us partakers of His heavenly glory. That it may please Him to grant this grace not only to us but also to all people and nations of the earth; etc.

11

THE PERIL OF APOSTASY

Sermon 159. Tuesday, 24 March 1556.
Deuteronomy 28:36-45.

36. The LORD shall bring you and the king whom you set over you to a nation that neither you nor your fathers have known, and there you shall serve other gods — wood and stone.

37. And you shall become an astonishment, a proverb, and a byword among all nations where the LORD will lead you.

38. You shall carry much seed out to the field and gather but little in, for the locust shall consume it.

39. You shall plant vineyards and tend them, but you will neither drink of the wine nor gather the grapes; for the worms shall eat them.

40. You shall have olive trees throughout all your territory, but you will not anoint yourself with the oil; for your olives shall drop off.

41. You shall beget sons and daughters, but they will not be yours; for they shall go into captivity.

42. Locusts shall consume all your trees and the produce of your land.

43. The alien who is among you shall rise higher and higher above you, and you shall come down lower and lower.

44. He shall lend to you, but you shall not lend to him;

he shall be the head, and you shall be the tail.

45. Moreover, all these curses shall come upon you and pursue and overtake you, until you are destroyed, because you did not obey the voice of the LORD your God, to keep His commandments and His statutes that He commanded you.

We know what kind of emotion led the people of Israel to choose themselves a king: pride, for they did not wish to be inferior to their neighbors (1 Sam. 8:20). Moreover, they thought it would make them very secure to have a head over them who would have all authority. And so we see that the children of Abraham were not content with their liberty, but desired to have a king. Because they saw that the Egyptians, the Syrians, and the Moabites, as well as the Tyreans and other like people had kings, they were certain that if they also had a head, all would go well with them.

Now, just as pride and ambition were the reasons they chose a king in Israel, even so they became hardhearted in it, supposing that they were out of all danger. Having such a defense, we see that they despised the prophets, believing that they were well guarded. The Spirit of God, foreseeing this though it had not yet come to pass, said that the king that they should appoint would be led captive into a strange country (v. 36). It is just as if God had said that they might well seek hiding holes to save themselves, but such would be of no avail at all against His hand. This is what we touched upon yesterday, namely that when God is our adversary, we may not imagine we can defend ourselves against Him by means of His creatures, knowing that He shall surely apply them to our destruction. Therefore, let none of us deceive himself; neither let us make our defense out of what is nothing but smoke and lies.

It is true that the king who was first chosen by the people of Israel, namely king Saul, was not brought into captivity, although he died in battle. The successors of David, however, were dealt with cruelly and with great reproach, even though God had ordained them, and even though they were a figure and image of our Lord Jesus Christ. And it is a horrible thing that the kingdom God had dedicated to Himself (as we see from the anointing) should be laid open to such reproach. You see how the successors of David, who had received the promise that their fear should be everlasting, and were also figures of our Lord Jesus Christ, were handled in such a way that they were led prisoners in chains, were arraigned as offenders, had their eyes put out, had their children's throats cut in their own presence, and were cast into a deep dungeon, there to rot or to be eaten to death with vermin.

And that, as you can see, is a very strange matter. But the vengeance of God extended that far, and it was necessary because of the rebelliousness of the people, for which there was no other remedy. The more God put up with them and patiently waited for them, the closer they came to the extremity of all confusion for despising such great goodness and for being so rebellious and hardhearted against it.

Now we may gather a good warning from this, that (as was declared yesterday) although in the eyes of the world we seem to stand in no peril, yet it is needful for us to seek to have God's favor. For if God is not on our side, and we under His protection, all the helps we think to obtain from creatures are cursed, for they will serve rather to overthrow us. And therefore let us take heed that we not put our confidence in the greatness of princes or in any other defenses, for we see how they are but means to blind such as might otherwise turn to God and obtain forgiveness from Him, and we see how in the end it will overthrow them utterly. Let us, then, be better advised, and though we seem to be well guarded by the world, yet let not that prevent us from always walking in the fear of God, knowing that all the favor we are able to purchase in the world amounts to nothing at all; and that if God but blows upon it, it all vanishes away in the minute of an hour. That is what we have to note from this text.

Apostasy Itself the Greatest of All Curses

Now it is expressly stated that both the king and the subjects shall serve foreign gods of stone and of wood; that is to say, puppets and idols. Doubtless God intended by these words to utter the dreadful extent of the punishment that was to come upon the Jews. For although the nourishment God gives us and all the testimonies of His fatherly love and goodness appertaining to this transitory life are to be highly esteemed, yet the most singular benefit that we receive as long as we live in the world is that we have religion well ordered, that His service be pure among us, that we call upon Him and that it be lawful for us to claim Him as our God, and that we be not corrupted and defiled with superstition and idolatry. That, I say, is the principal good thing to which the faithful should aspire; and we are truly but blocks and beasts if we do not prefer the same above all manner of riches and pleasures and before all our ease and comfort.

Now then, on the contrary part, the plague that ought to be the most dreadful to us, and the most horrible calamity that can fall upon us, is to be deprived of God's service and to have our mouth shut so that we cannot call upon Him; and not only that, but also through tyranny to be compelled to honor idols and to defile ourselves with their abominations, and to pervert what God has ordained for the magnifying of His name among us. When things are thus corrupted, let us understand that God has departed from us and has declared Himself to be our mortal enemy; that He has quite forsaken and refused us, and is loath that we should henceforth have any token or inkling at all either of His presence or of His favor.

And so, when Moses says in this text that the Jews shall serve foreign gods, he intends to threaten them more dreadfully than before. It is as if he should say, "It shall surely be grievous to you when you are famished and want bread to eat and water to drink, when your enemies will rob you of all your substance and make havoc of all your possessions, when you will pine away in grief and sorrow without any means to assist yourself — surely these will be very hard things for you, especially when you can obtain no favor from your enemies, who will be as wild beasts against you. All the same, this is all nothing in comparison to the other curse, which is that instead of honoring the living God and of confessing that He has chosen you to be His people (which is an immeasurable blessing) — instead of such things, I say, you should serve idols and become accustomed to the superstitions of the pagans, and have no more prayers, neither psalms nor offerings, but be dispersed and forlorn."

Now, seeing that we perceive the natural sense of Moses, let us understand that among all the blessings of God that we enjoy in this present life, this ought to be preferred above all the rest: namely, to have freedom to serve our God, to make confession of our faith, and to declare that we are His people, of His Church and of His flock. Certainly this truth is little enough acknowledged; it is not, however, in vain that we are admonished concerning it. Seeing, then, that it has been the will of God to plant His Church among us, and that we should have His Word and His sacraments, by which He declares that He dwells among us, let us accept such a blessing according to its worth.

Do Not Envy the Prosperity of Apostates

It will serve a double use to us. First of all, when we fare better every day as a result of the doctrine that is preached to us, such a treasure cannot perish except through our own unthankfulness; just as we see many folk who think that it is enough to be in attendance at sermons, and it seems to them that God has been given His due if they have but made a ceremonial appearance. Meanwhile, the seed of life perishes without yielding any fruit. Therefore, so that we may apply the blessing God bestows upon us — which blessing is that we have liberty to hear His doctrine, and be trained therein, and have the sacraments for an establishment of our faith, and may declare that it is the living God whom we worship and that He governs us — I say, for all this to profit us, let us acknowledge that our Lord cannot bestow any greater blessing on us than this.

And meanwhile we must take it patiently if other things fail us so that we lack comforts. Let us not be grieved at the children of this world, who have their delights and triumphs, revelling in their earthly pleasures. If the children of God have not the same, let them know that they enjoy something that recompenses double, yea a hundred-fold. And that is that they are able to serve God.

After all, what good does it do these wretched people who dwell in papistry to lie slumbering in their nests, if meanwhile they are banished from the kingdom of God, and Christ Jesus Himself and His Word are banished from the country in which they dwell? What does it avail for them to be served in their houses, if they are not permitted to serve God? What does it avail for them to have food and drink to consume until they burst, if they are starved for lack of spiritual food? What does it avail them to have honor and credit, if they are constrained to defile themselves with these treacherous dealings whereby God is despised and His honor spoiled and conveyed over to idols, they being guilty thereof? Alas, is this not a cursed condition?

Let us therefore take it patiently, even if we are held in contempt by the world and counted as underlings and castaways, lacking comforts and not having what our flesh desires. Seeing that God gives us this special freedom, that we may purely worship and serve Him and be delivered from this cursed slavery to idols, let us be content and esteem this benefit according to its worth, so that we are not grieved toward them that enjoy the goods of this world, but who are meanwhile destitute of the grace of God, which does remain among us.

Do Not Forsake Christ's True Liberty

Additionally,[1] here is a warning that, since God has put us in possession and fruition of this liberty, we must take good heed that we not be deprived of it through our own leadenness, for this threat that was made to the Jews is also directed to us. Let us understand, therefore, that since we have the gospel preached to us, if it does not prevail with us, God must deliver us into the

---

1. This apparently is the second part of the "double use" mentioned by Calvin above.

hands of other teachers when we refuse to obey Him. And in truth, we ought not to think that the horrible confusion that exists in papistry comes from any other cause than this: They were taught the pure doctrine of the gospel, but they have rebelled against God and have not bound their necks to bear His yoke, and therefore God could not do other than deliver them over to such tyranny as we see.

And truly this was prophesied to them by St. Paul (2 Thess. 2:11-12). It is proper, says he, that the world, since it will not believe the truth, should obey lies, and those who will not be subject to the living God should be obedient to the creature, even to idols. With such examples before our eyes and hearing the threat as it lies here, let us, while God keeps us in His school, learn so to walk in His fear and awe that we may not be bereft of the welfare we now enjoy, but that God may rather augment it and cause it to prevail.

Moreover, let us mark that those who serve idols shall not be excused for it even though it is itself a punishment from God. We know that one sin is punished by another, as it is said in various places in Scripture, and as we see it especially avowed in the first chapter of the letter to the Romans (1:24). Those who would not serve God by giving themselves wholly to cleanness of life were shaken off and given over to all manner of shameful lusts and retained no more understanding to discern between good and evil than the brute beasts, but ran into all kinds of evil. By this St. Paul shows very well that when God gives us leave to plunge ourselves into the depths of our iniquities, it is so that we should be more guilty before Him. Those therefore who worship idols, notwithstanding that they are compelled to it and sigh and desire to be at liberty, still offend God, and from this they should better understand how heinous their sins are, seeing that they must receive such correction for them. How so? Because when I should be glorifying my God, I offend Him instead, and He is ready to cast me off because I am not worthy to serve Him, and He must deprive me of the liberty and ability to dedicate myself wholly to His obedience.

Let all those therefore that are in the captivity of papistry and mingled among the superstitious understand that the vengeance of God lies upon them, and that they will be more and more guilty for their serving of idols. It is a poor reply for them to say, "We do not do it willingly. We wish that it might please God that the right and pure religion were over all." But for all this, our Lord does not exempt them from condemnation. And He is the competent judge. Let us therefore rest upon His Word, and seek no more escape routes, but let them that endure such a state understand that it is now or never when it comes to turning to God, since they are as good as drowned in their present condition and possess a token of wrath against themselves in that He is gone far away from them. Therefore let them think upon this, and be moved with it to the quick, according to the meaning of God in this text, and as we have touched on it heretofore.[2]

An Example to the Nations

Now Moses says that this people shall be an astonishment, a proverb, a byword, and a ridicule among the nations in which they will be dispersed. Here our Lord shows that as His goodness should be displayed among the people of Israel, so that every man should rejoice in the seed of Abraham, so should the very same people be abhorred and detested. The promise to Abraham was thus: All nations shall be blessed in thy seed. Of course, it is true that we must look to our Lord Jesus Christ, who is the very bond of the seed of Abraham, or else this blessing has no place or ground to stand upon. Yet notwithstanding, they who were descended from the race of Abraham should have been blessed by God so that they might have been an example, that everyone desiring grace might say, "O God, take pity on me, as upon the

---

2. Calvin does not make it clear what he thinks these people ought to *do* about their situation. By 1556, however, the Reform in Europe was pretty well advanced, and Calvin probably would have answered that anyone genuinely grieved by idolatrous worship should separate from the Roman Church and join the Reform. Those who remained in idolatry, and did no more than wring their hands over it, would be condemned.

children of Abraham," whom He had chosen and adopted. Such was the promise.

Behold here the threat that was laid against it: When men see how fiercely God smites the people whom He had chosen, they will be astonished at it and think thus with themselves, "Is it possible that they whom God chose should now be cast off and be persecuted and thrown under foot with all manner of reproach?" And upon this, men may say, "O God, keep me that I not fall to such a case as this people is in." Or else when they intend to curse, they might say, "God do to you as He did to those vile Jews." This much is to be understood from this place.

Now let us mark that just because the Holy Spirit spoke thus by the mouth of Moses, it was not His intention that this doctrine should serve only for two thousand years or thereabouts, which was the time the law lasted until the coming of our Lord Jesus Christ, but that we at this day must apply the same to our own use. Insomuch as God has come near to us, we must walk in His fear in spite of Satan, so that His goodness may shine in us and be perceived to remain upon us. And on the other side, when we are unthankful, and our God is as it were mocked by us, it is needful for us to think thus: "Well, we may shrink back from the way, but we shall gain nothing from all our plans, for in the end we shall surely come to shame."

In truth we see how it is said that the name of God will be blasphemed among the unbelievers because those who were counted faithful earlier have been so cast down that God may seem to have falsified His promise and to have deluded them, so far forth must the vengeance of God extend. Now, seeing that this is so, let us learn to submit ourselves to our Lord while He allures us to Himself with gentleness, and so hold ourselves under His obedience that we may not become a byword and a ridicule to all the wicked, who seek nothing but to blaspheme God and to make a mock of us. Let us, I say, look well to that.

Moreover, when Moses says that God shall disperse His people, it serves to confirm the matter, so that the Jews should not think that they were carried away by a storm, as it were by mere happenstance, but that they should understand that it was the hand of God that was upon them. And in that His warnings did not prevail with them, therefore what happened to them should cause us to stop short. For behold what vengeance we hear God threaten in this place! We see the same thing executed before our eyes. Is it not a horrible thing that the Jews are abhorred at this day throughout the whole world? Yet they were the people whom God had sanctified for Himself. They were His heritage. They were the royal priesthood, as they were termed in Exodus 19:6. They were the blessed generation. And yet for all this, they are rejected by all men, insomuch that men do as it were shudder to behold them as though they ought to be cut off from mankind.

If it be said, "Well, this might very well happen to the faithful, and similar things happened even to the holy patriarchs," this is quite true, but in another fashion.[3] For the faithful may well be put in fear, just as it is said in Isaiah 8:18, and people may point at them with the finger and shun them afar off, and that is because God is not known and His grace is despised.[4] But when we speak of the Jews at this day, it is very well seen that God is against them, for they are like rotten members, and their body is torn to pieces, and there does not remain any token of the blessing that God had bestowed on them. Therefore, when we look at such a mirror, let us learn to make a good use of it, and let their example serve to seal this doctrine and to confirm it, so that we do not test God, and so that we not continue hardhearted so long that He decides to wrap us up in reproach with all the rest of the nations of the world.

The Destruction of Food and Oil

After this, Moses returns to something he had touched upon before, which is that the people, having tilled their fields and possessions, would neither drink of the wine of their grapes, nor

---

3. In other words, the righteous also suffer as strangers in a strange land, ridiculed by men.

4. Isaiah and his children were signs to Israel. Calvin assumes that because Israel rejected Isaiah's message, they also shunned his family.

eat of the grain of their harvest, nor enjoy the fruits of their trees (compare v. 30). This has been spoken before, but there is here a certain difference to be noted. For before, God had stated that when the Jews had labored for grain and wine, the enemies would come and take it all away, and that all of it would be made a prey. But now He says that without any force of man and without any trouble of war, they should nevertheless not fail to be famished and to be destitute of all things that might do them good.

And how? Because worms, beasts, caterpillars, locusts, and all other things would eat up the fruit of the earth. Behold what armies God stirs up against the wicked! Again, on the other hand, they would be blasted and singed, so that all would perish. So that even if men do not touch the Jews, and leave them alone in rest, yet they are to understand that God has other means to punish them and that He is always armed in infinite ways. That is what God intends to declare.

And therefore let us take warning from this text, that when we have escaped one plague, God shall find another for us, and if we step aside to the left hand, yet He is nevertheless armed against us and before we have gone three paces He stops us in our way. Behold how well men succeed when they seek holes to hide in! We see it in the prophecy of Isaiah (29:15), how he mocks those who think by their craftiness to escape the hand of God. "Dream on. Dream to your fill," he says. "Yet will the curse always overtake you." And similarly, even though we have no enemies to trouble us and to rise up against us to spoil our substance, yet let us understand that God has other means, which we are not aware of, by which He can bereave us of what He has put into our hands. We shall be abashed when, thinking we have something wherewith to satisfy ourselves, the bread will be plucked out of our mouths; and that when we think to drink, we shall be dry.

And what brings this to pass? Well, it is our Lord who gives increase to the grain when it is sown in the ground, and it is He who sends the grapes. It is He also who causes all things to prosper for our nourishment. We are taught by this text, first of all, that when we till the fields, sow them and reap them, we must make prayers always to God to bless the earth, that we may be fed through His grace. And we must hold it for a certainty that it is His peculiar office to feed us as a father feeds his little children. So much on this point. I have treated it at large before, so that it suffices here merely to touch upon it.

God's Special Warriors

Now furthermore let us note then when God speaks here of locusts, worms, caterpillars, and other beasts, and when He speaks of blastings and of burnings that come from it, He shows that He has men-of-war of a strange sort available when He determines to punish men. This serves to pull down the pride of men. For if we are spoiled by our enemies, "Very well," men will say, "this was done by violence and plain force." For example, when war comes, the whole country is spoiled; the richest become beggars; and all this is ascribed to the war. Man is not blamed for it.[5] But when it comes to pass by other means – so that men do not know by what means their substance is wasted, though they see it melt away before their eyes, one year by hail, another by frost, and one time one way and another time another way, so that all things are consumed in their hands – God by this means makes it more manifest to men that He intends to confound them utterly.

Indeed, if we look at the way God dealt with the Egyptians, we shall see it much better (for we discern God's judgments better in other men than in ourselves). If God had stirred up a great army against the Egyptians, instead of lice and vermin, they would have continued on in their pride and presumption. And even if they had been a hundred times discomfited, yet they would not have ceased being stiff-necked to this very day. When they were persecuted with lice, which were God's soldiers in Egypt, they should have been confounded. Therefore, let us well note

---

5. I take it that Calvin means that the cause of the destruction is not ascribed to the immorality of man, but to the designs of the enemy.

that God, by sending men such chastisements as are set down here, is warning them to think on their frailty.

If Herod had been slain with a thunderbolt from heaven, it would not have been as fit a punishment for the blasphemy he committed in allowing himself to be called a God and not a man, as when God caused him to be eaten and consumed with vermin until he was as rotten as could be. Thus he was compelled to say (as one of his friends and contemporaries records), "Oh, behold here a goodly god, which is so rotten that he is forced to feel that the hand of God is persecuting him for his pride."[6]

Let us therefore mark well that God, after threatening the Jews to send against them enemies who by violence and force of arms would spoil the country of all manner of food, now adds moreover that although they were not vexed or troubled at all by the hand of man, nor was anything attempted by man against their possessions and land, yet notwithstanding they should not pride themselves in their labors or in their tilling well their grounds. And why? Because the vermin will waste it all.

And He says expressly, "You shall sow much, and gather nothing." He shows by this that no matter how good provisions men make beforehand, thinking undoubtedly that all will go according to their wishes, yet they will be never the better for it. And it serves to this end, that we should not fall asleep when we see fair prospects, according to our propensity to despise God, as if to say that if there is a good seed-time then we are out of danger. As if God had no more dealings with earthly things! Or if we have reaped and laid up the grain in our barns, we become more confident because we see no likelihood of any more danger. But instead of this, we should evermore have an eye to God, saying, "Lord, behold, the earth waits for rain as though it were athirst,

---

6. "A severe pain also arose in his [Herod Agrippa's] belly, and began in a most violent manner. He therefore looked upon his friends, and said, 'I, whom you call a god, am commanded presently to depart this life; while Providence thus reproves the lying words you just now said to me; and I, who was by you called immortal, am immediately to be hurried away by death.'" Flavius Josephus, *Antiquities of the Jews* 19:8:2, trans. by William Whiston.

and when You give it, it is to make it bring forth sustenance for our nourishment. Again, such storms might fall from heaven as would wash away all from us, and one war would be enough to bereave us of all that we have. Thus is all in Your hand, O Lord, and we must depend upon Your mercy, and be all our life long in Your custody, or else we must perish, and all the provisions that we have will profit us nothing." Thus, then, must we call upon God with diligence and walk in His fear, seeing He is so gracious as to be our foster-father and vouchsafes to stoop so low to us.

Therefore Moses has very well declared in this text that we must not be beguiled by such goodly prospects and fair provisions as we may have. As for example, when we see the grain is fair upon the ground, we must not be too joyful, as if all were won; no, not even when the grain is gathered in. For God wishes to be called upon at that time, just as we are bound to make our daily suit unto Him, saying, "Give us this day our daily bread, O Lord," that day by day He may feed us. For even if we have never so much today, yet tomorrow we may starve. For when it pleases God, He is able not only to destroy the grain and wine in the fields, but also He can make them to be worth nothing, even when we have them in our garners and cellars. Nay, we hear the threats that He makes, saying, "You shall carry grain to the mill by measure, and the bread to the oven by weight (Ezk. 4:16), and yet for all that, you shall still be empty and hungry. When you have eaten your fill, there will be no strength at all in the meat, neither will you be sufficed therewith." Seeing our Lord tells us that He has so many ways to famish us, let us not be hardhearted, but let it rather waken us, that we may altogether depend upon Him and walk in His fear and be His children, if we want Him to continue to do the office of a father toward us. That is the effect of these things, which we have to remember.

Here again Moses repeats these threats, which he had spoken before, saying that the Jews and their lineage shall be carried away into captivity (v. 41). Now certainly there can happen nothing more bitter to men than to see their children taken away by force, eaten and devoured by the enemies, and cruelly dealt with. They would a hundred times rather bury them. Now then let us mark in few words what God intended to declare in this text, which is that although He has been never so bountiful to us and filled us with His blessings, so that we are fenced in on all sides, yet He can very well bereave us of them all again, and that plague will be much more grievous to us than if we had never known what His goodness means. Wherefore the larger God bestows His blessings upon us, yea even those blessings that concern this transitory life, let us look that we are always so much the more provoked to honor him and to serve Him. For He for His part will not cease to do us good, if we do not turn tail and give Him over. But seeing that He allures us to Himself gently, if we are willing to come to Him, let us assure ourselves that His hand will evermore be stretched forth to augment the gifts and blessings that we have received of Him.

Comprehensive Judgment

In the end he returns to the matter we have dealt with already: All these curses shall come upon you; they shall seize upon you, and you shall be caught and besieged by them on all sides until God has completely consumed you, all because you did not hearken to His voice, to obey His statutes and the commandments He gave you.

I have told you before how Moses has repeatedly shown the Jews that no evil or adversity came upon them except by the hand of God. It is necessary for us to know the cause as well, however. It is true that sometimes God visits us and we cannot perceive the reason for it, for He does not do it on account of our sins (not that He might not do so, but because He spares us). Yet must we always look to this, that when we sustain any affliction, we ought to think upon our sins and enter into examination of them to condemn ourselves before God. Indeed, and we must not tarry until such adversity comes, but we must benefit ourselves from every calamity that we see throughout the world, knowing that God punishes men's sins by such means and bridling ourselves in the light of it.

So then, the matter to which Moses now returns is this: that having showed us how it is the Lord who withdraws all manner of blessings from us, how it is He who curses our possessions and the fruits of the earth, how it is He who sends vermin and storms and tempests to destroy all, how it is He who gives power to our enemies, he then shows why all this is done: It is because we have rebelled against Him, because we have despised His law. That is the very reason why these plagues of wrath do so pursue us.

Now then, let us bear in mind the teaching that has been sufficiently set forth about this already, which is that when God afflicts us, we must shut our mouths from replying or entering into argument, for we shall win nothing by being contentious with Him. No, rather we must condemn ourselves, confessing that He deals justly. Even if it is His purpose to prove our patience and to try us to the uttermost, yet all the same we must declare ourselves guilty before Him, and understand that our sins deserve to be thus roughly handled at His hands. Such an approach would cause to cease all blasphemies, murmurings, and complaints that are daily heard in the world. When any adversity or affliction happens to us, it is so that we should think on the sins we have committed. Mark that for one point.

And since mention is made of the commandments and statutes that God has ordained, the same expressly and purposely concerns us. For although the Papists have the law, yet it is buried in their midst. The Jews, as St. Paul says (2 Cor. 3:15), have a veil before their eyes. The Turks walk in their own ignorance, as do all the rest of the heathen. Now our Lord enlightens us and shows us the way. There is, therefore, a more villainous rebellion in us when we do not do according to what we have been taught. We deserve that God should use greater severity with us and pour upon us the plagues of vengeance that are contained here. Therefore, let us benefit ourselves by the things that are said here concerning the commandments and statutes that God has ordained. And seeing it is the case that He speaks to us daily, declaring to us His will so familiarly, let every one of us submit himself obediently to it.

And when Moses says further that these curses shall catch hold of us, and that we will be hemmed in round about by them until they have consumed us, it is a warning to us that we should not be self-willed against God. For we may well seek hiding places, but it will avail us nothing, as we have said before, for the end will always be unhappy for us. And therefore, let us remember the complaint that God makes through His prophet Isaiah. He says in Isaiah 1:6 that from the crown of the head to the sole of the foot, God must of necessity smite hard upon them that have rebelled. And having spoken thus by His prophet Isaiah, He says, "What more can I do? I have not ceased to chastise My children, insomuch that from the crown of the head to the sole of the foot I have so beaten them that there is no whole or sound place, and yet they continue hardhearted still. Alas, what shall I do? I must crush them and break them all to pieces."

So then, let us be afraid to take such a rebellious stance against our God, and let us prevent the condemnation here pronounced. And as soon as God begins to correct us, let us bestir ourselves to return to Him. And let us not tarry long, but being admonished by His Word, let us fall to bewailing our sins, being sorry for them, and let us ask forgiveness of them in the name of our Lord Jesus Christ.

Prayer

Now let us fall down before the majesty of our good God, with acknowledgment of our sins, beseeching Him not to allow us to be so blinded in this mortal life as not to realize that all the miseries and wretchedness that we suffer are warnings given to us, to make us think on ourselves and on our lives, and also to move us to repentance. And therefore that, if we are afflicted by His hand, it may not cause us to blaspheme His holy name or move us to impatience, but rather tame us so that we may fare the better by all His corrections and turn again to Him. And that when we see the wretched world at this day to be so full of wretchedness and horrible miseries, and thus behold the wrath of God for the sins that reign therein, it may be a means to hold us in awe, praying God not to use any such rigor toward us, but rather that we, fleeing for refuge to His mercy in the name of our Lord Jesus Christ, may be touched with true repentance and increase and prosper more and more therein until, being delivered from all our imperfections and sins, our God clothes us with His righteousness unto which we are daily called. That it may please Him to grant this grace not only to us but also to all people and nations of the earth; etc.

12

SIGNS AND WONDERS OF WRATH

Sermon 160. Wednesday, 25 March 1556.
Deuteronomy 28:46-50.

46. And these things shall become a sign and a wonder on you and your seed forever.

47. Because you did not serve the LORD your God with joy and a glad heart, for the abundance of all things,

48. Therefore, you shall serve your enemies whom the LORD will send against you, in hunger, in thirst, in nakedness, and in the lack of all things; and He shall put an iron yoke on your neck until He has destroyed you.

49. The LORD shall bring a nation against you from afar, from the end of the earth, as the eagle swoops down, a nation whose language you will not understand,

50. A nation of fierce countenance who will have no respect for the old or show favor to the young.

Because things are so greatly confused in this world, so that it is hard to tell which people God intends to punish for their sins and which He intends to show His love, therefore Moses expressly says that God shall send such plain signs upon them that are stubborn against Him, that they shall marvel at it. As a result, they will be compelled to understand that these come to pass neither by fortune nor by any ordinary means, but that they are extraordinary things, and that God is showing forth His power in them.

It is true, as we have noted before, that at first sight it cannot be easily discerned who they are whom God loves and who they are whom He hates, because as Solomon says (Eccl. 9:2), both good and evil are common to all. He that serves God sometimes prospers and oftentimes is afflicted. And the same is true of the despiser of God. This is why he says that men become hard-hearted, for it seems to them that they win nothing by serving God, or rather that it is but lost labor. Moreover, we often see that the children of God are sometimes handled more roughly than the most wicked in the world. From this the carnal-minded gather that it is much better to despise God. David confessed (Ps. 73:2) that he staggered as if drunk when he beheld the course of things to be such that the good, and those who endeavor to walk in all manner of integrity, are constrained to drink the water of trouble, to eat the bread of heaviness, and to moisten themselves with tears; but that meanwhile the wicked, who do not cease to do evil, live at their ease and in pleasure, whereby it should seem that God loves them. And what kind of dealing would that be? But our Lord declares in this place that in the end He shall make it apparent to them that are corrected by His hand that their sins are the reason why they suffer pain, even if it is not quickly perceived.

We have seen already among the other curses that Moses pronounces that they who cast off the word of God are constrained to borrow and to be always in need, but that the others [the righteous] who lend to them, have the wherewithal to help themselves. But we see how all the children of God fall into need, and do not find any that will comfort them. They make many turns before they meet with a man that will use gentleness toward them, and this seems clean contrary to the word spoken by Moses. But yet God is exercising His people after this fashion, and in that respect it is said that when we are afflicted, whether it be with poverty or sickness or in any other way, we must not fail to enter into account with God; that is, to examine our lives and to see whether we have not committed many faults. And then will every one of us find himself at fault.

But on the other hand, if we do not perceive the reason why God is moved to treat us rigorously, let us be content, recognizing that He knows it is profitable for us. If we have not already offended Him, perhaps we were on the way to doing so and He has prevented it. All these corrections are designed to bring us low, to the end that we should walk under Him in fear and that our flesh should not overcome us, as is its tendency. For God sometimes foresees the pride of a man, and then He takes away the occasions and the objects. Besides this, He knows that a man will be too cavalier in his pomps and delights, and therefore he cuts off the occasion beforehand, preventing a man from doing what he would. Seeing that our Lord provides beforehand for our welfare after such a fashion, let us think on the faults we have earlier committed.

Moreover, if there were no further meaning in it than to move us to repentance, even that would be plenty. But we must always consider how God cannot provoke us too much to come to Him, for every least straw is enough to hold us in this world, so that meanwhile we do not think on the heavenly life at all, or if we do think about it, we do it so coldly that we do not travel towards it with the kind of earnest affection we should have. Therefore, God finds it necessary to deal out to us many afflictions. This is how every one of us should deal with them.

Our Attitude Toward Others

Now, concerning others, we may not at first blush condemn those whom God is punishing. We must keep in mind what is said in the psalm (Ps. 41:1), that God shall bless the man who deals kindly with a man in tribulation. But we have an incredible way of jumping hastily to conclusions in this matter. As soon as we see any poor man in misery and wretchedness, we say, "Oh, God is plaguing him, and he must deserve it." When we do this, we are very rash judges. If God smites us, after He has bestowed many stripes upon us, it is still hard for us to admit that we have sinned; but concerning others, our tongues are ever so quick to condemn them.

But gentleness is what we should incline towards. For example, when we see the faithful suffer, we should think, "Behold, how God deals with His children, instructing us thereby that there is no rest in this world, and that our happiness is in heaven, and it is thither that we ought to lift up our hearts." And again, if this happens to a green tree, what will become of the dry wood (Luke 23:31)? If God does not spare those who have endeavored to follow His Word, as we see, what will become of those who scorn it, as the prophet says (Is. 51:21)? If judgment begins at the house of God, most miserable will they be who have hardened themselves against Him, as St. Peter admonishes us (1 Pet. 4:17). And so you see how we ought to deal in this situation.

Profiting From Suffering

Moreover, if we have patience and meekness and are teachable, it is certain that we shall always feel a taste of the goodness of God in the midst of the afflictions He sends us. It is true that often we shall be frightened by them. There will be a kind of disquiet in us that will so vex us that we shall think ourselves utterly forlorn unless God withdraws His hand very quickly. If He prolongs our afflictions, then we become wholly stupefied. Our courage fails us, so that if we are not constrained by the fear of God and by patience, so that we are wholly quiet under His hand, we shall be always wandering. But if we hold ourselves there and keep still, then we shall understand that He chastises us in His mercy and goodness. As it is said in the prophet Habakkuk: the faithful, after they have been in heaviness, do come to understand that God is always upholding them and does not forget them but always tempers and mitigates their afflictions, so that they feel His fatherly goodness toward them, and comfort themselves with it. They can say with David (Ps. 30:5) that the anger of the Lord is but for a moment, but His favor is for a lifetime.

So behold, here we may always have matter with which to cheer ourselves and to rejoice in the midst of our afflictions, so that we may perceive indeed that our Lord will always be merciful to us, notwithstanding that He uses some sternness in dealing with us, testing our patience and quickening us up to come to Him and to labor with a view to the heavenly life. But we must always take the long view, as David says in the thirty-seventh Psalm (v. 1), where he exhorts us not to be grieved at the prosperity of the wicked, for he knows that our eyes can be dazed by it. When we see a wicked person at ease and having all his desires, we conclude straight away that God has no regard to deal with men according to their worth. When we think thus, we stagger and are in such confusion that we do not know what will become of us. Now David says that in so thinking, he was acting like a beast, out of his mind, and he confesses that he was at that point devoid of reason and judgment, affirming that he did wrong to all the generation of God's children (Ps. 73:22), until he came to look into the sanctuary.

It is true that in the thirty-seventh Psalm, which I mentioned earlier, he says, "I passed by and saw the wicked flourish and grow high like a cedar tree of Lebanon, and when I looked again, he had been cut down like a tree that had nothing left but dry stock lying on the ground, so that there remained no sign of him at all" (Ps. 37:35-36). Such changes do we see in the world, but even if we saw none, yet must we enter into the sanctuary of God, as it is said in the seventy-third Psalm (v. 17). And there we must wait patiently until God makes it plain to us that all afflictions are profitable for His children, and also that He sends them as medicines for their health. And contrariwise, that the prosperity He permits to those who have contempt for His law and His justice will be converted to their great confusion. We must therefore learn to hold our wits and senses in awe, that we do not wander in the afflictions God sends us.

Strange and Unusual Punishments

But to return to Moses and his purposes, let us note it well when he says that the punishments God sends upon those that have utterly rebelled against Him, who have refused correction, shall be as signs and wonders to them and to their posterity.

That is to say, He will punish them after a strange fashion, in a way not commonly seen among men, so that they will be compelled in spite of themselves to say, "Surely this is the hand of God."

Indeed, can there be a more beastly contempt of God found than what was shown by Pharaoh? He was a man not only drunk with pride, but wholly senseless. He was a man who despised the majesty of God, a man so rebellious that he could not in any manner be dealt with. When he heard Moses and Aaron speak, he laughed them to scorn. When he felt the first strokes, he refused to yield. But in the end he needed no prophet to admonish him, for he himself could say, "Surely this is the finger of God." We see therefore how God often expresses His power in such a way that even the most fierce are constrained to perceive and to think that there is some majesty in heaven, which before that time they had not acknowledged, and as a result they enter into consideration of their sins and confess them, and are the more lively touched therewith. This is what Moses here means concerning signs and wonders.

This matter is worthy to be marked. For as I have said, if God begins to punish men, it is usually ascribed to fortune. This is agreeable to our state, for we know that man's life is subject to much wretchedness — so they think; yet all the while the hand of God is not regarded. And if He doubles the punishment, yet men continue to be dull and seem as if they could continue to hide themselves and escape away. They do not enter into their consciences to search out the sins therein. They don't want to know them. It is as if a man should go and hide himself in a dark corner in order to shun the brightness of the sun at noonday. Even so do we behave in all the chastisements God sends us to warn us of our sins and to draw us to repentance.

But in the end God augments His punishments in such a way that they become miracles. That is to say, they exceed the common measure, the ordinary order and course of nature, so that we might be ravished with astonishment, and thereby perceive that God is showing Himself as though His hand appeared from heaven. And this is more fully declared in the twenty-sixth chapter of Leviticus. For after He has pronounced the sentence upon them that reject the doctrine of salvation, He says, "I will send upon you seven times as much if I perceive that nothing prevails with you. If My punishing you fails to amend you, I will add thereto seven times as much" (vv. 18, 21, 24, 28) And He repeats this sentence again in the end, and says, "If you will walk contrary to Me, I will also walk contrary to you."

The Hostility of God

Now this word, "contrary," refers to the stubbornness that is in us, which we have touched upon before. For we see very well those adversities that befall us in this world, and wading in yet further we confess that it is God who punishes us. But to think on the matter in good earnest, and for each man to judge himself by calling his sins to remembrance as often as God gives any inkling of them — this is farthest from our thoughts. Let each man examine himself: How many afflictions do we have during the year that should be testimonies to us of the wrath of God, and as it were summons to appear before Him, warning us to sue to Him for pardon and [to beg Him] to have pity upon us? Scarcely does any one day pass, but that a man is warned five or six times. It is as if God should say to him, "Wretched creature, have you no concern for your soul? Why have you no care to beseech Me to receive you to mercy?" But scarcely once in a month will a man enter into examination of his life to condemn himself. And if we do it, it is but coldly. But we ought to be as ashamed and as vexed at seeing God's wrath as though we saw hell lie open before our eyes. But we see that very few actually think on these things, because each one of us forgets himself. That is the matter God intends by His threat to walk adversely to us.

Yet we tend to continue on our course as if nothing had happened to us. We swallow up our afflictions. They do trouble us, indeed, when they pinch us, yet we do nothing but shake our ears (as they say) and continue in our own way. Thus, we proceed in hostility, yea exceedingly so, when we fail to acknowledge the hand of God and do not perceive that He is a judge, so that we might condemn our sins and each of us labor and endeavor to withdraw himself from them.

Therefore, our Lord says that He shall come against us in all hostility. It is as if He should say, "I will cross you and thwart you. Don't think to gain anything by your hardness of heart and by your kicking against Me, and by your dullness in refusing to perceive that it is My hand you are dealing with. No, no," He says, "I will be as stout and as headstrong as you; yea, and more stout and headstrong, too. For I will manifest all sorts of hostilities. I will let My plagues run out at random, so that I will break your necks, and beat you on both back and belly, and that without pity."

Now we can see how much this word ought to weigh with us, where Moses says that the plagues shall be for signs and wonders to all scorners. When they have given the raspberry[1] at the threats of God, and have wagged their heads against the first corrections that He sends them, and have bitten on the bridle; yet He proceeds onward still, and does not cease to wring them, but drives them in the end to come to a reckoning. Having done their worst, they will say openly, "It is the hand of God that presses us; these are miracles, no ordinary thing, not according to the course of nature."

Now therefore let us learn not to provoke God's wrath so far against us. Let us allow ourselves to be tamed by Him, and let us yield ourselves tractable and gentle as soon as He has summoned us. Let us yield ourselves guilty without using any excuses, for we shall win nothing thereby. There is nothing better than to enter into pure and free confession, saying, "Lord, what will You do to these frail and wretched creatures? It is true that we have deserved a hundredfold to be sunk, but yet for all that we flee to Your mercy. Wherefore, have pity upon us." When we have thus condemned ourselves, it serves to pacify the anger of God, which will never happen if we harden our hearts. For then He will

---

1. In Golding, "bleared out their tongues at the threatenings of God."

always proceed farther, until He has brought us to these signs and wonders that are here mentioned.

Again, God will do the same thing when men prove slothful and negligent (or rather, utterly senseless). If we could be subdued at the first blow, God would take no pleasure in laying on us plague after plague. But when He sees that there is so much stoutness and presumption in us, that we will not stoop or bow our necks, He finds it necessary to hold on until He makes us to feel in very deed and after a strange manner that it is He before whom we must yield our account. Let us therefore mark well how the obstinate malice of the world is the reason why God sends such strange corrections, to put us in fear.

And if we considered well the state of the world at this present day, it would make the hairs of our heads stand upright. Certainly all men sigh at the feeling of the stripes, and they complain, but not to any amendment of life. Rather, they bite upon the bridle, insomuch that when those who are not wholly stupid enter into a comparison of the present with what existed before the wrath of God was provoked, they see a great gulf, and that ought to make us afraid. And so, let us come back again to what Moses declares, which is that the world must be very rebellious and hardhearted for God to augment His punishments in such a way. For such would never come to pass were it not that men were otherwise unreformable. Let us not accuse God of cruelty when we see Him using exceedingly great rigor in punishing us, but let us acknowledge that our stubbornness is so great that our Lord must handle us after that fashion, for otherwise He should never overmaster us.

That is what we have to bear in mind. That is not all, however, for we must always fear what is to come. And since we saw that God has thus increased His punishments not upon one man only, but upon the whole world, let us think upon it, and call ourselves home again lest He fall to striking us with many blows, to our confusion and utter undoing, without giving us any more opportunities to come to a knowledge of our sins. Let us beware lest God's vengeance proceed so far. And inasmuch as we see that the trials of these present days are very great, let us acknowledge that we have provoked God very much and that it is not for us to abuse His patience any longer. Thus you see in effect what we have to carry away from this text, especially when we see that sin is overflowing so that all the world is infected with corruption.

Even if a man does good, yet all the same it is so mixed with sin that he will be chastised.[2] Not immediately, however, because as I said before, God spares the wicked and waits for them, and meanwhile punishes the good that seek to walk aright. Yet in the end He always plagues the despisers of His law and majesty. And concerning the good, He will make them to feel His grace to their joy, so that although He exercises them with many chastisements and adversities, yet notwithstanding, they will always know Him to be their God and Father still, and will rest upon Him. As for the wicked, they are not disposed to taste or to feel the love and goodness of God, but rather are cold to Him.

But when iniquity has increased to the size of an ocean and all men are corrupted, then the vengeance of God must also overflow so that none may be free from it. We have seen already the threat that was made here before, namely that the people should be led into captivity with their king (v. 36). When this came to pass, were none carried away into captivity but the wicked, and such as strove against the prophets, and such as despised the true teachings, and such as were headstrong against God like wild beasts? No indeed. There was Jeremiah himself, who had called upon the people for fifty years altogether and never ceased to cry, "What are you doing, you wretched people?" Yet notwithstanding we see that while others ridiculed them, he wept and wailed, and not contented with that, said, "Who can turn my head into tears, so that my brain may be as a fountain gushing out continually, that I may bewail the sins and calamities of my people?" (Jer. 9:1).

---

2. Calvin apparently here refers to a wicked man who does some good deed, as the next sentence makes clear. Punishments come first, he avers, to the righteous, to train them. Only later are the wicked punished, permanently.

See how the holy prophet, after he had labored in the service of God and fought against all the wicked and made war against all manner of iniquity and stubbornness, is still led away captive along with the rest and is put to reproach — not of being carried away to Babylon, for that had been the best that could have been wished for at that time, but God gave him not the favor to be brought thither, but he was carried into Egypt (Jer. 43:6). Yet he had said, "Cursed be they that go into Egypt. Go into Babylon and serve the king of Babylon. Be quiet and obedient there, and bear patiently this punishment of God, and in the end He will take pity on you" (cf. Jer. 42). The holy prophet was not given the same privilege.

So we see then that when calamities come as a result of the general corruption of all men, the good are wrapped up among the evil. And why is that? Because it is virtually impossible to walk among such infections and not be somewhat spotted therewith. Although Jeremiah resisted the evil as much as he could, yet he savored of the public corruptions of the people, and therefore it behooved him to be punished along with the rest. God, however, did not execute such vengeance upon him, as He did upon the despisers of His law; no, not by a long shot. For Jeremiah always had a good testimony, that God was guiding him. And when he was in Egypt, he was by a special privilege free from the curse that he had pronounced upon all those that would go into Egypt. For they drew him thither by force. You see, therefore, how God wraps up His people among the rebels, but yet He saves them after a marvelous manner, which gives them continual cause of comfort in Him.

The same may be said of Daniel. Daniel is set forth to us as a mirror of integrity. Speaking of him, Ezekiel names him one of the three most holy men that can be found (Ezk. 14:14), yet he was carried to Babylon, and was it for the sins of others? He would have been a hypocrite and would have lied to God, if he had maintained that it was not for his own sins. For he says expressly in the ninth chapter (Dan. 9:20), "I have made confession as well of my own sins as of the sins of my people." He begins by saying, "Lord, we have offended You, and been disobedient. We have rebelled against You, both we and our fathers, our kings and rulers" (Dan. 9:5). These words of his are spoken generally, and it might be said that he is simply putting himself in with all the others. But so that there might be no such misunderstanding, he goes further and says, "I have confessed my sins and the sins of my people." Whereby we see that Daniel, despite his integrity and perfection, was nevertheless stained with the common vices and therefore deserved to suffer his part and portion of the punishments that God sent upon all the people.

Hereby we are also the better warned to stand in fear and to walk with greater wariness when we see the world so corrupted, assuring ourselves that in the end we must feel by experience that God has spoken in good earnest where He says that He will walk contrary to us, if we continue to walk contrary to Him. This is in effect all that we have to remember in this text, where Moses speaks of signs and miracles. For this reason let us open our eyes in this situation, and let us not linger until God compels us to come to Him by force, stretching out His mighty arm against us. But let us receive His Word, and let it serve us for binoculars [eyeglasses] to behold His judgments afar off, and let us not tarry until He comes to the point of executing His extreme rigor.

God's Gentle Dealings Spurned

Now he adds the statement, "Because you did not serve the LORD your God with joy and a glad heart, when you had an abundance of all things" (v. 47). Here he reproves the Jews, since they were unwilling to hear when God entreated them gently. And he was speaking not only to them but also to us. We have, therefore, a general doctrine to be gathered from this saying, which is that God, of His own nature, is inclined to allure us to Himself by gentle and loving means. God is like a father going about to win his children by being merry with them, and by giving them all that they desire. If a father could always laugh with his children and fulfill their desires, all his delight would be in them. Such does God show Himself to be toward us. Indeed

He is not subject to passion as men are. We may not think that God is like us. But in so far as we are unable to comprehend His majesty, because it is so high, He is happy to humble Himself and to use a kind of speech fit for our rudeness and for the weakness of our minds.[3] Nevertheless, it is certain that it is the property of God to win us gently, as a father endeavors to win his children.

What does God require? That we should serve Him with an open and free heart, and with gladness. And how so? Because He deals gently with us and gives us all things that we need; therefore, we ought to be quiet and well contented, and not be thankless. And so we may conclude that all the calamities, troubles, wretchednesses, and miseries that happen in this world are but the fruits of our sins, and that we drive God to handle us with such rigor. He is ready, you might say, to transform Himself, and to forsake His nature,[4] in order to master us, because He sees that sin is exceedingly great in us, and that we have no skill to turn to our own benefit the good that He is ready to do to us.

All the same, as I have said before, God does not always wait until we have offended Him. We have to grant that He prevents our sins sometimes. He sees that we are in danger of falling and

---

3. This is a somewhat unsatisfactory statement, though it is unfortunately typical of one strain in Calvin's thought. We should rather say that God created man in His own image, and that human fathering reflects Divine fathering. There is no humbling of God to the weakness of our minds involved when the analogy is used; rather, it is one of the analogies God ordained in the first place. Ultimately, to speak as if the finitude of our minds makes it hard for God to communicate to us is to deny the doctrine of creation, and to fall into an epistemological monophysitism. As God's creatures, and particularly as His images, we have no problem understanding what is proper for us to know. Our problems are ethical, and that is what Calvin is really getting at by means of his unfortunate choice of words. For a brief discussion, see Ronald Wallace, *Calvin's Doctrine of the Word and Sacrament* (Tyler, TX: Geneva Ministries, [1953] 1982), pp. 2-5.

Calvin's statement that God is not "subject to passions" does not mean God is devoid of emotion. Rather, it means God is not swayed by outside forces. There is, however, a bit of Stoicism in Calvin's view of emotions. See Peter J. Leithart, "The Iron Philosophy: Stoic Elements in Calvin's Doctrine of Mortification" (Th.M. thesis; Westminster Theological Seminary, 1987).

4. That is, it is God's nature to woo us by kindness. When He punishes us, that is against His nature, so to speak.

He takes steps to remedy it in due time. Yet notwithstanding this, all the corrections we endure in this world proceed from our sins, and the filth that is in us is the reason why God does not send us abundance of good things according to our desire. The fact is that men fall asleep and sap themselves in earthly pleasures, so that they are not able to consider what David calls them to, which is to satisfy themselves with the sight of God and to rejoice in His presence. Seeing that men cannot attain thereto, but are constantly wedded to these base things, do we not deserve for God to withdraw the plenty that He was ready to give us? For He perceives that it would burst us, and instead of sustaining us it would so overload us that it would bear us down to the ground.

This is the reason why our Lord does not give us gifts liberally, such as we desire. After all, He is not drained dry, nor does He fear being impoverished by sending us plenty of all manner of good things. We know that He is a fountain that can never be drawn dry. But He sees that we waste and devour His benefits, and are worse than drunken, and that in addition to our riotousness we are also unthankful, not only falling into forgetfulness but also spurning His majesty and turning our backs upon Him. Indeed, if we have the means to maintain ourselves well, we fall to gluttony, pompousness, whoredom, and other looseness. And to be brief, the abuses we commit in the use of God's blessings are as immeasurable as the sea. Therefore, when He sees such things, He withdraws His hand and stops showing Himself liberal towards us. This is the sum total of what we have to bear in mind.

And therefore, seeing that God for His part is always ready to multiply us, and to give us plenty of all good things, were it not that we are unable to bear it, we must understand that we are like sick people who may only eat a little food at a time, being constrained to a diet. And why? Because they are not able to keep their food down. From this we ought to understand what Moses is saying, that it is to our reproach. For what a shame it is that we cannot abide that God should deal gently and in a fatherly way with us! Behold, God offers Himself not only in words but also in deeds, and He offers to give us all that we desire. But what do we find? He sees us not disposed to receive Him. We despise Him, and thrust away His grace. Must there not be a horrible perversity in men? Let every one of us excuse himself as much as he wishes, yet this saying is true; and when we have kicked and spurned as much as we can, yet we shall at the last be convicted of this evil, that we could not find it in our hearts to permit God to deal gently with us, "nor have served Him with joy and a merry heart."

Therefore, let us not wonder when He handles us as we deserve, since we are so rebellious against Him. For when He sees that we kick against Him, He must needs break us, and deal with us in such a way that we may understand that He is our Master. It is not as if those who are punished wind up serving God, but that they understand that He has the majesty over them when the punishments come so fiercely as to be signs and wonders. When God appears to them as it were in a visible manner from heaven, then do they perceive the reality, "Alas, I cannot flee or escape the hand of God." Then do they understand that He has the lordship over them, not that they willingly yield themselves thereto, but that they lie languishing and astonished, as men locked up in prison.

What we have to remember, then, is that since we could not be content that God should handle us gently, by bowing under His hand that He might guide us, turn us, and return us whichever way He wished; therefore, we must be forced by tribulation and sorrow to understand that He has full sovereignty over us, and that His utter breaking and overthrowing of us is because we could not abide to be governed by His hand when He was ready to guide us. This is what we have to note here.

The Loss of Spiritual Blessings

We see the same thing in all humanity, and not only concerning the afflictions of this present life — we have this reproach laid upon us, that we are still as it were famished for want of spiritual blessings. For our father Adam was created in such a state that the world was an earthly paradise. The whole earth yielded him all good things to his wish. He endured neither heat nor cold, nor any grievous want. Thus was our father Adam appointed lord and master over all the world. All the elements and all the beasts of the earth served him quietly, and all fruits served his taste and savor. What was he in his person? He bore the image of God, and was of such a great nobility and worth that he was like the angels of heaven.

And he would have dwelt in this world with all his lineage, in a place in which he would have had no trouble, but he could not abide to be so gently entreated. When God had thus enriched him with His benefits, he had to ruin things for himself, for he could not serve God with a good heart and with joy. What could have grieved him? After all, God had showed him a fair and gracious countenance, and poured out the treasures of His fatherly love towards him. But Adam could not abide that, and through his ingratitude alienated himself from God.

And how is it with us today? We must serve God in hunger and thirst, in nakedness and reproach, for the earth is cursed to us. When we have tilled it, it must bring us forth thistles and thorns. We find the seasons contrary, so that when we wait for a good year, we see hail or frost, drought or rain, which serve to pluck the bread out of our mouths and to disappoint us of our food. We see the air troubled, and infections that often engender diseases. Great is the toil of men. For when they have gotten food with great distress, yet they lack something to clothe themselves with. See there, I say, what a state we are in. And why? Because we would not serve our God cheerfully and with a good heart, when He gave us abundance of all manner of blessings.

But this is not the chief matter, as I have said already, for we are destitute of the righteousness of God. Our very truest ornament was that we could have fashioned ourselves to all manner of rightness, and how we have ruined this! Then we had reason and understanding, but now we have become beastly, for the brightness that should shine in us is but darkness. Again, we are covered with reproach, and where the image of God should shine in us, now we have the marks of sin, so that even our very bare bodies must give us to understand the same thing, so that if a man is naked, he is ashamed of himself. And why? God by this means shows to us what infection there is in our souls, in that we find it necessary to hide ourselves, not being worthy to be numbered among His creatures. Finally we become like dry earth. True it is that we are overly fruitful in evil; but of goodness, what is found in us? Seeing that we are thus lacking in all graces, there is good reason why we should languish in this frail life, because we could not serve our God with joy and a good heart, at the time when He had poured out all His riches most perfectly upon us.

Now since we behold the evil that is in all mankind, let us also apply the same particularly to ourselves. Therefore, when our Lord visits us and makes us feel afflictions that are strange to us, let us cast down our heads and enter into such examination of ourselves as this: When God has given us the means to serve Him, how have we discharged ourselves with it? If there comes an ill year that brings dearth of grain or wine so that famine threatens us, let us look how we honored God in the time that He gave us plenty.

If we see that there is abundance of wine, then drunkenness will have full play, so that men cannot be restrained from breaking out into all sorts of disorder, and what is worse, they do not hesitate to blaspheme the name of God and to rush out into all disorder, in order to fill and glut themselves out of all measure. When grain is abundant we see the same thing. Men are so proud of it that they cannot abide either warning or discipline, but they kick against God. And their pride is moreover matched with cruelty so that every man rakes in everything he can unto himself. He that has the most will, if he can, play the tyrant over his neighbors, taking no pity upon them that are in want.

Wars and Rumors of Wars

At this point we are in a time of plenty. Therefore, we can expect our Lord to change His plenteous abundance and to manifest His majesty to us, in order to compel us to understand what

sovereignty and dominion He has over us, since we cannot find
it in our hearts to serve Him with a cheerful heart and with a
good will, and since we refuse to give ourselves over to Him. Are
we at rest? Yes, and so all our endeavors center on how to pluck
out one another's eyes and to torment each other like cats and
dogs. And if we are not warring with men, then we are warring
against God, something far worse. And if we keep this up, let us
not be grieved when we are confounded altogether, seeing we set
ourselves up against the majesty of Him under whom we ought
to bow.

After all, we see that most commonly men make war against
God when He gives them rest. We shall see both generally and
particularly that those who have leisure to do evil are the ones
who persecute the Church and torment the poor faithful ones. As
soon as God gives them any respite, they seek nothing but occasion to do hurt and to exercise their cruelty. And this is to be seen
not only in the enemies of the Church, but also in all others, both
great and small. When God has given us rest and we have made
an end of warring one against another, we fall to despising God
one way or another. Let us not wonder, therefore, if when a war
is finished, it begins again immediately. For it is necessary that
God should deal with us in such a way; otherwise, He cannot rule
us.

Thus it is said here, in verse 49, that God shall raise up a
barbarous people against such as will not be obedient to Him.
Such is God's rule over us that He desires to be like a father to
us, rather than to be a dreadful king or prince over us. It is true
that we must do Him homage as our sovereign Lord, and that
we must behave ourselves as His people in all subjection and
humility, submitting ourselves under His yoke. But all the same
He continues to perform the office of a father toward us, and
wishes to be acknowledged as a father. For He speaks to us in a
friendly fashion, so that although His commandments are hard
for us because of our malice and rebellion arising from the flesh,
yet notwithstanding, after He has declared His will to us, He
exhorts us, warns us, rebukes us, and does all these things with

such mildness that we must lack both sense and reason if we are not benefited by the goodness He employs.

But if we will not hearken to our God when He speaks to us in so gentle and gracious a manner, what then? Then He will speak to us with the heavy strokes of halberds, pikes, and hackbuts [or, battle-axes, bayonets, and pistols].[5] We shall find this hard to comprehend; their language will be strange to our intellects. And why does this come about? Because we had no ears to hear when God spoke graciously to us, indeed when He stooped so low as to teach us like little children that are taught their ABCs.

Let us then understand that when we are so deaf to God's word, He must speak with us in another language, and He must stir up some barbarous and brazen-faced people that have no fear, reason, or justice. When you petition such people for pity and compassion, it will be in vain. They will give no ear to you. You will find yourselves in such straits, whether you think so now or not.

And what is the remedy for all these evils? Let us enter, let us enter I say, into our consciences. Let us not grind our teeth at men, as we are prone to do. Let us not strive with them, for that is not where our combat lies. But let us understand that God intends to chastise us by means of men, because we have been stubborn against Him and refused to be edified by His Word according to His first intention. And therefore, let us benefit ourselves by these warnings and corrections God sends us. And let us not wait until we feel the strokes, but whenever God does us the favor of teaching us at the expense of other men, let us receive

---

5. *Halberd* — a military weapon, especially in use during the fifteenth and sixteenth centuries; a kind of combination of spear and battle-ax, consisting of a sharp-edged blade ending in a point, and a spear-head, mounted on a handle five to seven feet long.

Pike — a weapon consisting of a long wooden shaft with a pointed head of iron or steel; formerly the chief weapon of a large part of the infantry; in the eighteenth century superseded by the bayonet.

Hackbut — an early kind of portable firearm.

(Definitions from *The Oxford English Dictionary*.)

profit from it. And when He spares us, let us not abuse His patience. And since the means to reconcile us to Him is to accept the promise that He offers us in the gospel, let us embrace our Lord Jesus Christ, who is our peace, to the end that we may be entreated after a fatherly fashion at the hands of our God.

Prayer

Now let us fall down before the majesty of our good God, with acknowledgment of our sins, beseeching Him to make us to perceive them better and better, and to bear with us in such a way that His chastisements and corrections may be so fatherly and measured toward us that we may be reduced to the obedience of His righteousness. Let us pray that He evermore comfort us, so that we may have the ability to rejoice in Him and to glorify Him for His procuring of our salvation by all available means. And so let us all say, "Almighty God, heavenly Father, etc."

13

GOD OUR FORTRESS

Sermon 161. Thursday, 26 March 1556.
Deuteronomy 28:49-58.

49. The LORD shall bring a nation against you from afar, from the end of the earth, as the eagle swoops down, a nation whose language you will not understand,

50. A nation of fierce countenance who will have no respect for the old or show favor to the young.

51. Moreover, they shall eat the fruit of your herd and the produce of your ground until you are destroyed, who also shall leave you no grain, new wine, or oil, or the increase of your herd, or the young of your flock until they have caused you to perish.

52. And it shall besiege you in all your gates until your high and fortified walls in which you trusted come down throughout your land, and it shall besiege you in all your gates throughout your land that the LORD your God has given you.

53. Then you shall eat the fruit of your own body, the flesh of your sons and of your daughters whom the LORD your God has given you, during the siege and the distress by which your enemy will distress you.

53. The man who is so tender and very delicate among you, his eye shall be evil toward his brother and toward the wife of his bosom and toward the rest of his children who remain,

55. So that he will not give one of them any of the flesh
of his children that he will eat (since he has nothing else left)
during the siege and the distress by which your enemy will
distress you in all your gates.

56. The tender and delicate woman among you, who
would not venture to set the sole of her foot on the ground
for delicateness and tenderness, her eye shall be evil toward
the husband of her bosom and toward her son and daughter,

57. And toward her afterbirth that issues from between
her feet and toward her children whom she bears; for she
will eat them secretly for lack of anything, during the siege
and the distress by which your enemy shall distress you in
your gates.

58. If you are not careful to observe all the words of this
law that are written in this book, to fear this honored and
awesome name, the LORD your God. . . .[1]

We must remember what we touched on yesterday, which
Moses continues to speak of here, that if men are rough and cruel
toward us, it is God who stirs them up to it because He has found
us rebellious towards Him. And therefore, whenever men fail to
deal with us in as mild a manner as we wish, let us look to see
whether we have responded to God, and whether we have meekly
embraced all that He has commanded us. For if any of us finds
himself to have made war against God, by setting himself up
against Him, it is not to be wondered at if God pays him back
with the same, using men as His instruments.

But we shall never be persuaded of this doctrine unless we
understand that God holds the hearts of men in His hand; to
soften them when it pleases Him, be they never so hard-hearted;
and to harden them, though they formerly bore us never so much
good will. Let us not therefore trust to the love of men, unless we
walk in the fear of God. For He has the ability to change their
hearts, so that they bear rancor toward us and completely with-

---

1. This verse actually begins the next paragraph of Deuteronomy 28. Calvin
isolates it, however, and preaches on it in the second half of this sermon.

draw themselves from us for less than nothing, so that the world will see that those who were most forward to help us, now become most against us.

And, the reverse of this, let us understand that our Lord can easily transform all malice. Indeed, though they be as fierce as lions, He shall make them mild and friendly toward us. There was never a nation as proud and cruel as the Egyptians. In particular, we see how spiteful they were against the children of Israel. It seemed that this poor people would never find any mercy. And yet God wrought in such a way that the Egyptians gave them all their treasures and all that was fine in their houses. Neither gold nor silver was spared. And how did this come about? Because they had held the Jews in bondage and had vexed them exceedingly. They would have plucked the bread out of their mouths, and would have cut the throats of them all. A little earlier, they had killed their children as soon as they came out of their mothers' wombs, intending to destroy the entire race of them. And now, how does it come about that they are suddenly mild, and every man brings them those things that were most precious in his house? It is because God converted their hearts.

And returning to the other side, it is said that God hardened the hearts of kings when the people were to enter into the land of Canaan (Josh. 11:20). They should have been allowed to pass, but there were many who opposed them. How did that come about? It was because they [Israel, apparently — ed.] had resisted their God.

Let us therefore learn (as I have said before) so to behave ourselves in obedience to God that men also on their parts will be friendly towards us. For there is no one so great or mighty that he can avoid the misery that will rise up against him when he resists and strives against God. And we have seen that those who are drunk with their own greatness must in the end be punished, and not by those who are in authority or who are high in the estimation of men, but by riff-raff and dissolute persons; they will spit in their faces. And we have seen such happen even to princes, and to other men of great estate. For when they will not yield themselves to be governed by God, He is willing to stir up governors to the contrary, to shame such as will not be obedient to Him. Yet notwithstanding, when men refuse to yield themselves tractable, then we must understand that God is overseeing the matter in a secret manner, and that He does it in order to make us bow.

Therefore, let us not deceive ourselves by means of mere creatures, saying, "What fortune is this?" Indeed, we may say so, but we must go further and understand that nothing comes to pass without the direction of God. And understanding this, we must come to the remedy, which is that we must bow under the word and hand of God. And we must consider that if it pleases Him, He can turn the minds of men that were spiteful against us, and make them become friendly toward us. And this is something more than necessary. For when we have to do with those who are rough and intractable, we by and by lose heart, and wish to rid ourselves of all trouble, if possible, and that at the first dash. But, we should rather return unto God, acknowledging that those things proceed from His hand.

And so, when men show themselves so unfaithful and cruel toward us, handling us scornfully and wickedly, so that we cannot get one ounce of right or reason at their hands; when we see how their entire program is to get their feet on our throats, and that they have such a beastly shamelessness (as it is said here) that they are not ashamed of anything that is said to them; when we see that they take the bridle in their teeth and act like wild beasts so that there is neither grace nor honesty in them; when we see such barbarous beastishness, let us learn to resort to our God, and to acknowledge that we deserve to be tamed by Him. Moreover, the only way to appease such fury, and to assuage those who are hot and hasty, is to call upon our God, and to pray Him to touch inwardly by His Holy Spirit those who are so cruel and who are simply unable to do us any good because we have set up ourselves against our God. That is what we are admonished about in this text.

Sudden and Swift Enemies

Now Moses repeats something touched upon earlier, which is that God shall bring us enemies from a far country, and that they will be like eagles (v. 49). We should not think that God needs to make any preparations long beforehand. If a man should threaten us, we would look to see whether he had a sword in his hand, and whether he is ready to execute what he has threatened. But if God but whistles (as He says in the prophets), immediately He has His men of war in readiness. He does not need to muster them, or enroll them, or pound the drum. He needs none of this. At His mere whistle (for He uses this similitude) all the whole earth must needs be moved. Therefore, let us not look to see whether or not things are in readiness, or whether or not any hurt or harm may be done to us. Let us not look whether any worldly means have been prepared. But let us understand that before we can even conceive what evil might happen to us, we shall be overthrown.

And why? Because it is God who speaks. He makes men to fly like birds, even from one end of the earth to the other. Neither sea nor mountain is able to save us from the experience of what we never believed could happen. God has so ordered things, and even among the heathen is often seen an incredible swiftness when God is disposed to chastise the greatest part of the world. So much so that some one man has risen up with a small number of people to chastise an infinite multitude that did set themselves against Him. And that not for one time only, but twice or thrice, one after another; sacking towns and fortresses that seemed to be so well appointed and strong by reason of natural situation that they could not be approached unto, and yet they have been sacked as if God had meant to renew a great part of the world. It has been likewise seen that a people without renown or estimation have risen up and made the most mighty to tremble.

And thus God gives examples of what is written here, which is that He can surely bring our enemies upon us suddenly, and they shall make such dispatch that they will come swifter than the post. And when we suppose that we have some respite by truce, for one month or one year or even a whole lifetime, we shall be suddenly surprised in a morning before we can think upon it. Let us therefore understand that as soon as God speaks, we must have an eye to His infinite power (which is incredible to man's understanding), so that we tremble at His very word and yield to Him, knowing well that if we delay from day to day, we may be prevented from doing so, and it will then be too late. Let us therefore be advised to humble ourselves in due time, and to crave pardon when we have offended Him.

No Shelters From God's Wrath

Moses says expressly that those who are disobedient to God shall be besieged and shut up within their walls until their fortresses in which they trusted are beaten down (v. 52). Here we see how God reproves the false and cursed presumption whereby men deceive themselves, thinking that they are well protected against Him. It is a sacrilege whereby God is robbed of His honor, when we attribute to the creation the means of our defense. It is certain that God serves Himself by means, and we must also apply them to our own use, but to settle our *trust* upon them is to rob God of His majesty. For He will have us to maintain that all things are His, and to do Him homage for them.

So then, it is an intolerable presumption for us to put our trust in creatures and to ground ourselves upon them, and yet there is no fault more common in all the world. We can say well enough that it is not lawful, and that we ought not to do it, but meanwhile everyone does it. Now, let us remember ourselves, for there is nothing that God holds more dear or whereof He makes greater account than His honor. Neither is it sufficient for us to leave Him the mere title and name of God. He must be known as He is; that is to say, that all power lies in Him; that He is the fountain of all manner of grace and goodness; that it is His proper office to maintain and preserve us; that our life is in His hand along with all things that pertain thereto. When we have thought well upon this, let us take order to gather our wits about us, so that we are not grounded upon creatures.

Surely the mischief is doubled when we shield ourselves with the creatures against God, and thereby become stubborn when He threatens us, holding on still when he utters forth tokens of His displeasure. Let us consider that the offense is then much more grievous. Yet, this is exceedingly common. For while we do not perceive any danger toward us from the world, do we not continue in our sins? And do we not abide in stubbornness? God speaks, but we regard Him not. If men favor us, and if we have the means to fortify ourselves, we think that the hand of God cannot come at us. And therefore it is with good reason that our Lord reproves the wickedness of all such as are disobedient towards Him; that is to say, they that put their trust in their fortresses, in their high walls, in their munitions, and in such like things.

Now, since we are subject to these things, it were better for us if we have neither hedge nor anything else, than to be well fenced with walls and bulwarks. For they serve but to blind our eyes, when we have no more respect for our God, but are bewitched by Satan to put our trust in things that will be our confusion. However the case stands, let us advisedly hold this rule in general; that is, that God be our fortress always, as we see He promises in His prophet Isaiah in the twelfth chapter and also chapters 55 to the end, for that whole section turns on this point. Indeed, it is so common a teaching in the Holy Scripture that we can scarcely turn a leaf but we shall see some text in which God tells us that He will be our ramparts, our walls, our moats, indeed double moats, our towers, and whatever else is necessary for our defense. And why? Because (as I have said before), our minds rapidly slide into vanity so that God is not able to hold us back to Himself, and to count on our putting our whole trust in Him.

What must we then do? First of all, if we are destitute of human aid, let us bear in mind that God by Himself is sufficient, if we return to Him: "Ah, Lord, it is certain that we are the prey of men, and we do not have the wherewithal to save ourselves, for all the world fails us; but yet it is enough that You are our succor." After that manner should we learn to resort to Him. And thus we should take occasion to yield ourselves wholly to Him when the things of this world fail us.

And by the way [secondly], although we have walls and artillery, money and munitions, and all that we can wish for, yea and people also, and all things else; yet let us understand that we must meanwhile so use them that our Lord may be always our trust, and we give Him always this honor: that it is His office to defend us, and that we not wade in any deeper than this. It is certain that we may serve our turn with the things that He puts into our hands, but our hearts and minds must always be raised up above all the world, and He alone must be our Sheet-anchor.[2]

Thirdly, we must not put our trust in the power of the help that He gives us, for as they say, a thorn of a bramble is enough to make us believe that we are invincible. "What?" we say, "Is it possible that they should prevail against us?" All this is nothing; not even the peel of an onion as they say.[3] Yet we have to strain our wits in order to give it price and glory. Rather let us acknowledge our weakness and increpitude, that we may repair to God. And let nothing hinder us from yielding ourselves wholly unto Him and unto His protection. Let us not deceive ourselves with such vain confidence, as the Jews had in their high walls.

Human Shelters, Human Traps

Now with all this he also shows that whatever we may devise for our own strength and security, it will be impotent in the face of His power, and we shall continue to be besieged until we are totally wasted. Indeed, we may gather from this text that it would be much better for us to be delivered into the hands of our enemies from the first, than to have the means to resist. [Shut up in the siege] we are made so to languish that we are not permitted a simple and clean death. The poor folk who are abroad in the

---

2. From the *Oxford English Dictionary*: A large anchor, formerly always the largest of a ship's anchors, used only in an emergency. *Fig.*: That on which one places one's reliance when everything else has failed.

3. In other words, our human fortresses are as diaphanous as the outer, paper-like skin of an onion.

fields are struck at the very first, and are dispatched. Surely they are in a piteous state, with their throats cut and all their possessions set on fire, but all the same, by such means they are delivered from their miseries so that they do not pine away in suffering. But those who are in strong towns have to abide a long siege. They must languish and pine away piecemeal, not for a mere month or two, but until they can no longer hold out. The result is as if they should die a hundred deaths.

Thus does our Lord avenge Himself on those who think that they have escaped when God does not root them out at the first. "No," He says, "think about this. Which fruits are preferable? Those that are brought to the market in their prime and are eaten immediately, or those that are kept for a time and eventually rot? It were better then for you to be overcome and vanquished by your enemies at the first." Let us therefore consider well that when we have the means to defend ourselves against the world, where it ought to profit us, it will turn to our double confusion if we place our trust in it. We shall groan a great while under the burden, and be wasted little by little. For when we are disobedient and refuse to be reformed, our Lord will not let us go until He has utterly destroyed us, as He shows here so many times in this passage.

Cannibalism

This is brought home by what Moses adds in verse 54, that the man who is so tender and very delicate among you shall be grieved at his brother and at the wife who lies in his arms, because they shall demand a share of his children when he eats them. The woman who is so particular that she will not touch the ground with her bare feet (such are the words of Moses), shall seek to destroy and spoil her own children. Indeed, they shall no sooner be born out of her womb than she will desire to devour them, and if she has raised them to a larger size, she will still not spare them. These are dreadful things. For it is not simply said, "You shall be besieged, and remain a long time in famine, so that you will be driven to eat horses, rats, mice, shoe leather, and the very manure of birds (as it is said in 2 Kings 6:25), and all these things will be your meat." Nor is it said that men and women should be eaten, but that every man will eat his own children.

When God speaks this way it should make our hair stand upright. And in fact, everything here declared by Moses eventually came to pass. Let no man say, "This is not credible; it is repugnant to nature. A man would pluck the bread out of his own mouth when he is in extremity, in order to give it to his children. He would die to help them, just as we see that Hagar could not abide to see the death of her child, but left him alone and wished for her own death." But we don't need to get into an argument over such things, for the common affection of humanity sufficiently shows that any man would rather die than eat his own children. Yet, such cruelty was shown among the Jews. They who had been instructed in the law of God, and should have had much more humanity and compassion than the pagans and infidels, even they forgot all manner of true living and were overcome by this madness. It was fitting that this blindness, of which the prophets also spoke and which we see here already mentioned by Moses, should come to pass in them and that they should lose their minds. For when God takes away all reason and uprightness from men, then He leaves them to a kind of madness. Such fury must have been in them, for them to eat their own children.

By this we are particularly warned that those who are set aside for the last judgment are in no better situation than those whom God chastises long before. And this is a profitable warning. For as soon as God strikes some and leaves others alone, we want to know why. Weren't they equally deserving? We do not have the patience to allow God to execute His judgments in the order that seems good to Himself, but we surmise that those whom He leaves alone, and whom He forbears for a little while, are privileged more than we are. But it is the other way around. It would have been better for them to have been punished earlier than to be thus reserved for the end. And therefore, let us not envy those whom God forbears for a time, as though they were exempt from all plagues, but let us wait until God fetches them about at their time; for it would have been far better for them if they had been dispatched out of hand.

And with all of this let us every one look to himself. Let us not trust in the patience that God uses towards us, deceiving ourselves therewith. Indeed, when God has been patient and forborne us, it should give us a better disposition to resort to Him, and to hope to find Him merciful to forgive us our faults and trespasses. But we must not fall asleep therein, to dally with Him and to say, "O well, He has waited this long to deal with us. He will continue to wait some more." We see the wicked thinking this way. They don't worry, for when they see that God has spared them, they think that they are discharged. Let us beware of that. For we see how he says that when we are well appointed, and have fortresses as it were invincible, all must fall down on our heads, and we shall be so much the more grievously punished. This much we have to bear in mind from this text.

Now let us mark further that when we forget our God, we must also forget all the course of nature, and He finds it proper to strip us of our wits. For it is He on whom all human fatherhood depends; He is the wellspring of it. We would not know what the duties of parents toward their children are, or what reverence children owe to their parents and superiors, except for the fact that God is sovereign leader in this. If we do not refer all to Him, He shall make us to become idiotic, so that we will not understand what this fatherly affection toward our children should mean. This much for one point.

But we also have to note that those men who did so devour their own children were not so blockish as to be bereft of terrible heart pangs. They were vexed with furious fearfulness, that made them abhor what they did. It is true that they were carried away by force, and had no reason in them; but yet for all that, they had certain secret stings and prickings inwardly, and God held them as it were upon the rack of torture, as if He were saying to them, "What will you do, wretched creature? It would have been better for you to have been born before your time, and for the earth to have swallowed you up a hundred times, than that you should have committed so terrible a deed. All the same, necessity gets the upper hand with you." Let us mark therefore, that when we are not made meek under the hand of God, we must then fall into such a blockishness as will overmaster us and make us torment ourselves without the help of any other executioner, so that every one of us will execute God's vengeance upon himself, which vengeance he had earlier scorned and scoffed at.

I have said that there is nothing here mentioned that has not come to pass, to wit that fathers have eaten their children, and also have mothers (2 Kings 6:29; Lam. 4:10). But in that the Jews had most exceedingly provoked God, even so they came to the fullness of iniquity, and consequently it behooved God so to utter His wrath toward them with extremity, that it was seen when they were besieged by their enemies. For then did they eat pigeons' dung, buying it by gold weight. You will see that they committed acts against nature by eating one another. But when they had once rejected the Son of God, and had utterly cut themselves off from the hope of salvation by forsaking the Redeemer upon whom were grounded all the promises that had been made unto them concerning the goodness of God; then it was necessary that those things should be the more accomplished. For if you read the histories, even of those who were of that same nation, and which were present witnesses of the matter, you would think that you heard dreams or fables; and yet for all that, those things were then notoriously known, and noted to be true, and God intended as it were to set up scaffolds, that it might be seen how His threats directed against His people were not in vain, as we see, and that all men should take example thereat.[4]

For they are horrible things, and such as should make our hairs stand upright, when it is said that the husband shall deceive the wife and steal away the children that issued from their two bodies, and that the wife also shall seek some secret place to cut the throat of her child, as if to say, "I will set this aside for

---

4. The reference is to Josephus's accounts of the devastation of Jerusalem in A.D. 70.

myself." And both the husbands and the wives should be so mad as to say, "I will eat my own child." Seeing that all these things were accomplished, and that our Lord has executed such vengeance, let us understand that we ought not to read these things at this day without trembling, for it is even as if God should lay forth His previously uttered vengeance before us on a silver platter. Moreover, let us understand that when God had pronounced such sentence against the Jews, it was not executed at the first day. For He waited for them with long patience, so that it seemed that no mischief should light upon them. But when the sore was burst, then was the rottenness perceived that lay hidden before, and the disease was the more deadly. Also let us mark that if God does bear with us, and afterwards He corrects us in various ways, and yet does not strike so roughly as to come to extremity, we must not think that we have thereby escaped His hand, but we must return to Him, and not tarry till He sees our disobedience to be unreformable, and so finds it needful to proceed to the extremity of His threatenings. Thus much have we to remember touching this text.

The Fearfulness of God

Now finally Moses says, "if you do not keep all the words of this law to do them, and if you do not fear this dreadful and glorious name, the Lord your God. . . ." It certainly seems at first glance that what Moses requires of men is beyond measure, that it is not in their power, for who is he that can fulfill all the law of God? And again, though a man miss in some certain points, should God use such rigor? I have told you before that he directs this speech towards those that are wholly given over to evil, and to such as are despisers of God, who break His law by every means they can. To what end, then, does he require such perfection?

Let us first of all mark that God will not have His law chopped into pieces and sections, for He is setting forth His righteousness unto us in it. Men therefore must not chop things up at their own pleasure, as if to say, "I will, for God's honor, abstain from whoredom, but I will steal if I please; I will abstain from murder, but I will be a blasphemer." No, but seeing that He who forbids us to rob has also forbidden us to kill, and He who has forbidden fornication has in like manner forbidden blasphemy, let us learn to obey Him in all points and in all respects. Let us restrain our senses and bridle our affections, and to be short, let us come to the point to give ourselves wholly to the service of our God. That is what we ought to do, and that is what Moses is speaking of here. For if we miss in any one point, we are accursed of God, and deserve the rigor here mentioned.

Nevertheless, He of His mercy does not cease to bear with us. Yea, and He will never use the great severity that is spoken of here, but towards such as set themselves altogether stubbornly against Him. Yet notwithstanding, it is with good reason that Moses here exhorts the Jews to the perfect observation of the law. A physician prescribing an order does not permit his patient to eat whatever he wants, or to do anything amiss at all, no matter how little it seems, but he says, "I will have you to do such and such." Now if the sick man were to step aside to the slightest degree, very well, he is not yet incurable, the physician will still have care of him. But if he overturns everything, and casts off all order, and plays the madman, well, he will have payment as he deserves. In like manner will our Lord have us at His commandment in all cases, and for good reason.

Even so, there is such great infirmity (I mean even in those who are governed by the Holy Spirit, and who strain themselves to be obedient unto Him) that they fail in many respects, but yet however the world may go, sin never overpowers them, for they do not strive to transgress the law, but proceed forward, and even though they do it limpingly, yet they keep on moving toward God. And concerning these infirmities, they are borne along withal. It is true that God will chastise them, and in what manner? Even in forgiving them, according to this saying of His, "I will visit their iniquities, but it will be with the rod of men, and not with extremity. I will not deal with them as with enemies. I will not take away My mercy from them, although I correct them." Thus does God deal in that way. But if our hearts are utterly hardened, then will He war upon us, and destroy us without sparing, and even though He bears with us, yet will all turn to our confusion. That is one thing that we have to remember concerning this text.

It is also a notable point to be observed, where Moses speaks of the yoke of iron. For he says (v. 48) that the Lord shall lay a yoke of iron upon the neck of all unbelievers until they are wholly consumed. And that is to the end that we should learn to receive the corrections He sends and not kick against them. For we see what happened to Hananiah when he mocked at the threats of Jeremiah (Jer. 28), and tried to break the yoke that he had upon his neck, which was a yoke of wood and cords. The prophet wore that yoke to move the people to consider that they should all become captives, and so to behold their own state in the person of Jeremiah. Now this wicked one that was possessed by the devil (to make the Word of God to be ignored) came to break the yoke from Jeremiah, and said, "Even thus shall God break the yoke of Nebuchadnezzar; and even if he besiege you, and do what he can to carry you away captives into a strange land, yet shall you be preserved by the grace of your God." God threatened, and this fellow mocked all His threats, and for that purpose took the shadow of the name of God, and abused the people. Well then, what did he win by such rebellion? It was said to the prophet Jeremiah, "Take a yoke of iron" (Jer. 28:14), for whereas the bondage should have been gentle and tolerable, it must now be so cruel, that they will not be able to endure it. See here how He deals with all such as harden their hearts against Him, and refuse to abide and be meekened by His hand.

So then, let us be afraid of this yoke of iron. First of all, we know that God's yoke is amiable to all such as willingly yield themselves to it, and allow themselves to be governed by the hand of our Lord Jesus Christ. We have the testimony of the Son of God, "My yoke is easy, and My burden is light. Come to Me, and learn that I am lowly and meek." Seeing that our Lord Jesus declares that those who are teachable and obedient will perceive that there is neither burden nor weight nor grief in His yoke, to overpower them, it ought to move us to yield our necks unto it and to pray God to put us under it, and also to permit Him to chastise us when we have offended Him. Indeed, the strokes will be grievous to us, as the apostle says, and we shall never find the corrections pleasant during the time that God strikes us (Heb. 12). We are like little children when they are corrected; we feel it grievous, because our nature cries out against it. But whether we like it or not, God will use that fatherly means, and little by little teach us to return unto Him. But if we find it necessary to try His patience to the uttermost, He must then use the iron rod to break our heads with it, as it is said in Psalm 2. We shall be driven to feel the iron that will serve, not to reclaim us, but to break us in pieces and to confound us utterly. And justly, for we have heard what is said here, "If you will not fear the glorious and dreadful name of the Lord your God."

Where does this despising and contempt of all good doctrine come from, and our boldness in sinning, if not from this, that we are deaf to all admonitions? Indeed, if we could yield ourselves obedient to our God with a good heart and a good affection, and abide at that point continually, we should no sooner hear these threats but we should consider thus, "Alas, do we not deserve a grievous curse at God's hand, seeing we have thus striven against Him?" We see then that all the evil deeds and disobedience that are committed spring from ignorance and contempt of God, in that we have failed to regard His majesty. Certainly this kind of stubbornness is not always directly of set purpose and determined malice, but yet there is such rudeness in us that we do not yield such a reverence to God as is requisite, nor do we render the obedience whereby we should endeavor to submit ourselves to His Word.

And because we are so dull-headed that nothing can quicken us up, when we are called upon to submit ourselves to God, Moses says expressly, "this dreadful name, this glorious name," which is "the Lord, your God." Where he says, "The Lord," which is "the eternal, the everlasting,"[5] that term imports all glory

---

5. In French, the word "LORD" is rendered "the Eternal." The translation is based on the meaning of "I am that I am."

and majesty, and therefore ought to ravish us with wonder. Indeed, for we should not have this name of God so that we can use it coldly, so as to say "God, God," as they do who have it continually in their lips, and afterwards let it vanish as though it were a thing of nothing. But we must join both together thus: God, even the same that created us, the same that holds all things in His hand, the same that is honored by the angels, the same that is of glory infinite, the very same whom all the principalities of heaven cannot abide, at the sight of whom all manner of creatures must be fain to cast down their eyes, even the same which with one word alone can make all the earth to tremble, the same that can remove mountains with His mere blast, the same that gives being to all manner of creatures, finally the same that maintains and governs all things and orders all things well, righteously, and with wisdom; the same it is who speaks to us.

And so you see after what manner we use the words of Moses, where he says, "The Lord your God, He it is who speaks to you." Let us therefore hear Him speak, in such a way that His majesty may possess all our wits, and that thereby we may be so humbled under the same that when we have worshipped Him, we may so remain under His hand that we allow ourselves to be governed by Him to follow the rule that He has delivered to us.

Prayer

Now let us fall down before the judgment seat of our God, acknowledging the infinite faults of which we are guilty, if He inclined to execute the office of a judge against us; and with all this let us pray Him not to fail to be a Father to us for our Lord Jesus Christ's sake. And that since we are guilty of many offenses, we may allow ourselves to be daily cut off from our sins, so that nothing may hinder our coming to Him to yield ourselves in such a way to Him that we may renounce all our wicked affections more and more until we are thoroughly rid of them and are clothed with His heavenly righteousness. And so let us all say, "Almighty God, heavenly Father, etc."

14

A PLETHORA OF PLAGUES

Sermon 162. Friday, 27 March 1556.
Deuteronomy 28:59-64.

59. Then the Lord shall make your plagues marvelous, and the plagues of your seed, even great and certain [lasting] plagues, and sicknesses wretched and chronic [lasting].

60. Moreover He shall bring upon you all the diseases of Egypt, which you were afraid of; and they will cleave to you.

61. Also every disease and every plague that is not written in the book of this law, them shall the Lord bring upon you, until you are destroyed.

62. And you shall be left few in number, whereas you were as the stars of heaven for multitude, because you would not obey the voice of the Lord your God.

63. And it shall come to pass, that just as the Lord your God rejoiced over you to do you good, and to multiply you; so shall the Lord rejoice over you to destroy you, and to bring you to nought; and you shall be plucked from off the land whither you go to possess it.

64. And the Lord shall scatter you among all people, from the one end of the earth even to the other; and there you will serve other gods, which neither you nor your fathers have known, even wood and stone.

I have discussed already how slow men are when it comes to

learning from the chastisements that God sends them. For they continue to become more and more hardhearted, until they perceive the hand of God and are driven to understand that it is He with whom they have to do. And to make it worse, they labor to conceal from themselves what they ought to feel and see right before their eyes, which is that it is for their sins that they have been smitten.

Marvelous and Lasting Plagues

Since men will never willingly come to a knowledge of themselves, God finds it needful to force them to it. This is why Moses, in addition to what he has already said, adds that God shall make the plagues that He visits upon the despisers of His law to be marvelous (v. 59a). That is to say that they shall be so noteworthy that even in spite of their rebellion they will be afraid of them, as of things never before seen and never in use before. For we see that accustomed things are despised, just as the same is true concerning God's blessings.

For instance, the sun daily rises to lighten us, but who thinks of the change and alternation that God makes between night and day? Psalm 19 tells us that it is as if God should waken us every morning and tell us with a loud voice how reasonable it is that His infinite goodness, wisdom, and power are known (Ps. 19:2). But we have no ears to hear. And why? Because the sun appears every day in the same way, and we become hardened to it because it is ordinary and we make no account of it. It is the same with punishments; for the more our Lord provokes us to come to Him, the more do we stir ourselves up to become unreformable. Thus is it needful for us that His plagues should be a wonder to us, and we may be afraid of them in spite of our rebellion.

Again he adds that they shall be great and certain, or lasting (v. 59b). The last word Moses uses signifies true or faithful.[1] By this God causes us to understand that His plagues shall grasp us

---

1. That is, "certain" means "lasting, continuing, or true in the sense of faithful, enduring."

completely, just as He said also that they would cleave to them that were rebellious and could not be won by gentleness. These plagues must be rooted in them, and for that reason He terms them "certain." Here we must consider our own hardness, that every one of us may be more vigilant in looking to the hand of God, and benefit ourselves from it. And let us be afraid lest God should do what is threatened here in this text, which is that when His normal punishments do not profit us, then He must proceed against us after such a strange and horrible manner; indeed, such a way that will make us fearful and cause the hairs to stand on the back of the heads of all those who but hear of it, and as the prophet Jeremiah says, to make men's ears tingle when the reports of it come into foreign countries (Jer. 19:3).

Let us be afraid, then, lest God work on us after that manner, when He perceives such stubbornness in us that He cannot win us by measurable and tolerable correction. And with this let us also take warning by this phrase, "sicknesses wretched and chronic," or lasting (v. 59c).[2] When God has followed us to bring us to the way of salvation and we have fled from Him, then the plagues must also continue to the uttermost, both upon us and upon all our descendants, so that when we think we have seen an end of them, we shall find that we have not yet begun. Let us not, therefore, think that we shall escape when the plague has lasted for a while. For as we proceed on in our wickedness, so must God proceed with His rigor and augment it more and more, according as He sees us wax worse and worse.

When this happens, let us not do as we see most men do, who cry out and storm at it, saying, "When will this end? Why is it that God takes no pity on me, to ease my pains?" But when they say this, do they have any intention of reconciling themselves to God? Do they confess their sins and bewail them? No, rather they defy Him at this very point. All the while they talk about their feelings and make their complaints, but not one of them looks to the foundation of the trouble in order to set it right.

---

2. The same Hebrew word for "lasting" as in the earlier phrase of the verse.

Therefore, when we have been rebellious against God, let us not think it strange that He should pursue us with such rigor, but let us acknowledge that it is expedient for us. And meanwhile, let us not forget what is here written, namely that God threatens sinners for the purpose of bringing them back again, even though they have been like folk forlorn and past hope of recovery. For God is not speaking here to men who have committed only one fault, or some two or three faults. Nor is He speaking to those who, having done amiss, did not wholly give themselves over to wickedness. Rather, He speaks unto such offenders as have made war against Him for a long time, and despised His Word and been deaf to all His warnings, making a mockery of them. Yet notwithstanding, He does not cease to threaten them still. And to what end or purpose? Even to win them by His amiable goodness. So then, although we have gone astray for a time, yet it is better for us to turn late than never, and thus we shall fare well by what is here shown us by Moses.

The Plagues of Egypt

Now, next he says that God shall cause the plagues of Egypt to come upon the Jews (v. 60). We understand that God afflicted the Egyptians so much that they became a terror to His own people, insomuch that the Jews themselves were astonished at it, even though they were exempted from the evil. When the Egyptians were oppressed to the uttermost, the Jews understood from this that God was sparing them, and that He held them in His protection because He smote their enemies while He kept them in peace and rest. And this we see chiefly in His killing all the firstborn of Egypt. For God had commanded that the door posts of the houses should be marked with the blood of the Paschal Lamb (Ex. 12:7). In this, God gave a singular testimony to the Jews that He would spare them, and during that time He turned His wrath and vengeance against their enemies.[3]

But now He says here on the contrary that God shall cause

---

3. In other words, the Jews deserved to be punished the same as the Egyptians. God's sparing of them was solely of gracious election. If they do not live in accor-

these very plagues to return back. For the word that Moses uses means the same as if he should say, "Your fathers saw how God turned His wrath against the Egyptians, but now it must come back again upon you, because you do not care to honor and serve Him, who has loved you so much, and to whom you are so greatly bound." By this we are admonished that when God has borne with us for a time – indeed, moreover, for the love that He bears towards us, has punished our enemies and showed Himself their enemy in order to maintain us – we must not therefore flatter ourselves, but rather be more diligent to walk in His fear. For when we refuse to acknowledge such grace, but rather abuse it, God has good reason to cause to fall on us those very things that He had sent upon our enemies, thereby to show us that He held us in His defense and safeguard.

It is said that the people of God will be as a fire kindled to consume all the wicked and unbelievers. And God will surely bring this to pass. But if we kindle His wrath through our sins and transgressions, then the fire that should have fallen upon the unfaithful must fall on us, and we must perish therewith.

Let us therefore consider well this word, and let what is said concerning the land of Egypt be to us a mirror and an opportunity, that we at this day may apply it to our own use, since all these things are written for us. Let us mark (I say) what our Lord did in old time for the Jews, and let us understand that thereby He recorded what love He bears to His Church.

And yet, let us take warning to yield ourselves obedient to Him in such a way that He may continue to do us good, and that this covenant may be confirmed between Him and us, namely "I will be a friend to your friends, and an enemy to your enemies (Ex. 23:22). It is certain that this promise was given to Abraham, but with the intention that we also should enjoy the same. Now if we refuse to let God be our friend, but rather make war against Him and break the faith and alliance that is established between

---

dance with His covenant, then He will bring on them the judgment He originally spared them.

us; then whereas before He set Himself against our enemies, now He must be compelled to fall upon us and to make us feel His infinite power, until we are quite confounded and brought to nothing. Therefore while our Lord spares us, let us acknowledge His goodness and not provoke His wrath to make us feel His power in smiting us.

And moreover, when it comes to pass that, although the unfaithful are the ones who should be stricken by His hand, it is we who feel the first blows, let us acknowledge that it is proper that it should be so, because we have broken the peace He made with us. Let us not thereupon be discouraged, whatever happens, but let us stick by Him closely. Furthermore, let us not tarry till He proceeds to extremity. And if we are not so wise as to have that discretion at the first, yet at least let us benefit ourselves by the notices set down in this place. After that manner should we put this text in use.

Now Moses says expressly that the Jews feared the plagues of the Egyptians and that they had good reason to be afraid of them, for when they beheld them upon their enemies, they were then astonished at them. Therefore it was proper that they should magnify the goodness of God. But regardless of that, the plagues God sent upon the Egyptians were so great and so horrible that the Jews must have been amazed at them (although they themselves were free from them) because they beheld such an alteration of nature.

Now if they feared the wrath of God while it was upon their enemies, and had therein a testimony of His love and goodness, how should they then feel when God rushes upon their heads and they are compelled to feel the very same plagues that came upon the Egyptians? Must they not be doubly decimated? Yes, and therefore we see that this threat is not superfluous, but serves to wake them up, according as we have said here before. And as experience shows, we are far too deaf, yea and as it were senseless, when God warns us that He must smite upon us as it were with a hammer, or else we shall never understand what He says. And so you see the reason why this word is expressly set down.

Now when we see that God punishes the wicked, let us learn to have such fear of His vengeance that we do not tarry until He wraps us up in the same package with those whom we have seen punished before us. This is what St. Paul meant in saying, "Deceive not yourselves, neither let any man abuse you with vain words: for the wrath of God has been wont to fall upon the unbelievers and disobedient for such offenses" (Eph. 5:6). Hereby St. Paul shows to the faithful that they should not fear the hand of God only when they see it armed against them and when it touches their persons; but they ought to use the opportunity to reform themselves, when God is so good to them as to punish the reprobates and rebels before their eyes. Let us therefore be afraid when God punishes the wicked, and let us be advised to acknowledge Him for our judge beforehand, and that we have well deserved to be handled as severely as they, were it not that He of His goodness forbears us. Let this touch us to the quick, that we may be brought to repentance. Thus should we yet further put this saying of Moses in practice.

New and Unheard of Plagues

Now he adds that God (over and beside all this that He has declared) shall send yet other adversities and afflictions upon the Jews (v. 61). Indeed Moses had reckoned up many sorts of plagues already, and he thought it not enough to have said only once, "God will chastise you after such and such a manner," but he redoubled it, because he saw men so gross and heavy that they could not be moved at the first as much as was desirable. But our Lord's intent here is to declare that He has means of vengeance incomprehensible, and more than can be uttered by words; insomuch that if a man should make a list of them, and rehearse a million different kinds of them, yet should he not comprise them all for God has other hidden means unknown to men, wherewith to punish those who rankle full of malice against Him. And that is what we shall see in the thirty-second chapter, in the solemn song that Moses makes there. "These things are laid up in My treasury," says the Lord, "so that I have whole chests full of horrible plagues, such as have never been imagined or understood by men." Thus much is said in this text.

And so let us remember two things when we experience the power of God by His doing, or read the threats that He has made against the transgressors of His law and behold the practice and execution thereof. First, let us be amazed thereat and say, "How now? What a thing it is to provoke the Lord! For if He spares us on the one side, He can well assail us on the other; and when we are delivered from one hundred afflictions, He has three hundred others ready for us; and when we have escaped all those, yet have we gotten nothing." Let us therefore think upon these things.

Now let us look at what sorts of threats there are in Holy Scripture, how many sorts of deaths there are that God has denounced against the despisers of His majesty, and against all them that despise and set light by His word. It would weary us to recite them. And in reading the histories, we see the examples that God has given us of His wrath; and that not of one sort only. We should be at our wits end if we should think but upon the tenth part of them. And if we should set our minds to mark and to note them all, what a thing were it? The first thing therefore that we have to do, is to be diligent to call to remembrance all the threats whereby God would tame our wicked affections and hold us embridled, and along with that to compare the things that are set down unto us, how that God has not threatened in vain but has accomplished whatsoever He has said. Let us think on that.

And moreover [second] let us understand, that besides the means that are contained in the Holy Scripture, God has yet a great many other means to punish men, and we see how He daily sends new kinds of wrath. And that is for the purpose that I have touched on before, namely to make His plagues wonderful, that men may be forced to think upon them because they see that God works not after the ordinary course of nature but after a sort that was not formerly known. When each of us has well studied all the lessons that are declared to us in the Holy Scripture, and made use of the examples and punishments that are there mentioned, let us conclude that God has yet a great many more means than are expressed, which men never thought upon.

And He has made this manifest ever since the law was written; and He has never stopped making it manifest, in order that all manner of excuse may be taken from us. If a man looks upon the diseases that are currently in the world, he will see that there are many that were not mentioned in the law of Moses, or in the days of our fathers. How has whoredom been punished by diseases that have come up of late! Who knew the pox (syphilis) a hundred years ago? Surely that is one horrible plague God has sent upon the world! It is the same as if He had stretched His arm out of heaven and said, "So, they refuse to know Me any longer as their judge; they harden their hearts against all the plagues that men knew and experienced in earlier times; they make but a fig at it;[4] but now I shall make them to understand that in My coffers and in My storehouses there are yet other rods that are incomprehensible to them." God shows this; and we perceive that we cannot take a better course to profit by this doctrine than to fear those rods and punishments that are not written in the book of the law. And in everything it is proper that we understand that God is wholly our judge, no matter what happens.

The Rending of the Abrahamic Covenant

Now he adds that even though they were as many in number as the stars of heaven, God would waste them so thoroughly that there would but a handful remain (v. 62). Here must we remember what we touched on earlier. For when God uses this similitude of the stars of heaven, He has respect to the promise He had made to His servant Abraham; namely, that his seed should be in number like the stars of heaven. So God spoke. But now, so that the Jews should not presume to think that God was always bound to multiply them, He says "No, I will consume you whatsoever come of it, and you shall be but a handful of people."

It seems at the first sight that here is a contradiction. For when God promised so great a seed unto His servant Abraham

---

4. That is, treat it as nothing.

it was not grounded upon the merits of men. So then, seeing that the promise depends upon the free goodness of God, must it not be kept, even though men are wicked? Yes indeed, but we have to consider that God does not always accomplish His promises after our fashion or according to our carnal capacity. He has means that we cannot begin to comprehend, and that we do not understand until they appear by effect. Whereas He promises to multiply His Church, that is to say to make it to prosper, if He sees that under color thereof the hypocrites take liberty to do evil, He withdraws His hand.[5]

Let us therefore consider well that since the Jews were puffed up with a foolish presumption and thought it impossible for God to diminish them, seeing He had spoken the word that He would increase them; since, I say, they abused the goodness of God and falsified His promise through their hypocrisy, He consumed them and brought them to a small number. Nevertheless, of that small number there came a great offspring again; yea, and a very great one so that men might so much the better perceive His truth and mercy, although after another manner. Therefore He says by His prophet Isaiah in the tenth chapter: "Even though you are as the sand of the sea (for He always sent them back to the promise made to Abraham), and even though your seed (as I said) is as the sand of the sea; yet will but a final remnant be saved" (Is. 10:22). But when you are altogether consumed, yet shall that little remnant be dispersed over all the earth, as if out of a little fountain should issue forth a great river or a great lake, wherewith very many lands should be watered. So shall it be.

Now then we perceive that even though God punishes the hypocrites that abuse His promises, yet He never fails to perform His promises to the full, even if by an extraordinary means as we have seen it in the Popedom, and as it is still to be seen. For the

---

5. Calvin touches here on the "problem" of unconditional promises. Promises by their very nature have to be received by faith. God's promises are always, from that standpoint, conditional. Since God predestines all things, His promises will surely come to pass, in His own good time. Whether they come to pass in our own day, however, has to do with whether or not we are faithful.

Papists have overflowed the whole world with superstition and idolatry and all manner of evil. Yea, and moreover they harden their hearts in pride and scoff at God with open mouth. "How now," say they, "Are not we the Church? Is it not said that Jesus Christ will be with us unto the end of the world? Can He forsake His Church?" Yet they continually crucify Him as much as in them lies;[6] they spit in His face, and do Him all the reproach in the world; they make Him as if He were a prisoner or a bondslave among them;[7] and they do not consider that such a horrible destruction happens throughout the whole world, through God's just vengeance, for the shameless hypocrisy that has been in them that have rebelled against the gospel. Yet notwithstanding, God has continued to save His people, as it were under the earth. And in our days He has raised His Church, as if its bones of rotten bodies should recover flesh and strength again (cf. Ezk. 37). For what were we through our unbelief? You see how it is a miraculous resurrection that God has wrought in this way.

Mark well therefore that when our Lord promises to maintain His Church and to preserve it, this promise does not apply to them that abuse His name falsely or to them that come to despise Him because He is gentle and merciful. For they will evermore be disappointed of that favor that God has reserved unto His people, because they remove themselves from it through their own malice and unthankfulness. Yet notwithstanding, however the case stands, God is ever faithful and will find incomprehensible means to give place to His truth, by fighting against the malice of men. That is what we have to remember concerning this text, where He says that He shall waste the Jews though they were as the stars in the sky.

And in fact the same appeared even in Jesus Christ the Head

---

6. A reference to the perpetual sacrifice of the Mass, in which the transubstantiated bread and wine are seen as resacrificed. Calvin seems to have Hebrews 6:6 in mind here and in the next phrase.

7. A reference to the claim that the priest has some sort of dominion over God when he performs the "consecration" of the sacramental elements. The Roman Catholic Church has modified this type of claim in recent years.

of the Church. And therefore we ought not to think it strange that the members of the body should be fashioned like unto Him. Whence came Jesus Christ when God His Father sent him to be the Redeemer? The prophet Isaiah says that He would spring from a stock, as if a tree were hewn down and there remained but the stub within the ground, the sort that men might tread upon (Is. 11:1). It is not said that He would come out of the house of David, but out of the house of Jesse, who was a cowherd and a man despised. Such was the father of David: a man of no estimation. Although David was so excellent a king that he was chosen of God to be magnified to the skies, yet the prophet shows that when Jesus Christ would come into the world, it would not be with any show of that royal majesty that was in David, but He would come out of the house of Jesse, as if He came out of a herd. And that in addition he would not come from a tree, but from a stock that had been cut off. And in what manner? And after what fashion? As a little branch, says he.

Now seeing that God did thus to the Head of the Church, we must understand that all the body must be secure, but this does not mean that hypocrites will be partakers of what God reserves to His elect, whom He has chosen, who show themselves to be His children and are obedient to Him, as to their Father, and who also come not only with all confidence, but also are drawn with a right affection to honor Him. And when we perceive that at this day God is sending horrible destructions into the world, let us understand that He practices what is here declared. Yet, let us not doubt, but realize that He always preserves His Church. Let us not doubt, but realize that He upholds us as often as we have our recourse to Him, according to this saying, that whoever calls upon the name of the Lord shall be saved, yea even amidst the greatest trouble that may ever be (Joel 2:32). Though heaven and earth should run together, yet we are sure that by calling upon the name of God, we shall be preserved. But let us take heed that we do not abuse His name, to make thereof a false cloak, for He can waste us well enough. And if we boast that we are of His Church when He has cut us off, He can quickly raise

Him a new people and increase them in such wise as His truth will not be defaced, and yet we shall perish.

God's Delight in Their Destruction

After that, Moses adds that just as God had taken pleasure in doing good to the Jews, even so He would take pleasure in persecuting them until He had consumed them and utterly rooted them out (v. 63). Here Moses first of all shows what affection God bears towards these whom He has chosen out for Himself and intends to take for His flock. It is certain that God is not subject to any human passions,[8] yet He is not able sufficiently to manifest either the goodness or the love that He has towards us, except by transfiguring Himself, as if He were a mortal man, saying that He would take pleasure in doing us good.

Let us understand therefore that God holds us dear, as if a father should delight and rejoice to do good to his children. When he sees them behaving according to his mind, and doing him honor and obeying him, then when he feeds them and clothes them it is a comfort to him; and it does him good to see them in their bravery, for that is the very felicity of a father. God likens Himself to mortal men, and says that He will delight to do us good.[9] And therefore we cannot magnify the inestimable goodness of our God too much, seeing He stoops so low as to tell us that His whole delight is in making us to enjoy His benefits, and in that He demeans Himself towards us in such a way that we may have cause to praise Him, and finally in that He yields to all our desires. But what? We cannot endure it; we are not able to apprehend it, for we are not able to consider it.

We see that God is (as one might say) wayward towards us; we see that He not only bereaves us of His blessings, but is also angry with us; and to be short, we perceive in Him nothing but all manner of rigor. And what is the cause of it? Certainly we

---

8. On Stoic elements in Calvin's way of speaking, see note 3 in Sermon 160, on page 213 above.

9. It would be better, and clearer, to say that mortal men were created "likened" to God.

shut the gate against His goodness, and will not permit Him to use (as one might say) His natural disposition. Here is something that should make us the better acknowledge our faults, and not accuse God of any excessive cruelty when He does not deal with us after our liking. For it is certain that He will take pleasure in doing us good. But on the other side let us consider also that He must likewise delight to do us evil. And why? Certainly because He is just.

Indeed, if we permitted God to use His own inclination towards us, He would bestow infinite benefits upon us, and we living in this world should be as in Paradise. But because of our sins we must live here like wretched wanderers. We must languish in many miseries; we must dwell in continual fear and in doubt; and we must groan in great unrest. It must be so. And why? Because God is just.

This is the very pleasure that is spoken of in this text. It says here that God shall rejoice and be glad when He has punished the wicked and maintained His majesty against them, because they have despised Him and set Him at nought. Nevertheless, it is also true that He says by His prophet Isaiah that He does it unwillingly. Alas (says He), do I have to avenge Myself of Mine enemies (Is. 1:24)? God cries there alas, as if He were in sorrow and anguish for it. I must (says He) take comfort in avenging Myself of Mine enemies. Those whom He terms His enemies are the children whom He had adopted and who boasted themselves to be His people. And how does He comfort Himself in them? Even by giving them over, and by driving them away. But in the meanwhile, He shows that it is against His will when He must so beat men down with heavy strokes, although He cannot do otherwise.

Yet notwithstanding, God is surely able to tame the hearts of men without any great violence, for (as we have said) He is not subject to our passions. But hereby we are to consider how He intends to declare that our unreformable sinfulness is the reason why He is compelled to pursue us after the manner spoken of here, and that He is compelled to take pleasure in doing us harm,

wherein the order of nature is in a way quite altered and changed.
But all this is our own fault, and we ourselves are to blame for it,
and it is not for us to seek any other reason thereof than our sin,
which has kindled His vengeance to the uttermost. Thus much
concerning that sentence.

The Coming Diaspora

Now for a conclusion it is said that God shall root out this
people from the land wherein He had planted them, and then
He shall disperse them among all the nations of the world. And
that there this wretched people (which were formerly in a country
of freedom, wherein God had set them so that His service and
pure religion should dwell there) will serve strange gods, even
idols of wood and stone (v. 64).

First we see that even though the land of Canaan was given
as an inheritance to the people of Israel, yet they were surely put
out and banished when they abused the favor that had been
shown unto them. God had planted them there, even as though
He had set them with His own hand. Lo (says He), here is My
resting place and yours (Ps. 132:14). He intended to dwell among
them Himself, and thereupon He promised to give them rest here,
insomuch that although all other people should be displaced and
removed to and fro, yet should the children of Abraham continue
to enjoy the heritage of that land. Notwithstanding, this did not
prevent God from driving them out again and scattering them
abroad with the wind because they had defiled that land, which
should have been kept holy to His name.

Now since it is so, let us not think it strange when God at this
day sends many changes into the world; for He has given no such
privilege to any nation as to say unto them, "You shall inhabit
this land, as the land of Canaan was given to the lineage of
Abraham." But we see how God is offended. We see men's misdoings as heinous as can be. Now then, if God removes men, let us
understand that it is for their sins.

Moreover, let us return to the eternal rest, whereunto the
Apostle leads us in the epistle to the Hebrews. Having spoken of

the rest of the land of Canaan, He says that we must look unto a rest that is higher (Heb. 4:9; 11:16). For the children of God are commonly like wayfarers in this world as St. Paul terms them, putting himself in the number (2 Cor. 5:6); but let us evermore direct our course and endeavor to this heritage that is promised us in heaven, for we shall not be disappointed of that heritage if we continue in our calling whereunto God has called us. Nevertheless, it is said that they who give themselves over unto wickedness shall be wiped out of the Book of Life (Ex. 32:33). Not that God's chosen will ever perish; but it is spoken with respect to such folk as think it enough for them to bear the name of God's children, and to have been baptized, and to receive the Lord's Supper, and such like things, and make no further regard. But our Lord tells us that although it seems for a time that they are written and enrolled in His register, because they are taken to be of the company of the faithful, yet will they not fail to be wiped out.

The Greatest Privilege

So then let us advise ourselves, and as long as it pleases God to keep us in this world, let us walk under His obedience in such a way that His hand may ever be stretched out to preserve and maintain us. Let us so stick to Him that we may have freedom to honor and serve Him. For it is a dreadful desolation that Moses here speaks of, namely to be no longer of the body of the Church or to have any longer the appearance or shape of religion; and yet this is seen throughout the world at this day.

Therefore, let us mark that one of the greatest benefits God can bestow upon us in this transitory life is to let us have some little corner in which to assemble ourselves in His name, to call upon Him, and to profess ourselves to be His people. This ought to be esteemed among us more than meat or drink or anything else. Yet very few do think upon it. Notwithstanding, however, we must confess that even though we have sufficient food, yet if we forget God meanwhile, then our state is most miserable. And if we do not think on this, we betray our own beastliness. For God tells us that the benefit that is spoken of here is far greater than all the rest. That is, that we may worship Him in purity and be gathered together under the Head He has appointed to us, namely our Lord Jesus Christ.

And therefore, while we have such a privilege as to hear the Word of God, to call upon His Name, and to walk according to His gospel, let us hearken unto it, for fear lest God disperse and scatter us abroad in the same way as he has dispersed the Jews. And especially let us stand in fear of this threat, which is namely to be made such beasts as to honor idols again, as we see it has happened to others who are a good example to us of the vengeance of God, of which we ourselves have also felt our part.

For we have been bondslaves under idolatry, and underlings to the abominations of the Papal system, and that was for our sins and for the sins of our fathers. Seeing we have already felt such blows, and indeed have been as mirrors unto others, should we now be so brutish as to provoke our God in such a way that He should be forced as it were to deprive us of the grace that He has given us?

Let us then use this benefit and treasure of the gospel, while our Lord gives us a place wherein to hide ourselves as it were under His hand, while He governs and guides us, and while we are knit together in one body, that He may be magnified among us with one accord not only with the mouth, but also especially with our lives; to the end that as a result of our endeavor to honor Him, He on His side may continue doing good towards us, and that this threat not be executed upon our heads, which is to be dispersed here and there and to be constrained again to worship idols and other dead and senseless things.

Prayer

Now let us fall down before the majesty of our good God, with acknowledgement of our sins, beseeching Him to touch us with such repentance that, being ashamed of our sins, we may seek altogether to put ourselves wholly into His hands, and that by obtaining forgiveness of Him, we may also feel that He has reformed us, and that we are in His favor, to give over ourselves altogether to His holy will. And that even though there is always much to be amended in us, and our lusts and affections do draw us quite away from what He commands us, yet nevertheless we may not cease to strive against them, and to yield ourselves wholly to Him, and to enforce ourselves hereunto more and more, knowing that the same is our sovereign welfare. And that although He shows us now and then some tokens of rigor in correcting us, yet we may learn to profit thereby, to the amending of our sins, so that we may be brought to the perfection whereunto He daily calls us. That it may please Him to grant this grace not only to us but also to all people and nations of the earth; etc.

15

EXODUS UNDONE

Sermon 163. Saturday, 28 March 1556.
Deuteronomy 28:65-68.

65. And among these nations you shall find no ease, nor shall the sole of your foot have rest; but the LORD shall give you there a trembling heart, and failing of eyes, and sorrow of mind.

66. And your life shall hang in doubt before you; and you shall fear day and night, and shall have no assurance of your life.

67. In the morning you shall say, "Would God it were evening!" And at evening you shall say, "Would God it were morning!" — because of the fear of your heart with which you shall fear, and because of the sight of your eyes that you shall see.

68. And the LORD shall bring you into Egypt again with ships, by the way of which I told you, "You shall see it never again." And there you shall be sold unto your enemies for male and female slaves, but no man shall buy you.

Among the benefits that we desire in this present life, one is to have some resting place and some harbor to lodge in. Though a man be poor and troubled on all sides, yet if he has some little hole to hide his head to which he can resort, he cares not for all the rest. But if we know not where to go, nor have any friend to receive us or any nook or corner where we may rest, our state is then extremely miserable. That is why Moses now (after declaring that God would drive away and banish the Jews out of the land He had given them to inherit and to rest in forever) adds that they shall be as vagabonds and have no certain dwelling place, but be tossed from pillar to post.

How the Righteous Suffer

Now it is certain, as we have already said, that this often happens to the faithful; but [first,] it is for another purpose; [second,] God comforts them in it; and [third,] it is fitting that their patience should be tried in this manner. For our obedience toward God is displayed when He mingles us among the wicked, so that we do not appear outwardly to differ from them at all. All goes to havoc, as they say, and yet notwithstanding we continue sound in heart and commit ourselves into the hands of our God, knowing that He has not forgotten us, though He allows us to be so tossed.

On the other hand all despisers of the law bear their mark as if they were burned with a searing iron in their hearts. They know that God is against them and that their sins reprove them. Even though men do not accuse them, yet they feel a sufficient testimony in themselves to be confounded. And that is what Moses goes on to say, that concerning those who are hard hearted against God's Word, God shall give them a trembling heart, a sorrowful mind, and failing eyes, so that in the morning they shall say, "Would that it were night." And when night is come, "Alas how shall I get through it? Can I continue until the morning?" Their lives shall as it were hang before them, and they shall be in miserable distress. That is the thing wherein the faithful chiefly differ from the despisers of God, and where their state varies.

For although the faithful suffer much trouble in this world, yet they have much with which to comfort themselves — just as our Lord Jesus says in John 16:33, "You shall be vexed in this world, but yet you shall not fail to have comfort in Me." We must consider what is the ground of our comfort; namely that they who stand assured in the protection of God do evermore commit their life into His hands, as we see David did when he was beset on all sides. When he was threatened with a hundred deaths, he said, "Lord, I commend my soul unto Thee, Thou art faithful and Thou hast redeemed me" (Psalm 32:6). He knew that God had maintained him even to that hour; and that indeed without His marvelous power, he could not have lived so long. And thereupon he concludes that because God is faithful, "He will surely have pity on me, and therefore I commit my soul to His keeping."

Look at what point the faithful are. They very well perceive that their life is but a smoke that might vanish away out of hand. They see there are many ambushes laid for them, and that they cannot safely go forward one step without encountering some misery. The faithful understand, over and besides all this, that they are subject to all the changes of this human life and that they are as frail as all the children of Adam. They see that there is no resting place for them here. Yet in spite of this they know that God has care over them, and that He is their protector. That is what they rest upon.

Having such a stay, they keep on their way forward, yet they are not careless, for we must not be so stupid as to ignore perils. For we could not call upon God if we did not see the perils in which we find ourselves. And it provokes us to seek our God when we see that without Him we should perish during every minute of an hour. The faithful then must not be without fear, but resting upon the instruction of God they must stick to Him and assure themselves that He shall never forsake them. That is what they rejoice in.

Yea and they go yet further, for although they have to go among thorns, although they are driven to make many leaps, although they catch now and then some knocks, and although they are altogether shut up and have no way out, yet notwithstanding through the power of faith they evermore rejoice, even in the midst of all their sorrows and perplexities.

On the other hand, the despisers of God are as blind as is

possible and close their eyes lest they see their infirmities, and so they harden themselves. Yet for all this, God compels them to look at themselves, and then they are undone. They are over-wrought with fear and amazement. It is not their manner to make their recourse to God, for they understand nothing of His protection. No, rather they shun Him, and flee as far from Him as they can, because they conceive nothing in Him but dreadful majesty, which puts them quite out of heart. As for the wicked therefore, and all who have rebelled against God: they, after long hardening of themselves, when God wakes them, know not where to go. For they will not come to Him, but do rather utter their rage by spitting at Him and by gnashing their teeth at Him. And because they find no end to their miseries and have no rest, this terror that God casts upon them becomes an incurable disease. For to call upon Him, or to put their lives into His hands, is beyond their power; but rather since they know that they have warred against Him, they are likewise driven to understand that instead of helping them, He will sorely vex them. That is what we see here in this text where Moses says, "God shall give them a trembling heart, a sorrowful mind, and failing eyes."

Why the Righteous Sometimes Suffer Intensely

Now here we may ask a question. For we perceive that God's children — even those most dear to Him, who have served Him in the most right and sound manner — even they are often times in such distress that it bewilders them and leaves them besides themselves. What complaints does David make? That his eyes are worn out, that he is consumed with mourning, that the marrow of his bones is dried up, that all his strength is faded, that he is in such great fear that he seems to be swallowed up into a bottom-less gulf (Psalm 6). This happens sometimes to God's children.

How can this be? This is a threat made against those who despise Him, those who cannot by any good means be reclaimed, and who have always withstood God. I have already told you that God, in order to try His people to the quick, allows them to be in exactly the same situation as the wicked, so much so that

even they themselves think so too.[1] But yet God always reaches
to them with His hand, and although He does not overcome their
griefs at the first, yet He holds them so that they do not fall. There
lies still some seed of God's spirit hidden in them, which at length
manifests itself more fully, so they see clearly that God sustained
them in the midst of those extremities, and in the end it appears
to them as it were in a whole manner.

Let us mark it well then, that sometimes the children of God
are tossed and troubled with afflictions and have such grievous
and hard temptations that they think God has become their enemy, so that they dare not open their mouths to call upon Him,
but are utterly confounded. And even though He reminds them
of the promises of His grace, yet they cannot taste of them, but
sometimes even refuse them like unbelievers, as though they were
fully determined to shut themselves out of all hope of salvation.
When they are at this point, then our Lord works in them in such
a way as to cause them not to be overthrown completely with
temptation.

And that is what St. Paul means when he says, "We are
afflicted, but we perish not; we are oppressed, but yet no matter
how the world goes, we are not overcome, for we bear the mortifying of Jesus Christ in our flesh" (2 Cor. 4:8-10). Whereas he says
that the faithful may indeed be pent up in afflictions, he says also
that even so they do not fall. For even though they stoop under
the burden, and groan as though they were crushed and broken,
yet all those heartbreaks do not cause any deadly fall. He adds
the reason, namely, that it is the mortifying of our Lord Jesus
Christ that they bear. That is, that God always separates us from
the unbelieving and from reprobates, and from the despisers of
His majesty, and that He prints in us the marks of His only Son.
It is true that in this case they seem as dead, but the same death
is holy, for God sanctifies it because they are members of our
Lord Jesus Christ, and thereby they attain to the resurrection.

---

1. That is, the righteous themselves cannot see how their lot differs from the
wicked.

True it is, that St. Paul speaks not only of the last resurrection, but he begins at the comfort that God gives presently to His children to train them to arrive at the port of salvation. Now then, they enter into the midst of death even while they are alive.

And therefore let us remember that although God does now and then so afflict such as have walked in His fear and have put their trust in Him, so that they are stricken with terror and tossed with unquietness, yet notwithstanding He holds them up by the secret operation of His Spirit. And moreover He comforts them and makes them glad in the end, accomplishing what is said in another text, that the more they were distressed, the more did He set their hearts at liberty, that they may freely come unto Him and so consequently makes them understand that He never forsook them (Rom. 5:3ff.). Behold how our Lord tempers the troubles and afflictions of the faithful, so that although they endure ever such great pains, and do even pant in coming to Him, as people scarcely able to open their mouths to call upon Him, yet when they have ended their conflict against their temptations, even though at the first they cannot get the upper hand, yet will they get the victory in the end.

But as for those who have acted like restless horses, they remain pent up in their miseries without any remedy, because God continues to set Himself against them more and more until they become frantic and gnash their teeth at Him, and finally fall into utter despair. In short, we see what is spoken by the prophet Isaiah daily accomplished; namely, that there is no peace for the wicked, but that their minds are tossed like the waves of the sea (Is. 48:22). When there is any storm, the waves are troubled and the water is full of mud. It is the same with those who despise God. Because they make war against Him, therefore must He also trouble them — insomuch that even without an enemy, yea and without anybody to frighten them, they of themselves are frightened and beat and bounce themselves as if they were at war within themselves, so that there is no calmness at all in them, but they are full of trouble and disorder. For the faithful are enlightened in the midst of their darkness, and God still comes to them to give them some little spark of light, so that they may see Him. And although they attain not to it at first, yet they still strain themselves and hold on their way. But the unbelievers are troubled at the very root of their heart, and cannot otherwise conceive, but that they must perish in despair. And when they are at the last cast, then they fall to spitting at God and blaspheme Him with open mouth.

In brief, here we see that the worst curse that God can send upon men in this transitory life is that they cannot rest upon Him, to acknowledge Him to be the keeper of their lives, but contrariwise are cast up at adventure so that they are ever in doubt of their lives, and are so carried away with mistrust that they do not know where to go. When men are in this situation, it is the greatest curse that can light upon them. With good reason, therefore, Moses here declares for a conclusion, as it were by way of summing up the rest of all the curses we have heard heretofore, that there is nothing so dreadful as when men have become so stupid that there is no understanding in them. It is as if God no longer reckons them as His creatures, and they may well perceive that He neither guides nor governs them any more.

When men are come to this point, so that their life, even though allowed by men, is nevertheless heinous and detestable before God, and moreover they have no taste of His fatherly love or of the care that He has for other men, but are in the dungeon of despair; when men I say are come to such an extremity, it is better for them that they had been born before their time, and that they had never enjoyed this present life. And that is the reason why we hear it threatened that they will say, "O you mountains fall upon us" (Rev. 6:16), and that they will wish that the bottomless pits had swallowed them up. And why? For they find that all creatures are against them when they have no more access to God. When men perceive that He will not maintain them, but shows Himself to be armed against them, then they understand that all creatures are their enemies, and it grieves them to see the sun. Then are they so possessed with fear that they wish there were no world at all, or rather that they were rooted out of it.

Godly Fear

Now since we hear such horrible threats, let us learn to walk in the fear of our God. For there is no other way to live in rest, and to be comforted in the midst of our sorrows and adversities, except to come with a free will to yield ourselves obedient to our God, and to do Him such reverence as is due to Him. For when we acknowledge Him to be our judge, we shall not act as rebels, but shall be willing to be reclaimed, so that we do not wind up included in the number of them that have refused Him. You see then that we must willingly hearken to God when He menaces us, be moved by it, and be touched to the quick. Based on this we must endeavor to serve Him and to obey His Word. For it may well be that we shall sometimes be vexed with fear and unquietness, but God will deliver us from them. It is certain that we shall be weakened by that means, and it is good for us so to be. But yet however we fare, God will so keep us that we shall not fall into utter despair.

Moreover, when we sometimes feel any disquiet in ourselves, and we lack the power to call upon God but are tormented with distrust, let us understand that it is the fruit of our sins. And let us desire God to make us perceive that we have not kept touch with Him as we ought, and that this is why He casts us into vexation and distress. But let us not so tempt our God, lest He should proceed to the rigor here mentioned, namely, that we should have no power to commit our life into His hands.

So then, whereas mention is made here of a trembling heart (v. 65), let us consider wherein our true rest remains: that God is our father and that we are His children. Likewise mention is made of failing or sunken eyes. Let us understand that we must look upwards as often as we are in any fear, and that there is no other remedy to assuage our griefs but to lift up our eyes to heaven. For as long as men look downward, what will they find there but an infinite mass of miseries able to scare them out of their wits, so that they will not know where to turn? Let us therefore seek this means, which is to lift up our eyes to heaven, knowing that God has His hand stretched forth to uphold them that return unto Him. Where mention is made of a sorrowful mind, let us understand that it is the proper office of God to set our hearts at liberty so that no temptation can utterly vanquish and overwhelm us. And this will be treated of yet more fully.

Hanging by a Thread

Now we come to what Moses adds, that in the morning they shall say, "Would God it were evening," and in the evening they shall say, "Would God it were morning." For your life, he says, shall be hanging in doubt before you, as by a thread. Here we see even better what has been noted before, for why are men thus in continual fear except that they refuse to commend their lives into the hand of God?

Now in truth, and to speak properly, all of our lives are constantly hanging by a thread as it were. But those who despise God are the ones who most particularly find it so — and well they should, because they have gone to war against Him who alone could have set them in peace and safety. Their lives are as it were hanging by threads, because instead of life there is constantly this fear of death in their hearts, and with good reason. After all, what is the life of man, but a smoke that passes and vanishes away? And moreover, let us behold how many kinds of death beset us on all sides.

So then, as long as we remain in our natural state, without respecting God, our lives will always be hanging by a thread as it were. And indeed, even if we are never outwardly touched, how many diseases do we bear within ourselves? A man does not need to go out of himself or seek very far to learn how many miseries and wretchednesses he is subject to. Even in his own person he can immediately find an infinite number of deaths. Seeing then that it is so, let us realize that until we have learned to rest ourselves in the providence of God, our lives must of necessity be as it were flittering before our eyes and altogether uncertain. And in brief, we bear it continually as it were in our own hands, just as it is said in Job (13:14) and in Psalm 119 (v. 109).

Now, when it is said that we carry our lives in our own hands, it is to show that whereas life should bear the man, the man bears the life; that is to say, the life is left up to the hazard of all misfortunes.[2] This is how it is with all men by nature.[3] At the same time, as we have said, the faithful are not free from it, as we see in the examples of Job and David. Notwithstanding, it is those who despise God who most feel that their lives hang by a thread. And why is this? Because God, in spite of their rebellion, forces them to perceive the perils that beset them. They see very well that all manner of creatures are their enemies, and because of this they start when they hear but the falling of a leaf, and they are afraid when no one pursues them, as it is said in Proverbs (28:1).

Thus does God open the eyes of those who are puffed up with pride, and are drunk with the delights of this world, especially those who have hardened themselves in stubbornness against Him. He opens their eyes that they may know how their lives are less than nothing, and that all these shadows, lies, and vain hopes upon which men are wont to rest are but baits to beguile them. Behold here, I pray you, where they come to who have scorned God and His Word and are wholly given over to this world, reposing their trust on earthly means and on creatures. At the last they will be caught with such fear as will teach them double and triple to understand their own condition.

Driven by Fear

Having spoken thus (v. 66), Moses then adds (v. 67) what they shall say: "Who will assure us that we shall see the morning? How can we be sure we shall come to the end of the day?" When men understand once how frail they are, and with how many perils and miseries they are enthroned, they then have no more

---

2. This is a bit obscure. Calvin seems to mean that men should not have to worry about life, since it should be a gift from God. The sinner, having taken matters into his own hands, now must worry about his own life.

3. That is, by sinful nature.

happiness. Indeed we may well say that there is nothing more certain than death, nor is there anything more uncertain than its hour; but while we say this, in the meantime we do not regard it until God puts us in the wringer and forces us to think about it. For when that happens, those who act as if their lives should last forever, find out the contrary. (And we see how men deceive themselves by fancying an immortality in this world, imagining that they will live a hundred years after they are dead.) And therefore, because men are so blockish, God acts to constrain them to behold a present death continually pinching them and holding them at bay. As a result, they are in continual fear, and although they may utter nothing with their mouths, yet in their hearts they wonder, "Who can assure me that I shall see the morning?" In brief, it looks to them as if the very earth sinks under them. And although this does not always appear, yet notwithstanding those who despise God feel that this threat is not in vain or without effect.

So then, let us not fritter away time until God decides to execute such a judgment upon us, but let us rather prevent it by having the kind of willing fear that is spoken of in Proverbs (28:14), where Solomon says, "Blessed is the man who fears in his heart," that is to say, who calls upon himself and does not wait until God forces him to fear whether he wants to or not. When each one of us stirs himself up, it is the greatest blessing we can have. The worldling makes himself a dull head, and wanders away after his own imagination, and flings beyond the moon (as they say), trying to live in peace and rest without feeling any grief or trouble – this, I say, causes them to fall asleep. But let us look to ourselves, and gather our wits into some fear, and let every one of us stir himself up. And if we do not stir ourselves up in this manner, then must God torment and vex us, and make us a lively picture of what is mentioned here.

After those who despise God have acted like mad beasts and spat upon all manner of sound doctrine and ridiculed all threats, and like mad bulls have rushed against God and all His judgments, then at the last they will come to feel themselves vexed and troubled with disquiet. We see how the great tyrants, who make all the world shake under them, experience this without measure so that whereas they make others to drink a little glass of fear and terror, they themselves must drink up a whole jar full. They drink it down to the dregs, as the prophets say when they speak of the greatest punishment God sends. When those whom God chastens[4] have drunk more than their fill in swallowing up great stores of sorrows, then they who have lived at their ease and pleasure must drink the lees, which is the bitterest of all and will make them burst.

And indeed, we have an example of a heathen tyrant who bore witness and declared that all his whole life was continual torment. For being flattered by one who said to him, "O sir, how happy is your state," he replied, "Yes, and I shall make you to understand it for yourself." And thereupon he made him a feast, and when he had set him at his table, he put a sword over his head, hanging by one hair, to show to him what kind of state it was that he had accounted so happy. The man, seeing himself in this situation, said, "Let this kingly state be taken away from me, for I had rather die a hundred times than be in such unquietness and perplexity." This I say was the confession of a heathen tyrant — as if God had held him under torture — that it might be a general lesson against all such as make war with God and trouble the world with terror. They must, in spite of their rebellion, be made afraid themselves, and find no rest. After many tossings and much turmoil, hell must always await them, they must see their graves open into which they are to fall, and they must behold the great gulf ready to swallow them up — and in the meantime they make no recourse or refuge to God, but flee from Him still, whereas in fact He is the only person to whom they should have fled for succor.

Peace With God

Now beyond what we have said already, there is another

---

4. Because He loves them.

consideration. As we have noted, we ought to prevent this judgment by fearing God of our own accord. We must bear in mind that we are all wretched sinners, and there is no one, regardless of how well and right minded, who ought not to understand that he is greatly threatened by God. But, it is also true that when we have our Lord Jesus Christ, who is our peace, and when we can by His means rest upon the fatherly goodness of God, then we can be sure that He counts us as His children and that He watches over us and procures our welfare. And that is why St. Paul says expressly that when we are once justified by faith, then we are at peace with God (Rom. 5:1).

He says that we must be justified by faith, which is to say that we must have embraced the grace offered to us by the gospel, knowing that God forgives us our sins and is merciful to us in that He bears with us for our Lord Jesus Christ's sake. Until we come to this, we must always be in doubt and perplexity. But once knowing that God has buried all our sins, so that we put our trust in the death and passion of our Lord Jesus Christ, then we are at peace – yea in peace and not in dullness like the wicked. The unfaithful and despisers of God may have some peace for a certain time, as we have said before, but since they forget themselves and follow continuously on their wicked track, they utterly besot and bewitch themselves. But St. Paul says that we, acknowledging ourselves undone without Him, may boldly press unto Him and say: "Seeing God is my Father and He has shown Himself so gracious to me in this present life as to grant me some rest here, surely there is a more blissful rest prepared for me when our Lord Jesus Christ will come to meet me, to guide me, and to bring me up, that I may seek my God." And that indeed is the place we must come to, if we intend to have a place to rest ourselves in.

The prophets speak with the same effect when, prophesying the kingdom of our Lord Jesus Christ, they always say that every man will then sleep under his own fig tree and under his own vine, and nothing will make him afraid. The prophets were true expounders of Moses, and as the renewers of the law, bringing it to remembrance again, they showed the people the unbelief and rebellion they saw in them. And having shown the vengeance of God that was ready to fall on them, according to the threats set down by Moses, the prophets then brought the people back again to Jesus Christ. And although it was necessary for them to suffer smartingly for a while because of their sins, yet they gave them hope that God would make a covenant with them, and that then they should sleep every man in his vineyard and under his fig tree. By this, the prophets caused the people to understand that even if they slept not in a locked chamber but lay in the midst of the fields, yet they would be safe enough because they were under the protection of their God, and for this reason they might sleep in ease and safety.

Since we have such assurance then, we ought to be well settled in our minds. And since we have understanding of the reconciliation that is made in our Lord Jesus Christ, we now have a good reason to rest in our God and to be still and quiet — provided we do not forget such a great benefit. And we see that our Lord Jesus Christ desires to reign among us. Let us therefore allow ourselves to be governed by His hand, and as ewes and lambs let us follow our Shepherd, and then shall we do what our Lord has appointed for us, so that nothing may hinder us, but we may attain unto Him. Although we see things confused about in this world, so that all goes to havoc, yet we shall be able to take breath again and say: "Yet has my God still showed me the way, so that although other men have run to and fro, I have always stood fast. And although I have been in various ways troubled and vexed, yet I know, Lord, that Thou dost evermore govern Thy people." Thus you see that being stayed on our Lord Jesus Christ, we may be assured that God will never fail us.

Seeing that this is so, let us return to Him, and pray Him to defend and deliver us from all evil. The way, then, for us to be sure of our lives is that even if we see nothing but continual war, yet we must force ourselves to fight and persevere until we have obtained the victory. And if He takes us away to Himself, He will then be the keeper of our souls. He will guide us in this present life, so that both day and night we shall feel His grace. When the enemy comes, even if the night brings exceedingly great fear with it, yet shall we be in safety. Why is this so? Because God is our fortress during that time, and we will not be forsaken by Him. Therefore, let us tarry until the morning. Thus we are always more and more to refer our lives to Him.

And although we may not be strong, yet we shall always have something to hold us up when we see our own infirmity. For example, when a man perceives that he is not able to stand, but his legs quake and totter under him, he either leans on something or sits down in a chair, or else stays himself upon some staff. Even so it is with us. For we do not possess the strength of giants. We lack the power to defy our enemies, for we see quite well that we are far too weak. But, in all this we continue to lean on God, and that is our refuge. Nor is this faith good only for this present life, but we have it for the life to come also. Thus, even if our Lord does put us into the hands of our enemies, yet He will not fail to be our Savior even in the midst of death. Let us not doubt, but that not only will He safely convey us from the morning to the evening and from the evening to the morning, but also that even in the midst of the darkness of death we shall always be lightened with His goodness and He will show us that the life He has promised to His people will never fail.

Therefore David uses this manner of speech, in Psalm 23 (v. 4): "Lord, Thy staff, or Thy shepherd's crook." He uses the similitude of a shepherd with his staff or hook. "Lord," he says, "as long as I see Thy staff before me, I am safe, so that if I were to go into the darkness of death, yet being in that dark and irksome dale, yea even if it might seem I had been cast into hell, I would not cease to rejoice." Such must be our attitude as well, as we consider this teaching.

Back to Egypt

Finally, it is said (v. 68) that God would bring His people by the way whereof it was said "thou shalt never see it again," and that they would be carried in ships, and that coming into Egypt they would be for sale as slaves, but no one would buy them. They would not be esteemed, but would be regarded as a people utterly cast away, and everyone would disdain them.

Now this means that God would cut them off, saying, "Remember how marvelously I delivered you out of the land of Egypt, when I made you to pass through the wilderness and to go through the Red Sea (or the Sea of Bullrushes, which they call the Red Sea; but properly it is the Sea of Bullrushes because of the bullrushes that grow in it),[5] for I caused that arm of the sea to shrink back that you might pass on dry foot. But now you shall return thither in ships. You must pass that way again, even though I prohibited you from doing so and enjoined you expressly that you should not go that way any more. Yet, whether you like it or not you shall return thither. Indeed, the first time you were in Egypt you wept because of the oppression you suffered, and I took pity on you and removed you from it. But this time, when you shall need for someone to buy you as a slave, in order to yield your life up to miseries as great as any that may be, you shall find no buyer at all." Thus God says, "Seeing you have despised the deliverance that was wrought for you, and have forgotten such a benefit, it shall be well known that you are an unhappy and a cursed people, and that I have forsaken and rejected you utterly."

This threat could not help but be exceedingly terrible to the Jews. And when the prophets expounded Moses, we see likewise how the people gnashed their teeth against them. All the same, they were not rendered any more meek by it, but rather they doubled their rebellion, so that it was always cast in their teeth that their iniquities proceeded to such an extremity as was intolerable. Even though all the threats of the law were pronounced against them, they still disregarded them, but kept going on and became much more hard-hearted, as if they had a set purpose to make war on God.

Consider: These people were of the household of God, the

---

5. The Hebrew name for the Red Sea is *yam suph*, or "sea of weeds." In his *Harmony of the Pentateuch* I:205 Calvin discusses this more fully (comments on Exodus 10:19).

holy generation, the children of Abraham, who from the beginning had been trained up in the doctrine of the law and had possessed the sayings always laid before them that were written by Moses, so that their ears were continually beaten with them. Truly it is a horrible thing and against nature that these should yet notwithstanding never be the better for it, but still go on from evil to worse. Was that not a horrible thing? Yes indeed, and yet we see the same thing today.

Let us then benefit from it, and beware that we not wax so hardhearted, lest we be possessed by Satan and forsaken by God. Let it not be that no matter what is told to us and shown to us, we are touched with no manner of fear but become like wild boars that of their own willfulness do cast themselves to death. Let us take heed that we not provoke our God in such a manner.

And moreover, where it is said that God would bring this people whom He had redeemed into a double captivity, more reproachful than had been the first, let us trust in that redemption which was once and for all wrought by our Lord Jesus Christ. And that we may be partakers thereof, let us freely serve Him who purchased us so dearly. And seeing that our God has redeemed us in the person of His Son, to such a state that now we are fully free from the bonds of sin and Satan, let us henceforth fear Him and serve Him all the days of our lives, according as Zachariah speaks in his song recited by St. Luke (1:75). Seeing then that this is the case, let us learn to walk in such obedience to our God that He may always make available to us the redemption wrought by our Lord Jesus Christ. And let us serve Him in all holiness and righteousness, that we be not bereft of the favor He has purchased for us, as we see this people were, who after they had been settled in the land of Canaan were put out again for their unthankfulness.

Therefore, let us be careful lest God dispossess us of the grace He has bestowed on us. But let us learn to take such profit thereby that all may yield fruit to His glory, so that He may make us to understand that in life as well as in death He is always our Savior and Redeemer; and that we may make our boast that He has not

redeemed us in vain but with the condition that we should henceforth live in liberty, despite death and the devil, just as the example of St. Paul shows.

Prayer

Now let us fall down before the majesty of our good God with
acknowledgement of our sins, beseeching Him to touch us more
and more to the quick, that being stricken with such a fear as
may make us see that of ourselves we are dead and forlorn, we
may yet for all this not fail to flee for refuge to His mercy. Let us
therefore seek the way thither, which is that we acknowledge
ourselves to be reconciled by Jesus Christ, and that He is our
peace unto the end, according as He continually declares and
testifies to us by the teaching of His gospel. And that in the
meantime it may please our good God to give us the spirit of
mildness and meekness, to the end that we no longer rebel against
Him or have our affections straining and rebelling against His
law, but rather that we may commit ourselves to His guiding and
be confirmed in the assurance He has given us that He holds us
for His people, so that He may show by effect that He watches
over us and that He will continue with us to the end to preserve
us both in life and in death. That it may please Him to grant this
grace not only to us but also to all people and nations of the earth;
etc.

SCRIPTURE INDEX

(Page numbers in **bold face** indicate the places where Calvin preaches directly on a verse or passage.)

OLD TESTAMENT

275

NEW TESTAMENT

GENERAL INDEX

(See also the Annotated Table of Contents, which follows, for a listing of Calvin's major themes.)

ANNOTATED TABLE OF CONTENTS